SOCIALIST PROPAGANDA IN THE TWENTIETH-CENTURY BRITISH NOVEL

SOCIALIST PROPAGANDA IN THE TWENTIETH-CENTURY BRITISH NOVEL

David Smith

ROWMAN AND LITTLEFIELD
Totowa, New Jersey

First published 1978 by
THE MACMILLAN PRESS LTD
London and Basingstoke

First published in the United States 1979
by Rowman and Littlefield, Totowa, N.J.

Library of Congress Cataloging in Publication Data

Smith, David J., 1938–
    Socialist propaganda in the twentieth-century
British novel.

    Bibliography: p.
    Includes index.
    1. English fiction—20th century—History and criticism.
    2. Socialism in literature.   I. Title.
PR 888.S636S6   823'.03   77–29211
ISBN 0–8476–6023–0

Printed in Great Britain

FOR BARBARA

Contents

Acknowledgments

The author and publishers would like to thank the Hutchinson Publishing Group and Schocken Books Inc. for granting permission to reproduce the extracts from *A Scots Quair*, by Lewis Grassic Gibbon, and Lawrence & Wishart Ltd for permission to use the extracts from *The Ragged Trousered Philanthropists*, by Robert Tressell.

Introduction: Definitions and Limitations

'If one faces facts', wrote George Orwell back in 1937, adopting a devil's advocate stance, 'one must admit that nearly everything describable as Socialist literature is dull, tasteless, and bad'.[1] Sometimes it seems that British critics, particularly those concerned with the novel, have taken Orwell's deliberately exaggerated sentiment a little too much to heart. For despite the recent growth of interest in socioliterary studies and a corresponding proliferation of attempts to trace the interconnection between politics and literature, there still remains one promising area of study virtually neglected: namely that of Socialism and the British novel. There have been several examinations of Socialism and British poetry, particularly the poetry of the thirties, but to date nobody has attempted to do for the British novel what Walter B. Rideout did for its American counterpart back in 1956 in his book *The Radical Novel in the United States 1900–1954*. The following study—a survey of twentieth-century British novels which include as one of their primary purposes the advocacy of a species of Socialism—is an attempt partially to fill this gap.

But what, it may well be asked, is meant by the term Socialism? Its meaning in Edwardian Britain in terms of practical politics will be discussed in the opening chapter; what I would like to do at this stage is to arrive at some more theoretical definition. Obviously, no such definition could encompass all the details of every variety of Socialism. The nineteenth and twentieth centuries have seen the accumulation of a large and often conflicting body of Socialist tactics and theory, and the gulf in the twentieth century in particular between the Marxist parties on the one hand—with their fairly rigid economic and historic doctrines, their revolutionary approach—and the Labour Parties of the British variety on the other—with their gradualist, parliamentary, and basically empirical approach—has often seemed virtually unbridgeable. But if it has seemed so, there has nonetheless remained some common ground, and it is this which can serve as a basis for a theoretical definition. It is in fact possible to see that in the years covered by this study, there were two minimal factors to which the major Socialist sects paid at least lip service. The first was that Socialism was seen, whether by common sense or by historical laws, to have most relevance to the working class. The second, and more important, was that the moral and economic ends of Socialism were seen as the elimination of social friction and injustice by the common ownership of the means of production, distribution, and exchange.

It is this minimal theoretical definition which I have constantly borne in mind as a guide to the selection of novels to be studied. An ultimate Socialist objective may well be, and frequently has been, forgotten by a Party in the immediate practical demands of the moment, but if a novelist forgets or chooses to ignore this objective then his novel can hardly be said to be advocating or—to be more precise and to use the terminology of my title—propagandising Socialism. It is for this reason that I have excluded such novels of social protest as—to take two famous examples from the thirties—Lionel Britton's *Hunger and Love* (1931) and Walter Greenwood's *Love on the Dole* (1933), which certainly rail against the system or part of the system but which fail to proffer any radical alternative. It is for this reason also that I have excluded novels which could be classified as propaganda only from extraliterary evidence, such as George Orwell's *Animal Farm* (1945). According to Orwell the latter book was written '*against* totalitarianism and *for* democratic socialism',[2] but it is in fact the negative side of his purpose which emerges, and as a result this anti-Stalinist parable could be and has been seen as a condemnation of Socialism *per se*.

At the same time, however, it should be stressed that I have not always excluded those novels which in the body of the work nominally advocate Socialism, but which turn out on closer examination to fall somewhat short of the ideal. In these instances I have indicated the divergence and tried to show its relevance to the period under discussion. Indeed, it has been part of my purpose throughout to view these books against the background of the political, and where necessary, the social conditions from which they sprang. There has been no attempt at comprehensiveness (just as there has been no attempt to discuss *every* Socialist novel of the period), but where I have felt such extrinsic material would cast light on the novels themselves, I have included it.

But this study is ultimately and primarily a study of the works themselves, of what they say, and more importantly, how they say it. The word 'propaganda' is commonly used in a pejorative sense when applied to the novel, and, indeed, the majority of the books examined bear this out. Nonetheless, at the risk sometimes of producing the effect of breaking a series of already maimed butterflies on a wheel, I have throughout applied the criteria: to what extent is this book conveying its author's own conviction, and to what extent is it a satisfactory work of art? The answer to these two questions, the nature of the relationship between them, and hence something of the nature of the political propaganda novel itself, will hopefully emerge in what follows.

There remains one final comment to be made, a comment concerning the chronological boundaries of this study. I have chosen to confine it to the twentieth century, and furthermore, while I have mentioned novels published as recently as 1974, the main body of the work deals with the fifty years between 1906 and 1956. The reason for the tailoring-off point, 1956, will be apparent later, but why 1906? In a sense that date is chosen as much for its limiting convenience as for its significance. Just as British Socialism itself has its origins buried deeply back in the nineteenth century and beyond,[3] so too one can find scattered examples of the advocacy of species of Socialism in fiction before this time. Charles Kingsley's Christian Socialist *Alton Locke* (1850) is perhaps the most famous of these, although his book is less an onslaught on Capitalism than an onslaught on Chartism, with the final plea that Capitalism and competition must be Christianised. Chartism itself inspired several attempts at the propaganda novel— ephemeral works serialised in the pages of Chartist journals, and borrowing heavily from the conventions of popular fiction.[4] Equally ephemeral was Mrs Lynn Linton's *The True History of Joshua Davidson* (1872), wherein the eponymous hero, a latter-day Christ figure, joins the International Working Men's Association and is even involved in the Paris Commune, on the grounds that 'the Communistic doctrines' are 'the logical outcome of Christianity in politics'.[5] There were in addition several middle and later Victorian books featuring 'radicals'—such as George Eliot's *Felix Holt* (1866) and George Meredith's *Beauchamp's Career* (1876)—but their radicalism is usually of a fairly mild kind or at least eventually becomes so. Even Mark Rutherford's *The Revolution in Tanner's Lane* (1887)—in which Zachariah Coleman's final words are to reiterate his belief in 'insurrection'—is concerned in the latter half of the book with the changing attitudes of the religious dissenters rather than with political radicalism. Perhaps the first notable British Socialist novel with any kind of ideological basis was George Bernard Shaw's *An Unsocial Socialist* (1884), and, six years later, there appeared what has remained the most enduring Socialist utopia of them all, William Morris's *News From Nowhere*.

Although there are these and other earlier examples, then, they are far too scattered to make the decision of confining this study to the twentieth century a serious limitation.[6] And the first few years of the century saw little change. At a time when Socialist fortunes were recuperating after a decline in the mid-nineties, the sole book of note to appear during this period was Bart Kennedy's *Slavery* (1905), a novel of working-class Manchester life almost anarchic in its insistence that Revolutions 'are the periodic purifyings of civilisations'.[7] It is in fact only with the year 1906, a year which saw the election to Parliament of thirty members of the Labour Representation Committee (a loose federation of trade unions and Socialist societies formed in 1900 to facilitate the election of working-class MPs), and which marked to some extent a growing revival of interest in Socialism, that sufficient novels appear to make a study of them something more than a series of individual essays. Even so, it should be stressed that this type of fiction was still very much in its formative stages. Indeed, it should be said now that the story of Socialist fiction in Britain is sometimes as interesting for what did *not* appear as for what did.

1 The Nature of the Beast

Towards the end of the first decade of this century a middle-aged housepainter who had adopted the pen-name of Robert Tressell added a preface to his curiously titled manuscript, *The Ragged Trousered Philanthropists*; a preface which in part explained his reasons for writing yet one more book on Socialism:

> . . . not only are the majority of people opposed to socialism, but a very brief conversation with an average anti-socialist is sufficient to show that he does not know what Socialism means. The same is true of all the anti-socialist writers . . . The thing they cry out against is not Socialism but a phantom of their own imagining.
>
> Another answer is that 'The Philanthropists' is not a treatise or essay, but a novel. My main object was to write a readable story full of human interest and based on the happenings of everyday life, the subject of Socialism being treated incidentally.[1]

While it may well be objected that to 'know what Socialism means' is, considering the varieties on the market, an act of faith rather than a matter of knowledge, Tressell's points are basically sound. The British Socialist of his time was indeed encircled by hostile, often misleading critics, and fictional counterattacks to this criticism were sufficiently limited to make Tressell's novel, when first published in 1914, interesting for that aspect alone. *The Ragged Trousered Philanthropists* stands, in fact, in this pre-thirties period, not in isolation, but certainly as a lonely peak in a sparsely mountained country.

Before any attempt can be made to survey this peak and its less lofty surroundings some preliminary exploration is in order. It is particularly necessary that we should first examine rather more closely the state of Socialism in Britain at the time Tressell began writing. For such an examination should not only help to explain the scarcity of Socialist fiction at this stage; it should also, and more usefully, cast some light on those novels that were written.

II

It has already been pointed out in the Introduction that the election to Parliament of thirty candidates of the Labour Representation Committee (LRC) in 1906 was to a limited extent symptomatic of a Socialist revival that had been gathering momentum over the previous two or three years. To some hostile onlookers, however, it seemed far more: an event, indeed, that brought Socialism ominously close. The fact that this Committee had made no reference to Socialism in its manifesto, and, after the election, quickly renamed itself the Labour Party, was construed by these same critics as mere deceit: did not the Party contain within its ranks a considerable proportion of rabid Socialists? The newly founded *Daily Express* was typically one of the first to attack, running a long anti-Socialist campaign, and persistently referring to the Labour Group as the Socialist Party.[2] Arthur Balfour, the leader of the defeated Conservatives, was also troubled: '. . . what is going on here', he declared, 'is the faint echo of the same movement which had produced massacres in St Petersburg, riots in Vienna, and Socialist processions in Berlin'.[3] The election of Victor Grayson as an independent Socialist at the Colne Valley by-election of 1907 further aggravated this feeling, and anti-Socialist tracts and novels, displaying a combination of sophistry, fear, and hysteria, proliferated.

That there was at least some basis for all this anxiety is undoubtedly true, but it is now easy to see—as it was for many at the time—both that the hysteria was ludicrously overplayed, and also that Capitalism, to say the least, was still very much in business. Not only did the LRC, or Labour Party, fail to make any reference to Socialism in its manifesto: it also gained many of its thirty seats by an informal *entente* with the Liberal Party, and was not in fact to be committed to any kind of Socialist policy until twelve years later. It is quite true, as its detractors were quick to point out, that just over half the successful LRC candidates were, in theory, Socialists, members of the Independent Labour Party (ILP), the largest Socialist Party in Britain—but even membership of this body was no guarantee of any firm Socialist commitment. Founded in 1893, the ILP had an ultimate Socialist objective—the collective ownership of the means of production, distribution, and exchange—but almost no Socialist theory. It would certainly have little to do with Marxist theory: Capitalism, said one of its founders, Keir Hardie, in 1904, was 'the product of selfishness' and Socialism would make 'war upon a system, not upon a class'.[4] Its inspiration was in fact 'ethical rather than economic'[5]; it was animated by a strong non-conformist religious spirit rather than by any coherent body of doctrine. At the same time its emotional nature did not prevent it from being essentially pragmatic in its immediate objectives. Indeed its most frequent slogans were for the eight-hour day, the minimum wage, and the right to work, for it believed in a gradualist constitutional

impermeation of the present social structure, rather than in any revolutionary change, violent or otherwise.

Something of the quality of its emotional, essentially undoctrinaire
nature may be gauged from the answers to a survey conducted by the
editor of the *Review of Reviews*, W. T. Stead, in June 1906.[6] He asked the
new LRC and Lib–Lab members (working-class candidates elected under
the aegis of the Liberal Party) which books had been most useful to them in
'the early days', and apart from a few scattered acknowledgements to
Henry George, Robert Blatchford, the Fabian Tracts—and two references
to Marx—most of the answers stressed an indebtedness to the Bible or to
such nineteenth-century authors as Carlyle, Ruskin, and Dickens. Apart
from this, the strongest link between the majority of the MPs concerned
was, as Bealey and Pelling have observed,[7] their reference to a non-
conformist upbringing. From this, however, it should not be inferred that
the ILP would in fact exclude anybody with dogmatic views: 'Fervent and
emotional . . . [its Socialism] could accommodate, with only a little strain,
temperance reform, Scottish nationalism, Methodism, Marxism, Fabian
gradualism and even a variety of Burkeian conservatism'.[8]

Of the other Socialist Parties, the only one of any importance at this
stage—and much in the shadow of the ILP—was the Social Democratic
Federation (SDF), which was also the only Marxist Party of any size in
Britain. Originally founded as the Democratic Federation in 1881 by
Henry Mayers Hyndman, it had disaffiliated from the LRC in 1901 when
it had failed to persuade that body to adopt the doctrine of the Class War.
Two even more aggressive splinter groups, calling themselves the Socialist
Labour Party and the Socialist Party of Great Britain, had broken away in
1903 and 1904 respectively, but were too small numerically to be of any
effect. Not that the SDF, for all its comparatively greater numbers—6000
in 1907[9]—had any greater practical success. Before the election, which
it had fought on a moderate rather than a revolutionary platform, it had
received the vocal encouragement of George Bernard Shaw and the
generous financial aid of the Countess of Warwick,[10] but it had still failed
to win any seats in its own right, and was clearly a negligible force in
politics. It should be pointed out, too, that Hyndman's brand of Marxism
did not meet with the approval of the more orthodox Marxists. Although
he did have his periods when he talked of militant action and would not
have been surprised by the onset of a revolution, and although he
consistently opposed the piecemeal reform tactics of the Fabians, for most
of his career he saw the revolution as being accomplished by peaceful,
constitutional means, a series of immediate, wide-ranging 'palliatives'
acting as stepping-stones to the eventual social revolution. His 'anglo-
marxism'—which consisted of picking out the segments of Marxist theory
he favoured, such as the doctrine of the Class War and the Theory of
Surplus Value, and rejecting or modifying those portions he disagreed
with, such as the materialist conception of history[11]—was , hardly

calculated to endear him to the purer Marxists.[12] Finally it needs to be said that although the differences between the ILP and the SDF appeared large to Hyndman, it was apparently not so to all converts, whose choice of either one or the other was often arbitrary and accidental.[13]

In addition to the organised political parties, there were several Socialist groups, not distinctly affiliated with any party. One could include amongst these the Christian Socialists, although they were hardly a very homogeneous group. A less élitist development of the early Christian Socialists of post-Chartist days, their beliefs in fact varied from the advocacy of Trade Unionism to a wholehearted support for a thorough, but gradual change of society. More will be said of them in the following chapter, and more too will be said of the inspirer of another much larger group of Socialists, Robert Blatchford. At this time his tremendous influence, through the Socialist *Clarion* newspaper, his tracts, and the various *Clarion* organisations, was declining, partly because of his support for the South African War, and partly because of his adoption of the Secularist cause. Again it should be pointed out that though he was a definitely committed Socialist—*not* a Marxist—and made many thousands of converts through his tracts, a large part of his following was probably attracted not so much by any clear Socialist principles as by the spirit of friendship and fellowship existing in the *Clarion* organisation.

There was, finally, the Fabian Society, a fundamentally middle-class group which had been formed in 1884. It was to this body that intellectuals with a social conscience or with an itch to rearrange society more methodically were in the main attracted; just as in the thirties they were attracted somewhat more startlingly by the Communist Party. Although some of their members were also members of the ILP, and although their ideas to some extent influenced that body, one can make the initial distinction that their touchstone was efficiency rather than ethics (at this stage), and that, even more strongly than did the ILP, they envisaged the process of social and economic transformation in terms of the gradual and progressive modification of the system by democratic, parliamentary means—largely by increased taxation and greater municipalisation.[14] They were later to play the role of brains-trust to the Labour Party, but at this stage they believed in 'impermeating' all and any organisations—in practice, predominantly Liberal organisations—where useful Socialist work could be done. Indeed, their *immediate* objectives, which took the form of demands for municipal gasworks or better parks and housing, and enabled 'a church-warden, or an English trade unionist, to call himself a Socialist',[15] were frequently indistinguishable from those of the more progressive members of the Liberal and Conservative Parties.[16] As the Fabian H. Bland wrote, with some slight exaggeration, to Shaw in 1910: 'If everything that we have been proposing were carried out tomorrow we should be no nearer or very little nearer to Socialism or to anything worth fighting for than we are today. The working people's children would be cleaner, and have better teeth; most of them would be wearing spectacles, and the wives of them would have comfortable lyings-in; but the capitalist would still be ramping over them as he is today and making even more profit out of them than he makes today'.[17]

III

Such, then, were the general characteristics of the still relatively small body of British Socialists in the early years of this century—characteristics we should expect to find reflected in the books of propaganda. Paying much less tribute to Marx than did the large continental Socialist Parties, their views were in the main inspired by ethics or efficiency rather than by dogma, their approach was moderate and gradualist rather than re-volutionary. Indeed, there is good reason for assuming, as this survey has in fact implied, that the aims of a large number of them—particularly of many intellectuals drawn towards the Fabians—could be merged safely and painlessly into the wider stream of social protest fiction; and it is this, far more than their small size, which perhaps helps to account for the small number of books produced.

One final aspect needs to be elaborated, however, if we are to understand the contemporary attitude to Socialism, and that is the nature of those hostile, often misleading attacks which sprang up after the 1906 elections, and of which Tressell complained so bitterly. As representative of the tracts, a single characteristic example will perhaps suffice: a bulky volume issued in 1908 by the London Municipal Society, hopefully entitled *The Case Against Socialism*. Bearing an introduction by Arthur Balfour, this work very early abandons the distinction between evol-utionary and revolutionary Socialism. 'It is by means of revolution alone that Socialism can ever be carried into practice'[18] the anonymous authors decide, and as for the transitional stage envisaged by the Parliamentarians, that would mean nothing but anarchy: 'The present state of unemploy-ment would be accentuated a thousand-fold, and Socialism's first citizens would be a desperate, workless, starving mob. Indeed, the leaders of the new movement would be fortunate if they escaped a hanging on the nearest lamp-post'.[19] Were this stage ever passed, and the Socialist State brought into being—a possibility the authors can contemplate, despite their emphasis on its undoubted 'impracticability'[20]—it would result in a 'glorified "workhouse"', the only material difference being that work would be a 'stern reality' in place of the 'light manual labour' that is called for in the present workhouse.[21] This Socialist State would, furthermore, abolish all private property, 'except perhaps what a person carries on his back',[22] take away the small man's investments, 'breed the poor idler in overwhelming abundance',[23] 'intensify both poverty and misery',[24] remove all freedom, and most probably lead to 'an active persecution of all

branches of the Christian religion'.[25] Finally the Free Love which would
be an inevitable part of this society would destroy the concept of the family,
'result in an unrestricted reign of brutish lust',[26] and replace the 'present
home life, which has hitherto been regarded as one of the institutions on
which the British have most cause to pride themselves', by a 'universal
system of Foundlings' Hospitals for the children, and not improbably a sort
of barrack accommodation for the parents'.[27]

Bolstering this kind of tract there also appeared between 1907 and 1912
numerous anti-Socialist satires and tales of the future.[28] They ranged—if
that is the word—from John D. Mayne's *The Triumph of Socialism and How
It Succeeded* (1908) which foretells the disastrous consequences of the
election of a Socialist Government in 1912, and its fortunate overthrow by
a *coup d'état* the following year, to Horace W. C. Newte's *The Master Beast*
(1907) 'being the true account of the ruthless tyranny inflicted on the
British people by Socialism, A.D. 1888–2020'.

Such dire prognostications did not of course go entirely unanswered.
What should be said at once, however, is that while no Socialist responded
to Horace Newte with *The True Account of the Ruthless Tyranny Inflicted by
Capitalism*, the Socialist novels that were written at this time were often
unfortunately no less crude in their responses. For this reason it is not
intended in the following chapter to examine them all at any great length,
but rather to discuss most of them briefly before considering in some detail
the only really convincing example that appeared in these years, Robert
Tressell's *The Ragged Trousered Philanthropists*.

2 Love and Utopianism

It was clearly to disarm any searching literary criticism that the Reverend James Adderley noted in the preface to his *Behold the Days Come* (1907): 'This is a tract, not a novel'.[1] One is tempted, in fact, to leave it at that and pass on to the novelists who were, perhaps, less frank. But when Adderley goes on to say that his novel 'will tell of very ordinary people' who 'will talk quite ordinary language. That's where I am no novelist',[2] he obviously lays himself open to some kind of examination. Furthermore, as he was one of the most prominent Christian Socialists of his time, his book inevitably invites—but unfortunately does not sustain—comparison with Charles Kingsley's *Alton Locke*.

Adderley was, in fact, a wellborn High Church Anglican who had been converted to Socialism during the Great Dock Strike of 1889.[3] He subsequently became a strong supporter of the Reverend Stewart Headlam, a Fabian who twelve years earlier had founded the Guild of St Matthew, a society made up of Church of England priests and active laymen with a Socialist outlook. It was a more militant and less élitist group than the early Christian Socialists: although Headlam never advanced much beyond a belief in trade unionism and Henry George's Single Tax, and frowned on the emergence of the ILP, other members involved themselves rather more adventurously in Labour affairs.[4] Later, indeed, these more radical members, feeling that neither the Guild nor its milder offspring, the Christian Social Union (1889) was Socialist enough for their taste, were prominent in the founding of the Church Socialist League (1906), which stood for an ultimate Socialist Commonwealth.[5] Adderley was one of this more radical group, believed that 'the present capitalist system has got to go',[6] and wrote several tracts – which the publisher 'always insists on calling . . . novels'[7]—expressing his views. *Behold the Days Come*, he claimed, was one of the best.

It recounts the story of Vincent Heathcote, who, as the son of a leading member of the National Secularist Socialist League, is clearly ripe for enlightenment. This soon comes in the shape of 'Father' John Ball,[8] a High Church Christian Socialist who makes frequent forays into Hyde Park to attack the secularists and the idle rich. In a scene mixed with intended and unintended humour, he concludes a swingeing criticism of the aristocracy with the words:

'There's time yet for the old standard of Christ to be raised again in London. It rests with you whether or not the coming Revolution shall be for God or against him. Repent ye, for the Kingdom of Heaven is at hand.'

He burst into tears, and leaning on Kesterton's arm, stepped down from the chair.

'What a disgustin' exhibition!' said Lady Loafer. 'Worse than the popery at St. Clara's.'

'A horrid fellow, my dear,' said the Duchess of Derwentwater. 'Come back to lunch at once. It's nearly half-past two, and the Dean must be famished. Why do they ordain these men of the lower orders? It's an insult to religion.'

'Are the clergy often taken like this in London?' said the meat man.

'Oh no, Mr. Vandertrust,' said Mrs. Market Hatcham, blushing through the paint. 'He's a lunatic, a sort of Dissenter, I expect.'

'He's good copy, though,' said Lord Haypence. 'I must find out his name.'

'Father, isn't he grand?' said Vincent. 'I feel inclined to kneel down and say the Lord's prayer for the first time in my life.'[9]

Dedicated hereafter to the principle that while the Socialist Party can use the forces of the State, it must be Christianity that prepares the people for Socialism, Vincent is ordained as a priest and works for a while in the East End slum parish of Father John Ball. He meets some other Christian Socialists: Kesterton, who is elected to Parliament as a 'Christian Progressive', and Lady Spicebox, who thinks that Socialism is 'most interesting and all that, you know'.[10] Of the parish itself we learn nothing, beyond the fact that all its young inhabitants are, through Ball's example, thoroughly versed in the ritual of the church.

A General Election sees a new and widely accepted programme of social reform laid before the country by the Labour Party. 'There was no animosity against the rich as such. The bulk of them simply did not count in the national life. They seemed to the masses to be bent on pleasure. Let things go their way. The mass of the people intended to strike for a new social life of which it dreamed.'[11]

For no apparent reason Kesterton is made the first Labour Prime-Minister, while the Labour leader Bill Bunks—who except for Mrs Buttles, 'one of the best-known "characters" in St Martin's district',[12] is the only representative of the working class in the book—becomes Home Secretary. Vincent has meanwhile married Cissy Vandertrust, a phenomenally wealthy window who, of course, promptly gives away all her money. A final stunning piece of wishful thinking sees Vincent made a Bishop at the age of thirty by the grateful Labour Government.

Despite the occasional touches of humour, *Behold the Days Come* is clearly vitiated from the outset by the very naivety of approach. There is, however, particularly when one recalls *Alton Locke*, another rather more disquieting element: the essentially remote attitude Adderley reveals towards the people and the conditions about which he is presumably most concerned. One is left with the impression of the East End as a place where people may or may not go to Church, and with almost no impression of its inhabitants at all—beyond the fact, as Bill Bunks says, that 'some of them were drinking themselves drunk for want of a little restraint and letting their own houses reek in filth which a few pence spent in soap and water could have set right'.[13] It is this fundamentally middle-class attitude—unrelieved by the efforts of imaginative identification made by, say, Charles Kingsley or, moving away from the official Christian Socialists, Mrs Gaskell in the first part of *Mary Barton* (1848)—which also mars an otherwise interesting novel by Richard Whiteing, *Ring in the New* (1906).

Whiteing had, to be precise, come from a lower middle-class background: his father worked for the Inland Revenue Office, and he himself had started out in life as an engraver, working for Benjamin Wyon, Chief Engraver of Her Majesty's Seals.[14] After becoming a successful journalist, he had turned his hand to writing novels, of which the most avowedly Socialistic is *Ring in the New*. He had, however, given an earlier indication of his sympathies in the popular *No. 5 John Street* (1899). In this novel a wealthy middle-class gentleman undertakes to give a report on the manners and customs of English Society to the Pitcairn Islands, Empire territory ' "run" on principles of almost primitive Christianity by a handful of men and women'.[15] Feeling incapable of reporting on the poorer sections of the population, he decides to live and work as a member of the working class for a while, and so takes up residence in an East End tenement. Shocked by the poverty he finds here, and revolted by the ostentatious wealth of his own class, he concludes in his report to the Governor of the Island that the latter has little to learn from England at present. What England needs, however, is not the creed of the anarchists, nor the revolutionary doctrines of the social democrats, but a new ethical 'Democracy'. 'As a mere economic formula, democracy must ever fade off into Bellamy visions of a glorified Poughkeepsie with superior drains. The underground system of the human being is the thing that we must first set right'.[16] If one substitutes 'Socialism' for 'Democracy', his message is essentially the same as Adderley's.

And, like Adderley, for all his concern, and for all his more intimate acquaintance with hardship, the picture that he gives of working-class life is essentially superficial and sentimental. It is a world where a flower-girl can say to a visiting princess: 'Oh, Milidy, it 'ud be like the Bible if you could come and walk down John Street Saturday nights. Don't you believe 'em when they say the men won't mind nobody. They'd mind you. Oh, Milidy, that's what I'd do if I looked as though I'd got wings under my bodice and could talk French'.[17] Underneath this Dickensian sentimentality[18] one can also detect at moments something of the distaste that is often revealed in Arthur Morrison's turn-of-the century books on working-class life.[19] It is this superficiality and distaste that permeates and debilitates *Ring in the New*.

Making clearer the synonymity in Whiteing's mind of 'Democracy' with 'Socialism', *Ring in the New* is basically an elaboration of his plea for a more ethical Socialism to buttress its gas-and-water Fabian foundations. (As far as the ILP was concerned, he was, as we have seen, preaching to the converted.) His agent this time is Prudence Meryon, a young middle-class girl who has to struggle to keep herself from destitution. Finding the role of companion to a demanding maiden aunt too intolerable, Prudence throws herself, innocent and untrained, into the sea of London's unemployed girls. She tries postcard painting, window modelling, and even for a short time goes on tour with a travelling play company led by Mary Lane, who believes, as Whiteing does, in bringing art to the masses. Her struggles, however, are all curiously unconvincing, as unconvincing as the young man's sojourn in No.5 John Street. One rarely feels that she has a hair out of order, while her encounter with the home sweating trade is treated with an almost detached serenity. There is, indeed, an air of detachment, of impersonality, present throughout; the kind of feeling contained in the following description, for example, as Prudence on her way home 'met a ghostly procession winding through the streets in the dusk—the "unemployed" returning to their lairs after the daily round. The scene was dismally suggestive of a gang going down to "Plutonian shores" . . . in their shabbiness, and even, in some curious way, by their shuffling gait'.[20] It is symptomatic that the only genuinely working-class character is a charlady, Sarah, who is throughout exploited for her comic possibilities, with little regard for her as a human being. Clearly part of Whiteing's purpose in this first section of the book was to show Prudence's snobbery, her lack of sympathy for the masses, her fear of failure, but in the process he has so distanced her from her surroundings that one feels no sense of involvement in her problems. One cannot help feeling also, as this detachment continues to pervade the book, that Whiteing—whatever his present allegiance, and whatever his past struggles—partly shares her lack of sympathy.

When Prudence meets George Leonard, editor of a Socialist newspaper called *Branding Iron*, he is soon able to convince her that her attitude is basically selfish. He takes her round London, and stirs her social conscience by showing her such examples of Socialised property as the Galleries and the British Museum. She then plunges into a course of self-education at the County Council lectures along with many other poor scholars, and in common with some of them attends meetings of the Fabian Society. She hears a member—H. G. Wells?—plead for a return to 'the old fire and the impulse of your earlier and greater day',[21] and hears him backed up by an old workman who makes an even more rousing call for the old religious spirit of Socialism: 'Socialism was not—what d'ye call it now?—a doctrine: it was a religion, if it wasn't always made on the same last as what they've got in the churches now. There was a good deal of "Our Father" in it, though it was set to the tune o'the Marsilase'.[22] For all the passion behind this, it is still curiously detached, partly because of Whiteing's mannered style, partly because he is unable to resist making the Socialist who pleads for a return to the Chartist spirit into a 'character', a 'phantom' who disappears into the mist.

Prudence's Socialist attitudes grow stronger, but she is still looking for a set of definite beliefs. The answer, she feels, is certainly not in the church as at present constituted: 'The parsons are paid to keep people quiet—that is the ruling idea'.[23] It all comes back to the religion of Socialism, not the economics of it, but the spirit of humanity and selflessness: 'Love something, your race or a fellow, with or without return, and let others love you in the same way. Love is sacrifice willingly borne, sacrifice is blessedness—bliss'.[24] After this preciously expressed triuism one returns with a sense of shock to the outside world and the triumph of Labour at the 1906 elections. George and Prudence profess their love for each other, and Prue expresses once more the hope that Socialism will not become only another 'party in Parliament—perhaps another class interest',[25] but will retain the religious spirit she feels is a necessary part of it.

For a book pleading such a case—a Socialism based not on economics or on the class struggle, but on love of one's fellow-men—the world presented is again a curiously limited one, in which the unemployed are allowed only to enter gingerly enclosed in inverted commas or as poor wretches to be subdued; in which the only working-class characters *are* characters, or, like George, have risen so far above their class that they are no longer recognisable as such; and in which privation and penury are lightly sketched over. Whiteing's own explanation for the weakness of the novel certainly does not get to the heart of the matter. Comparing himself with Upton Sinclair (and more specifically with the latter's *The Jungle* [1906]) as an 'apostle of Socialism' he stated: 'he [Sinclair] goes in for it with his coat off, in the American way; I have to go in for it with a thousand considerations for the state of society and the state of opinion about me'.[26] That perhaps partially explains the cautious nature of Whiteing's Socialism: what it does not explain is why he weakens and blurs even this message by keeping at so remote a distance from the great mass of the people for whom he is pleading and from the conditions he wants changed.

II

Needless to say, neither of these books just discussed pays any noticeable homage to Marxist thought, and neither, again as would be expected, shows any militant leanings. In fact Marxist influence is at a premium in

Socialist novels throughout this period, while physical revolution is never seriously suggested. This is not to say, however, that it is always entirely discounted. Indeed, in an otherwise undistinguished book by Edith Moore, *A Wilful Widow* (1913), the heroine has a dream in which she is conducted around 'Fairland' by a guide who tells her 'it was not until the people themselves who suffered most rose up and fought that we got our Fairland'.[27] But even here the tone of the book would seem to suggest that the 'uprising' is intended to be taken figuratively rather than literally.

There was one book of the period, however, which in the name of Socialism and Anarchism—or so it seemed to some—not only failed to rule out violence, but virtually sanctified it. The book was *The Bomb* (1908), and the author, extravagant in this as in so many other ways, was Frank Harris. Written in a period when Harris's London fortunes were declining, this novel was set mainly in America and based on the actual incident at the Haymarket Riot in 1886 in Chicago, when a bomb thrown by an unknown person killed eight policemen. Eight anarchists were accused of the crime: one of them, Lingg, committed suicide in prison, four were hanged, and three were reprieved. Several years later Governor Altgeld of Illinois decided that there had been a gross miscarriage of justice, and in 1892 pardoned the two remaining survivors.[28] Harris, somewhat belatedly, also decided that there had been a miscarriage of justice, and that the deed had been committed by the anarchist Schnaubelt, who had fled shortly after the incident. Harris was concerned, however, not so much to establish the anarchists' innocence—for his novel approves of the violence—as to express his sympathy for them as fellow-suffering outcasts of society, a role he was himself increasingly assuming.

At the time this eminently readable but ultimately unconvincing novel was seen in some quarters plainly and simply as a tract for Socialism and Anarchism; but a closer examination shows, in fact, that the sympathy displayed for these two creeds falls somewhat short of that of the believer. Harris was indeed a member of Hyndman's Social Democratic Federation for a short time after he settled in London in 1883,[29] and throughout his life he displayed an intermittent sympathy for Anarchism, but it was an emotional rather than an intellectual sympathy. As he states clearly in *The Bomb* and in *My Life and Loves*, what he did believe in was a form of modified Capitalism, an 'equilibrium', as he put it, between the forces of Socialism and Individualism. When the anarchist hero, Lingg—who in actuality was distinguished for his 'revolutionary fanaticism', and believed in a completely authority-free society, in which production was to be communistic and co-operative[30]—stands up to state his beliefs, it is clearly neither Lingg nor indeed any feasible anarchist speaking, but Frank Harris. There is no need to 'subvert' the social structure, he explains: what is needed is some municipalisation, some nationalisation, and 'many more Government appointments at small salaries for people with extraordinary peculiarities or gifts which enabled them to see and do things that other men did not see and could not do'.[31] Only once does Lingg give any idea of the vision behind this violence, when he says that 'We want to govern ourselves, and neither govern others nor be governed by them . . .'.[32] Elsewhere he has the unmistakable and disconcerting ring of Harris explaining—against a background of suitable appreciative noises—his plans for a mixed economy. As Harris later remarked, with due artistic modesty if nothing else: '. . . I idealized Lingg beyond life-size, I fear. No young man of twenty ever had the insight into social conditions which I attribute to him'.[33]

But *The Bomb* was not the only 'Socialist' novel of the period which helped, perhaps, to give its readers a somewhat odd view of Socialism. In 1906, for example, the publishers of Maxwell Gray's semi-utopian *The Great Refusal* proclaimed that the hero of this novel, 'fired with the sense of the cruel and crying wrongs of the modern industrial and commercial systems, turns Socialist' and founds a 'Socialistic brotherhood' in Africa.[34] However, when one has penetrated the dense and florid prose of this monumentally lifeless book—which actually includes a character who says 'Never darken my doors again. Go!'[35]—it becomes clear that it is not Socialism that Miss Gray is propagating, and, furthermore, that she had no intention of doing so. Her 'Colony of Brothersland' founded in British East Africa is, rather, a wholesale return to medieval conditions, an almost nightmarish extension of Ruskin's Guild of St George,[36] complete with religious dominance, feudal stratification, and Guilds of, amongst others, Victuallers, Millers, Sempstresses, and Domestic Servants. Commerce is here 'pursued not for gain alone, but for the good of man and service of God first and for moderate profits afterwards. . . '.[37]

At least Harris and Miss Gray were aware, whatever the opinions of their publishers and reviewers, that they were hardly advocating a full-blooded Socialism: the anonymous author of *An Amazing Revolution and After* (1909), however, seemed a little less clear about his motives. This utopian tract, following an initial bout of sheer implausibility, in which the armies of the world 'quietly melted away and disappeared' and a 'sudden palsy' fell over Emperors, Kings and other rulers,[38] settles down to a long and extremely arid exposition of what the author describes as a 'sane collective socialism'. As in H. G. Wells's utopian schemes it is a sanity imposed from above, but with the willing acceptance of the workers.

> Once satisfied that their interests and ours were one, they accepted us not merely as comrades, but they accepted and have loyally followed those of us who were captains of industry as their captains and leaders. And those of us who were foremost in affairs, either in finance, or law, or administration, they also accepted as teachers and leaders with a simple trust which has indeed made our labour a labour of love.[39]

Industry is collectivised, but the land, except where it can be shown to have been improperly acquired, still remains in private hands. It will apparently also be possible under this 'sane' Socialism to make a fortune as an administrator or trader. The author is, finally, quite blunt about his belief that there must always be a superior class, 'largely composed of those who have inherited or won titles or high social position', although he does make the proviso that this class will rigidly exclude anyone, 'however high his rank or position, who does not conform to its very strict conventions as to conduct and manners'.[40]

III

If our interest in *The Great Refusal* and *An Amazing Revolution* lies primarily in their departures from orthodoxy, the interest excited by another utopia published just two years before *An Amazing Revolution* is of a rather different nature. For this book, *The Sorcery Shop*, was written not by a dabbler in the field of propaganda, but by one of the most successful and influential of the Socialist propagandists of the nineties and early twentieth century, Robert Blatchford.

Blatchford's proselytising was truly amazing. His admirers ranged from the Countess of Warwick, who became an ardent supporter of the Social Democratic Federation through his influence, to the future leader of the British Communist Party, Harry Pollitt, who later claimed that he knew Blatchford's tracts off by heart.[41] By far his most popular work was *Merrie England*, a series of letters to 'John Smith', originally published in his Socialist newspaper, the Manchester-based *Clarion*, and brought out in book form in 1894; it eventually sold nearly two million copies. Blatchford, who had come from a travelling actor family and spent his pre-journalistic days first as a brushmaker and later in the army,[42] wrote essentially for the more intelligent but not exceptional working-class man, was a 'populariser' of 'other men's ideas' rather than an original thinker,[43] and brought a much needed element of gaiety and humour to the Socialist movement.

Although Blatchford was quite certain about what was wrong with society, and was reasonably sure what Socialism represented, he was far less clear about how it would come into being, and exactly what form it would take—other than that he frowned upon physical revolution, and paid little heed to Marxist thought. He ended his two lively tracts *Britain for the British* (1902) and *Merrie England* with exhortations to vote for Socialist candidates, and was involved for a time with the ILP, but he was never very concerned with practical politics. 'Convince the people and never mind the parties',[44] he is reported as saying, and in *Merrie England* he admits that 'The establishment and organisation of a Socialistic State are the two branches of the work to which I have given least attention'.[45] In fact, *The Sorcery Shop*, apart from being his only attempt at Socialist fiction,[46] is also his only attempt to forecast a future Socialist society at any length.

It opens in a London businessmen's club, where Mr Samuel Jorkle, Liberal MP for Shantytown East, and Major-General Sir Frederick Manningtree Storm, Conservative MP for South Loomshire, 'a distinguished and richly decorated professional homicide',[47] are found talking with great disgust of the new creed of Socialism. Sitting nearby is an old man, who overhears their talk, reveals he is a wizard, and then takes them by magic to 'an impossible country, inhabited by impossible people, who do impossible things, and are impossibly happy'.[48] The country is still England, but the city is now Manchester: a Manchester which is part of a teetotal, vegetarian, Socialist anarchy. In this 'Paradise regained',[49] where the smell and smog of factories has disappeared, the people, like those in William Morris's *News from Nowhere* (a book whose influence is strong throughout) are bronzed, beautiful and happy.

The wizard now guides his two bewildered MP's over the city, allowing them fleeting contact with its inhabitants, but reserving most of the dialogue for himself. It seems that while there is no government and no legal code in this society, there is strict monogamy, and womanhood is held in honour and reverence. The family, and particularly the mother, is in fact at the heart of it all, and it is from the mother that the child receives its education. Gone are the forcibly fed 'scraps of mathematics, and history, and Latin, and Greek'[50]; the mother instead teaches her child 'to be truthful, and clean, and kind. With kisses, and songs, and stories, with silver precepts and a golden example, with gentleness, sagacity, and affection, she makes them happy and good . . .'.[51] Later the child casually makes his choice of a career, and 'goes to his work without a scrap of anxiety as to his wages [money, indeed, has been abolished], or his situation, or his future. . .'.[52]

Indeed, he will usually learn several trades. 'When a new road is to be made, or an old one mended, all the men will pour out of their workshops and houses and set about the job as if they were preparing a lawn for a garden party. They can all work, and they all like to work. To them work is a sport.'[53] As for the problem of deciding which men will do the less pleasant, less creative tasks, 'Do you ask me if it is fair for a man to do the work he is best fitted for?'[54] replies a bridgeworker with some surprise.

Away from their three or four hours of work a day—short hours made possible by the greater number of people working, by the absence of the waste of competition, and, paradoxically enough, by the greatly improved machinery—entertainment and sport are open to all. To confirm the point, the two men attend a ball, and then listen in to the conversation of a gang of navvies who are discussing the books they have read and the countries they have visited.

From here onwards Blatchford abandons all pretence of peopling his utopia, and conducts an argument on lines very similar to those found in

Merrie England or *Britain for the British*. When he is asked how such a Socialist State could be established in England, the wizard carefully avoids committing himself. He does not overlook the possibility of revolution, but says: 'I hope it will never come to fighting. I feel sure it never will. If it does, I hope you will be beaten'.[55] He then launches into a hideous picture of contemporary England, supported by statistics and quotations, and finally takes them on a balloon trip across the England of the future: '. . . this is a planned and ordered society',[56] he tells them proudly—and incidentally clearly establishes that for Blatchford, if for nobody else, this is not, as his subtitle asserts, *An Impossible Romance*.[57] 'These people . . . make the country and all its resources the property of the whole people. And besides that they make the welfare of every citizen the care of the whole people.'[58]

Arguing to the last, the two men suddenly find themselves falling out of the balloon and back into the London of their day. Jorkle remains unrepentent, but the General, who has throughout been drawn in a more sympathetic light,[59] is clearly impressed by the wizard's arguments and is so far moved as to put several sovereigns into the collection box of a passing unemployment procession.

Perhaps part of the reason for *The Sorcery Shop*'s undoubted lack of popularity in the Blatchford canon is that by 1907 some of his admirers had fled, disgruntled at his support of the Boer War and his attacks on organised religion in *Not Guilty* (1906) and *God and My Neighbour* (1903). But there are, of course, much more solid reasons for its lack of success. It was mentioned earlier that this utopia recalls, in many of its details, William Morris's *New From Nowhere*. Apart from such similar incidents as, for example, the gang of roadmenders that are encountered in both books,[60] the general basis of Blatchford's utopia is clearly derived from the earlier work. There is a similar stress on craftmanship, a similar inclination to keep machinery strictly in the background,[61] a similar somewhat casual educational system, and a similar impression of men setting willingly and apparently spontaneously to whatever work has to be done. But there are also some very important differences. In the first place, while Morris's vision is of the ideal, it is an ideal tempered by contact with reality: one needs only mention the long central section detailing realistically its revolutionary establishment, the account that Morris gives of its actual government, his admission that the majority rule, and that force had, in the past, to be used on malingerers.[62] Blatchford, on the other hand, discards this altogether: he makes no mention of the government of the country, and skirts very uneasily round the establishment of this state, making it seem even more remote and unlikely than 'Nowhere'.

But far more importantly, as even this short summary should have established, he possessed only a fraction of Morris's imaginative powers. When, to give but one crucial example, William Guest-Morris 'wakes up' from his dream, so intense has been his vision, that it is he rather than the inhabitants of Nowhere who seems to be fading into nothingness, and there can have been few readers who have not felt to some extent the strange sense of disorientation involved here. There is nothing of the same involvement in *The Sorcery Shop*. Interesting a writer as he always was, Blatchford is nonetheless here clearly out of his imaginative depth. Once one has struggled past the fairytale opening, one is presented with a narrative which, though not without its charm, is simplistic in the extreme and with characters that are, except in the crudest sense, almost characterless, existing mainly to be fed utopian pills by Blatchford in the guise of a wizard. Indeed, instead of underlining the irony of the 'impossible' in his subtitle, Blatchford has in effect produced an 'impossible tract'.

IV

For all the catholic nature of his admirers, Blatchford's most considerable audience remained the working class, for it was to this group that he primarily addressed himself. The middle-class Socialist of the period was far more likely to invoke the name of another writer altogether, a writer of infinitely greater literary ability: H. G. Wells; and it is with the latter that we may appropriately conclude this survey of pre-Tressellian Socialist propaganda.

In the middle years of the first decade, when Blatchford's influence was declining, Wells seemed, in fact, to be *the* Socialist writer. His tracts, *A Modern Utopia* (1905), *This Misery of Boots* (1907), and pre-eminently *New Worlds for Old* (1908), all reached a large audience that had already been attracted by his immensely successful science romances. If not all who picked up *New Worlds for Old* 'tumbled straight into Socialism overnight' like Margaret Cole,[63] they could hardly fail to be impressed by his persuasive arguments for a world-wide 'Constructive Socialism'. The ruling idea of Socialism, according to Wells in this tract, is the ruling idea of Science, in that each attempts 'to replace disorder by order'.[64] The revolutionary Socialists, the Marxists, have rescued this idea from its utopian, localised beginnings, but have provided no practical means of transition and no practical means of administration. The Fabians have outlined that transition and that administration; but they too have woefully fallen down in that they have paid no attention to the 'breath of life'[65] behind Socialism. This breath of life, this animating purpose and at the same time end-in-view, is 'the development of the collective conscious-ness of humanity'.[66] Only by developing this self-consciousness, this collective mind of mankind, by teaching, by changing man's ideas, can Socialism ever be achieved, for Socialism is the temporal embodiment of that collective mind. Socialism, therefore, cannot, and does not reside in one man or in one party. 'There can be no official nor pontifical Socialism; the theory lives and grows. It springs out of the common sanity of mankind.'[67]

Indeed, though Wells does in this tract urge that the Socialist who wishes to engage in active political work should support the Labour Party, as it is 'through intelligent Labour . . . that Socialism becomes a political force and possibility',[68] he was in fact never involved actively with a political party for any length of time. He did, it is true, join the Labour Party after the First World War, and even stood—unsuccessfully—as a Labour Candidate for the University of London in 1922 and 1923, but he soon withdrew from active involvement after the disappointment of the first Labour Government. For most of his writing life, Wells was a confirmed anti-democrat, believing that this massive reorientation of human thought leading to the collective world state had to be directed, and once the state was established, controlled by a revolutionary élite, a spiritual aristocracy. From 1906 onwards he tried to turn the Fabian Society (which he had joined in 1903) into the beginnings of such an élite, but retired, defeated, in 1908. At times he saw his revolutionary élite among the titular rulers of the world, that is to say among the kings, emperors, and presidents. More commonly, however, he saw it emerging from the industrial managers, the scientists, the engineers, and the intellectuals. It was this idea that he propagated particularly in the twenties and thirties, with his scheme for a worldwide 'Open Conspiracy' of such men. It is important to note, too, that although he continued to hold more or less Socialistic views, and stated in 1934 that 'the establishment of the socialist world-state' was his 'religion and end',[69] it is almost impossible, and certainly becomes increasingly impossible after 1914, to categorise him simply as a Socialist. He is, rather, the advocate of a world plan and a world religion—sometimes comprehensive in its practical details, sometimes almost purely mystical—the Socialist content of which varies considerably over the years. As he also said in 1934: 'World planning takes Socialism in its stride, and is Socialism plus half a dozen other equally important constructive intentions'.[70]

Even in this, his most avowedly Socialist period, his fiction is characterised by an expressed disapproval of the official Socialist sects, of their narrowness and their impracticality. It is characterised, too, not only by a rejection of the class-struggle concept of Socialism, but also by a virtual rejection of the working class itself. Few proletarians—as distinct from lower middle-class characters like Willie Leadford—cross Wells's pages, and when they do he views them sometimes with condescension, sometimes with distaste, and even sometimes, as Christopher Caudwell has implied, with what appears to be an almost conscious fear.[71] Clearly, then, his novels, as distinct from some of his tracts of the period, could give small comfort, certainly in the doctrinal sense, to any of the orthodox Socialists. But do they in fact give much comfort to any Socialist, however vague and latitudinarian his creed? One can only answer this by glancing briefly, with the possible risk of digression, at each of the novels in turn.[72]

Ann Veronica, in the novel of that name, certainly feels that the 'general propositions of Socialism' are 'admirable',[73] and that the female position of almost helpless dependence on the male can only be changed by a change in 'the whole order of things—the whole blessed order of things'.[74] But she can find nothing admirable in any of the Socialist sects,[75] and indeed once she has found her own happy solution in marriage to Capes, she expresses no more her desire for radical change. In *Tono-Bungay* (1909) George Ponderevo, after a short disillusioning venture into Fabian territory, and a spell as a disciple of the 'crude form of Democratic Socialism',[76] opts instead for 'Scientific truth',[77] finding Socialism 'a little bit too human, too set about with personalities and foolishness'.[78] It may well be objected that Science, for Wells, was often synonymous with Socialism as he conceived it, but this certainly does not emerge from the context. Moreover, the symbol chosen to represent this impersonal science is nothing constructive but the completely destructive destroyer, surely chosen by Wells, as David Lodge suggests,[79] with an awareness of its pessimistic implications. In *The New Machiavelli* (1911), Remington very early decides on his conception of Socialism: 'Order and devotion were the very essence of our socialism, and a splendid collective vigour and happiness its end . . . the organized state that should end muddle for ever. . .'.[80] Feeling strongly that one should not 'confuse Socialism with the Socialists',[81] he joins the Liberals, associates briefly with the professed Socialists, and then moves on to the Tories, all in his efforts to find a 'receiver' for his ideals. Only by developing a 'collective mind'[82] behind individual lives will Socialism ever emerge, and the best place to start developing that collective mind, he feels, is among the 'finer individuals'[83] he will find in the Tory Party. But eventually, partly in reaction to his disillusioning realisation that the Tories have no more sense of collective purpose than have the other parties, partly because of his disorderly passion, he throws overboard his ambitions, and runs away with Isabel Rivers. We are told at the beginning that he still has his constructive ideals, and, of course, the automatic ending of his career is meant by Wells to be a comment on the very absurdity of the present social attitudes, but it is also—and it is this which emerges most strongly—Wells's own ironic comment on the possibilities of a racial collective purpose ever emerging from the present basically individualistic human material. The following year in *Marriage* (1912)—a far inferior book to these first three—the scientist hero, Trafford, goes through the usual Wellsian process of rejecting the present Socialist sects,[84] and then tells his wife, Marjorie, that if ever the human spirit is to be released from the individualistic struggle, a goal towards which 'the primitive socialism of Christianity and all the stuff of modern socialism that matters is really aiming',[85] then it is necessary to 'get the emerging thought process clear and to keep it clear—and to let those other hungers go. We've got to go back to England on the side of that delay, that arrest of interruption, that detached, observant, synthesising process of the mind, that solvent of difficulties and obsolescent institutions which is the reality of collective human life'.[86] But even against this vague, attenuated, and essentially 'spiritual socialism', Trafford's wife has the last pessimistic word: '. . . you can't alter people fundamentally, not even by half-freezing and half-starving them. You can only alter people fundamentally by killing them and replacing them. I shall be extravagant again and forget again, try as I may, and you will work again and fall away again and forgive me again'.[87]

The point is that Wells believed for the greater part of this period that political activity was at the most incidental to the fostering of Socialism as he conceived it. Only by a complete change in the hearts of men, or at least in the hearts of key men, could he visualise a 'great-spirited Socialism'[88] ever being given any temporal embodiment. Because he is dealing in the main with real men and women who have traditional ways of thinking (and after all, he as a persistent advocate of the collective racial mind, had the constant and chastening reminder of his own inability to work collectively with anyone), it is only by, in Anthony West's words, 'shouting down his own better judgment',[89] or, in his utopias, enlisting the aid of some cataclysm, that he allows his 'Socialism' to dominate.

Indeed, in this period only *The Passionate Friends* (1913), and the two utopian romances *In the Days of the Comet* (1906) and *The World Set Free* (1914) end on what could be called a positive note. The first of these, *The Passionate Friends,* is one of Wells's distinctly minor productions; its narrator, Stratton, is for most of the book quite blatantly an authorial mouthpiece. Forced to leave England because of his involvement with a married woman, Lady Mary Justin, Stratton journeys round the world and sees at first hand the muddle and injustice everywhere. We are obliged to accept that this short trip, undertaken by him as a wealthy and essentially uninvolved tourist, is enough to convince him of the need for a universal 'great-spirited Socialism'. Henceforth, he will devote his life to publishing knowledge in order to create 'a world-wide sense of human solidarity in which the existing limitations of political structure must inevitably melt away'.[90] Eventually a vaguely defined world-state embodying peace and justice will emerge from this dissemination of knowledge. The need for such a change is driven home to him even more forcibly by the suicide of Lady Mary Justin: a suicide brought about by his and her husband's jealousy and sense of proprietorship. He ends on the stridently optimistic note—and the book creaks under its weight, as there has been absolutely nothing in the story to justify it—that 'I know that a growing multitude of men and women outwear the ancient ways. . . . The ripening mind of our race tires of those boorish and brutish and childish things. . . . I give myself . . . to the destruction of jealousy . . . both in my own self and in the thought and laws and usage of the world'.[91]

The 'great-spirited Socialism' of *The Passionate Friends* could of course result in little more than an ennobled form of Capitalism, but in *The World*

Set Free Wells is rather more explicit. The cataclysmic event which brings about the Change is atomic warfare, which Wells envisages in the year 1956, some twenty years after one of his characters discovers artificial radioactivity. The book is full of Wells's imaginative inventiveness, and has some very striking scenes, particularly in the war episodes, but he makes no pretence of its being a novel. Ranging widely in time and place, it is, rather, a panoramic prophetic history of the twentieth century, and the few characters that Wells does settle on have little chance to develop. Indeed, for a book that culminates in a world state, it does seem strangely underpopulated. The main sufferers of the muddle and chaos before the Change—the greatly increased mass of unemployed—are seen through the eyes of a rich man fallen onto bad times, and are dismissed at one point as a 'multitudinous shambling enigma'[92]; instead Wells concentrates—in so far as he does concentrate on people at all—on the important men, the powerful men who direct the Change. One such is the French statesman, Leblanc, who, as the atomic war is threatening to obliterate the habitable world, calls together a conference of kings, presidents, statesmen, and leaders of thought to discuss the world's problems. Another is the completely improbable King of England, Egbert, whose prophecy that 'All over the world . . . we shall declare that every sort of property is held in trust for the Republic',[93] is borne out by the decisions of the Conference. Feeling that the dramatic progress of science, and in particular of atomic science, has laid before mankind the stark choice of extinction or adaptation to the new conditions, the members of the Conference cheerfully and quite unbelievably proceed to transform the world social and economic systems into a collective world state. Many years later, having disposed of such melodramatic opponents as the 'Slavic Fox', and having accomplished most of its work, the Conference voluntarily submits itself to the democratic process. The book ends on a note of sustained prophetic optimism, as the Russian Karenin predicts the future limitless possibilities in store for man, including his eventual conquest of space.

In *In the Days of the Comet* Wells confined his ground and time to rather more manageable proportions. Supposedly written by Willie Leadford about fifty years after the 'Great Change', the first half of this book is set in the industrial midlands at the time when the comet—whose green vapours play a similar role to the atomic warfare of *The World Set Free*—first made its appearance. From the outset the emphasis is on the muddle, the complete disorganisation of the lives of the pre-Change people. There is suffering and injustice, certainly, but this is only a symptom of the chaotic confusion which is also reflected in their houses, their streets, their clothes, their law, and their thoughts. At the moment, through their absurd mismanagement of economic affairs they have allowed yet one more industrial crisis to blunder into being, and are facing the most 'monstrous' of all the 'irrational phenomena of the former time',[94] war with Germany. Against this background of muddle, looming war—and the daily approaching comet—moves young Leadford, an office clerk. His reaction to this chaos is, he retrospectively comments, typical of the unmethodical thinking of the time. Poorly paid, overworked and underfed, he can see salvation only in political Socialism: 'The Working Man would arise—in the form of a Labour Party, and with young men like Parload and myself to represent him—and come to his own, and then—? Then the robbers would get it hot, and everything would be extremely satisfactory'.[95]

When Leadford finds his sweetheart, Nettie Stuart, involved with another man, his unhappiness reaches its peak. The man is Edward Verrall, the son of a great landowner and industrialist who is, even worse, the employer of Nettie's father. In a fury of class hatred and thwarted passion, the young clerk buys a gun. As the industrial crisis worsens, and war begins, the lovers elope. Leadford pursues them across the country-side, the comet all the time moving closer. He finally corners them, but as he starts shooting wildly, the green vapours of the comet envelop the earth and mankind falls into a brief, transforming sleep.

The sleep, Wells later explained, represented centuries of Socialist education and legislation.[96] When Leadford and the rest of mankind awake, it is to find the world bathed in a wonderful beauty. All living things have been affected, but it is men's minds which have been changed most notably, and given a new morality: a morality in which the problems and confusions presented in such books as *The New Machiavelli, Ann Veronica,* and *Tono-Bungay* are miraculously capable of solution. The war stops, as everywhere men throw down their arms and recognise their past stupidities. In this atmosphere of sanity and peace, the leaders and statesmen of the old time, such as Melmount, the British foreign secretary, gather together to reconstruct the world on a new sane collectivist basis.

One must, of course, accept the comet and its green vapours as symbolic if one is to read on with any interest; and to some extent Wells's imaginative powers do enable us to do this—even though he proves to be almost as vague in his account of the functioning of this state as Blatchford. Indeed, Wells bypasses the question of the structure of his utopia with a few unsatisfactory, ambiguous generalisations[97]; instead he devotes most of his detail to outlining how all the paraphernalia of the past muddle is disposed of: how the old dirty inconvenient houses, clothes, and ornaments— 'amidst which . . . there were sometimes even *stuffed dead birds!*'[98]— become things of the past. To further compound this vagueness, one has the uneasy feeling at times that in this emphasis on the removal of muddle, the people of the utopia have been almost lost to sight. We hear much about Leadford, admittedly, but the considerable interest aroused by his lively portrait in the first half is allowed to lapse into the rather limited problem of whether he will or will not live in a *ménage à trois* with Verrall and Nettie. It was this tentative discussion of the freer love relationships possible in Wells's new world that accounted for much of the attention paid to the book at the time,[99] and, no doubt, led to the strengthening of the feelings of the embryonic authors of *The Case Against Socialism* that this doctrine would lead to a reign of untrammelled lust. Of Leadford's relationships with other men, however, we hear nothing—beyond the stated fact that he feels an instinctive inferiority before Melmount. Even worse, all the other characters who make brief appearances are, by the logic of Wells's premise, put into the essentially negative posture of flagellating themselves for their past mistakes, such as Melmount's almost risible: 'All my life has been foolishness and pettiness, gross pleasures and mean discretions—all. I am a meagre dark thing in this morning's glow, a penitence, a shame! . . . No more of this !'[100] Ultimately, in fact, we really know only a little more of the human quality of this utopian society than we do of *The World Set Free*: and certainly not enough to convince us of either its possibility or its desirability.

v

In an otherwise appallingly vapid novel of Christian Socialism published in 1909, Guy Thorne's *The Socialist,* one of the characters, complete with a mustard-coloured beard, 'coal black' eyes, cheeks 'pale as linen', and the name of James Fabian Rose, complains of the Socialist movement's lack of outstanding support in the field of the novel. What the movement really needs, he says, is a 'supreme' preacher who will 'wield the magic wand of fiction and reach where no others can reach'.[101] While the literary quality of this novel might raise some serious doubts about its author's interpretation of 'supreme', there should be few doubts by now about the contemporary validity of his complaint. Most of the books we have examined in this pre-Tressellian period—nearly all of which were written from a middle-class viewpoint—are little more than tracts, and, interesting, even fascinating as they may be, not very convincing tracts at that. The two positive books by the most gifted writer of them all, H. G. Wells, not only fail to rise very much above this level, in their allout utopianism and lack of believable human characters, but are, as we have seen, actually antagonistic to the political Socialist movement.

Had Tressell read any of these works—any, that is, that were written before 1911—the effect could only have been to spur him on to finish his own novel, which was, in its passion and conviction, to tower over them all.

3 The Philanthropists of Mugsborough

I

... it was from a friend [wrote the publisher Grant Richards in his book *Author Hunting*] that I heard of that mountainous manuscript, *The Ragged Trousered Philanthropists*. . . . One day I heard that Miss Pope had learned from a neighbour that her children's nurse, knowing that Miss Pope was a writer of books, had confessed that her own father had written one—well, not exactly a book since it wasn't in print, but a story in the sense that it was a novel, the novel of his own life that wanted to get itself into print and to be a book. Politeness and curiosity made Miss Pope promise to read the manuscript, and it was brought to her. It *was* a manuscript![1]

So large was it, in fact, that when Grant Richards finally did see it, he asked Jessie Pope to shorten its thousand-odd pages into a more manageable form. At last, almost a year later, on 23 April 1914, *The Ragged Trousered Philanthropists* by Robert Tressell[2] was published. A second even more abridged version was brought out in 1918, and for the next thirty-seven years these two editions sold steadily, both of them ending on the pessimistic note of the hero, Frank Owen, contemplating suicide. The original manuscript had meanwhile passed from Grant Richards to his secretary, Pauline Hemmerde, who herself at some unknown date sold it to a stranger in a London teashop for ten pounds.[3] Many years later a Socialist workingman called F. C. Ball was sufficiently interested to start tracking down the manuscript, and eventually he too bought it across a teashop table, this time for the increased sum of sixty guineas. Finally in 1955 the complete manuscript was published and has since attracted a whole new generation of readers.

In his biography of Tressell,[4] Ball was able to establish only a very few facts about his subject that were not already known. He decided that Tressell may have been born of middle-class parents in Dublin, that his real name was probably Robert Noonan, and that he worked for a time in South Africa. He also confirmed that Tressell earned a precarious living as a housepainter and signwriter from about 1902 to 1910 in Hastings, where the novel is set, and that he either took part in or heard of most of the experiences recorded in the novel. In 1910, after having apparently left the manuscript for safekeeping to his only child, Kathleen, he went to Liverpool, where in the following year he died of tuberculosis at the age of forty. More recent research by Ball,[5] and the rediscovery of Kathleen herself,[6] has added little to this somewhat hazy picture, beyond the theory that Tressell may have been the illegitimate son of two Dubliners, Mary Noonan and Samuel Croker.[7] However, while this enigmatic element could well have contributed in some small measure to the success of the book, there are, of course, many more solid reasons for its continuing popularity.

It must be stressed first that it is fundamentally a work of propaganda. The world of *The Ragged Trousered Philanthropists* is a world born of the desperate passion of Tressell, who felt that his own life, the lives of his fellow workmen, and of their children, were to be wasted away under the Capitalist system, and, what was far worse, found that these same workmen were prepared to defend Capitalism to their dying breath. On his representative group of housepainters working in Mugsborough from about 1907 to 1908 he shows the enslaving effects of this system and the position of prominence it had assumed in their minds. With a mocking laughter that at times has a note of hysteria he scorns their misplaced philanthropy, and flays the world of Sweaters and Didlums they so unthinkingly worship. At the same time he shows in their actions and in the many harangues of his Socialist hero, Owen, some hope for the future: the possibilities of a better, Socialist world. It is, then, a work of purely polemical intention—and yet somehow it triumphantly survives. Long after the amelioration of most of the abuses it attacks, it is read as a moving, human document, and is still capable, one feels, of making converts.

Certainly this survival is not owing to any originality of political thought on Tressell's part. Indeed it might well be argued that part of his appeal lies in his very unsectarian willingness to borrow from various strands of Socialist ideology. For his Socialism is an eclectic, at times surprising, but always interesting combination of ideas of the time. In the outline of the Socialist Commonwealth, for example, given by Barrington towards the end of the book,[8] he borrows fairly heavily from Edward Bellamy's classic American utopia, *Looking Backward* (1882).[9] Elsewhere his arguments are often echoes of, or similar to, the arguments found in such contemporary tracts as Blatchford's *Britain for the British* and *Not Guilty*, Wells's *New Worlds for Old*, and the various Fabian publications. There is present, too, the influence of Morris, in Tressell's stress on the necessity of work being creatively satisfying: indeed, Owen's lecture on the 'Oblong' is virtually a direct dramatisation of the arguments presented by Morris in his lecture 'Useful Work Versus Useless Toil' (1884).[10] And, finally, there is a sympathy for the ideas of Marx: in his emphasis on the importance of the workers' class-consciousness, in his reference to the role of the state and of religion, and in such economic arguments as The Great Money Trick,[11] which seems to be a simplified version of the Theory of Surplus Value.

The juxtaposition of these names should be sufficient to indicate the impossibility of placing Tressell in any ideological niche. In the first place, he is obviously not, despite this debt to some of their ideas, a Fabian or a follower of Bellamy. Unlike these two groups his political appeal is directed primarily to the working class, with the assumption that they must make the specific effort for their own emancipation, and he clearly envisages, unlike the Fabians, a complete—though peaceful—change of society in a fairly short time. Nor can he be classified as a Marxist. If it is true, as F. C. Ball claims, that he was a member of the Social Democratic Federation from 1906,[12] then his Marxism must have been even more anglicised than Hyndman's. He never employs any Marxist terminology, and it is symptomatic that when Barrington gives a short summary of the history of societies, it is from Froude that he quotes to support his case.[13] More importantly, however, Tressell clearly rejects the idea of a final class war leading to a class dictatorship: both in Barrington's section (his workmen will be 'part' of the Community[14]), and earlier, where his words at one point sound very similar to those of Keir Hardie's already quoted in chapter one: ' . . . the present system compels selfishness. One must either trample upon others or be trampled upon oneself. . . . As long as this "Battle of Life" system endures, we have no right to blame other people for doing the same things that we are ourselves compelled to do. Blame the system'.[15]

Tressell, then, is certainly 'unscientific' in the Marxist sense, and he borrows heavily from other writers. Nonetheless, he does have a definite set of beliefs: he is not preaching some vague Socialism of sweetness and light.

The *Socialist* writer with whom he seems to have most in common—in attitudes, rather than in specific ideas—is Robert Blatchford. The hero's son, Frankie, at one point in fact says that his father's favourite books are *England for the English* and *Happy Britain*[16]—clearly transpositions of Blatchford's tracts, *Britain for the British* and *Merrie England*. By itself, however, this would be no evidence of affinity, for as we have seen, Blatchford's books were popular with most Socialists. But in certain definite ways they can be linked. Both writers have a simplified approach to a firmly held but undogmatic set of beliefs,[17] both are primarily concerned with the working class, both attack Christian theology, and more particularly, the professing Christians,[18] and both, in varying degrees, use humour and the human element as the basis of their polemic. And, most important of all, despite Blatchford's expressed intention to remain calm and sensible, there are many moments in his tracts when there emerges a passion approaching that found in *The Ragged Trousered Philanthropists*:

Imagine this man, anxious, worried, overworked, poor, and bled by a horde of rich parasites. Imagine him standing in a well-dressed crowd, amongst the diamond shops, fur shops and costly furniture shops of Regent Street, and asking with a bitter sneer where John Burns got his new suit of clothes.

.   .   .   .

How the Duke, and the Coalowner, and the Money-lender, and the Jerry builder must laugh!

Yet so it is. It is not the landlord, the company promoter, the coalowner, the jerry-builder, and all the other useless rich who prey upon his wife and children whom he mistrusts. His enemies, poor man, are the Socialists; the men and women who work for him, teach him, sacrifice their health, their time, their money, and their prospects to awaken his manhood, to sting his pride, to drive the mists of prejudice from his worried mind and give his common sense a chance. *These* are the men and women he despises and mistrusts. And he reads the *Daily Mail*, and shudders at the name of the *Clarion*; and he votes for Mr. Facing-both-ways and Lord Plausible, and is filled with bitterness because of honest John's summer trousers.[19]

The above passage, from *Britain for the British*, might well have been written by Tressell.

There the resemblance ends. For Blatchford, despite the qualities in his tracts which made them so outstanding in their time, never intended them to be more than tracts, and what was his only attempt to fuse the tract and the novel form for a Socialist message—*The Sorcery Shop*—turned out, as we have seen, to be another extended Blatchford essay. Tressell's intentions, however, were quite different. *The Ragged Trousered Philanthropists* was to be a novel, 'a readable story full of human interest and based on the happenings of everyday life, the subject of Socialism being treated incidentally'.[20] Had the subject of Socialism really been treated 'incidentally' we would hardly be considering the book here, but the words do illustrate the difference of approach. Blatchford's elements have, in fact, been given a wholly new depth and dimension. His simplified approach to his beliefs has been retained, but his emotional commitment, humour and human approach have been intensified and transformed by Tressell to make *The Ragged Trousered Philanthropists* both a masterpiece of polemic and also an extremely good novel. It is at many points repetitive and overbearing, and Tressell's harangues on occasions threaten to sink the book, but so powerfully has he communicated the justice of his passion, his sense of life—both in its comic and tragic aspects—and his sense of the possibilities in life, that the book triumphantly lives through it all.

Nowhere are these lifegiving qualities more eloquently realised than when he is dealing with his philanthropists, the housepainters of Mugsborough. I am not thinking here primarily of the graphic nature of his account of the social hell in which they live, although this is certainly impressive enough in its delineation of the uncertainty, the meanness of their existence, and their pathetic attempts to keep some signs of respectability. So too is the meticulous detail, which in this respect makes it very much a novel of its time. There are admittedly occasions when one recalls Virginia Woolf's strictures, when the massed particulars, marshalled with little skill, read like so many lifeless inventories. But generally the detail strengthens Tressell's passion. One thinks, for example, of the way in which the Lindens' prized clock—which Owen first notices when he visits them, which is later reluctantly sold to Didlum by Mary Linden when she is near starvation, and which finally turns up in a corner of the room in the Cave, ironically complementing Owen's own decorations—has acquired something approaching the force of the motifs in Joyce. The point is, surely, that the Philanthropists' few belongings occupy, far more than the static possessions of the Edwardian middle-class gentleman, an integral, almost an active part in their lives.

But if such details involve us in the affairs of the Philanthropists, even more so does Tressell's treatment of and attitude towards the Philanthropists themselves. It is an attitude which could only come from one like Tressell, who was one of them, and yet at the same time had enough imaginative and intellectual comprehension to see them as a whole. He *could* be extremely sentimental (one has only to think of the scenes between Owen's son, Frankie, and his mother, or of the maudlin role of Barrington in the final chapter) but he is never sentimental towards his workmen. Nor does he show the slightest trace of that paternalism tinged with fear that Morrison, Whiteing, and Wells display towards their proletariat.[21] His ultimate attitude, as we shall see, is that of an acute sense of them, not as comic or tragic 'characters'—which had been the usual treatment of the English workman up to this point in fiction—but as human beings who matter and are a vital part of society. It is this attitude which guarantees our indignation, our sympathy, our involvement in their lives, and, ultimately, our involvement in (but not necessarily our acceptance of) Tressell's social philosophy.

There is no doubt, in the first place, that his unrelenting observation of their weaknesses could lead him to be quite remorseless, as in the following extract, for example, where Crass the sycophantic chargehand is regaling the others with an account of his no-nonsense policy towards the foreman, Hunter:

'Last Thursday night about five o'clock, 'Unter comes inter the paint-shop an' ses to me, "I want a pail o' wash made up tonight, Crass," 'e ses, "ready for fust thing in the mornin'," 'e ses. "Oh," I ses, lookin' 'im straight in the bloody eye, "Oh, yer do, do yer?"—just like that. "Yes," 'e ses. "Well, you can bloody well make it yourself!" I ses, "'cos I ain't agoin' to", I ses—just like that. "Wot the 'ell do yer mean," I ses, "by comin' 'ere at this time o' the night with a order like that?" I ses. You'd a larfed,' continued Crass, as he wiped his mouth with the back of his hand after taking another drink out of his glass, and looking round to note the effect of the story, 'you'd a larfed if you'd bin there. 'E was fairly flabbergasted! And wen I said that to 'im I seen 'is jaw drop! An' then 'e started apoligising and said as 'e 'adn't meant no offence, but I told 'im bloody straight not to come no more of it. "You bring the horder at a reasonable time," I ses—just like that—"and I'll attend to it," I ses, "but not otherwise," I ses.'

As he concluded this story, Crass drained his glass and gazed round upon the audience, who were full of admiration. They looked at each other and at Crass and nodded their heads approvingly. . . .

. . . .

'For my part, I'm a bloke like this,' said a tall man with a very loud voice—a chap who nearly fell down dead every time Rushton or Misery looked at him. 'I'm a bloke like this 'ere: I never stands no cheek from no gaffers! If a guv'nor ses two bloody words to me, I downs me tools and I ses to 'im, "Wot! Don't I suit yer, guv'ner? Ain't I done enuff for yer? Werry good! Gimmie me bleedin' a'pence." '[22]

Throughout the book Tressell scrupulously records this and worse characteristics: the workmen's toadying, their occasional viciousness towards each other behind the other's back, and the lack of concern that some of them show when one of their number gets into any trouble at work. It is their 'philanthropy', however, which most arouses his scorn: their acceptance of their inferior status, and their mindless support of their oppressors. At many points this ignorant passivity, which Owen feels is condemning generations more to misery, arouses him to explosions of rage and contempt:

They were the enemy. Those who not only quietly submitted like so many cattle to the existing state of things, but defended it, and opposed and ridiculed any suggestion to alter it.

They were the real oppressors—the men who spoke of themselves as 'The likes of us,' who, having lived in poverty and degradation all their lives considered that what had been good enough for them was good enough for the children they had been the cause of bringing into existence.

. . . .

No wonder the rich despised them and looked upon them as dirt. They *were* despicable. They *were* dirt. They admitted it and gloried in it.[23]

However, existing simultaneously with this scorn—indeed, it is the reason for his scorn—is another feeling altogether: a feeling of concern, of respect for them as human beings and for their value in society. This attitude can be said to emerge in one sense in the very fact that whether boasting like Crass or shouting down Owen's attempts to enlighten them, the workmen remain constantly, intensely alive. Philpot, for example, with his mock-elaborate introductions to Owen: 'Genelmen, with your kind permission, as soon as the Professor 'as finished 'is dinner 'e will deliver 'is well-known lecture, entitled, "Money the Principal Cause of being 'ard up" . . .',[24] or Harlow with his philosophical titbits: 'It don't seem right that after living in misery and poverty all our bloody lives, workin' and slavin' all the hours that Gord A'mighty sends, that we're to be bloody well set fire to and burned in 'ell for all eternity!',[25] are full of an exuberant vitality which belies their professed inferiority. But perhaps Tressell's feeling in this respect is most clearly shown in that aspect of the book which gives roots to this vitality: the relationship that he establishes between the Philanthropists and their work.

It is a relationship on a scale and of a depth rare to English fiction up to this point, and certainly rare in any treatment of the proletariat. Other writers, such as Kingsley, Disraeli and Dickens had shown their readers brief, horrifying glimpses of sweatshops and factories, but the concept of work as an integral part of human life is almost entirely lacking.[26] One certainly does not think, for example, of Alton Locke, Tailor and Poet, as a tailor, while one important reason for the fuzziness of the picture of Stephen Blackpool in *Hard Times* is that one has almost no idea of what he does for most of his conscious life. Tressell most assuredly does not laud work *per se*—his painters are no less driven than the inhabitants of a sweatshop, and their hatred and resentment of the manner and conditions in which they do their work is no less strong—but he does present their function with respect, and not just as an item for social reform. He is able, for example, to show that Jack Linden's pretensions to being a 'free' workman are mockingly absurd, but a few pages later when Linden is sacked for having been caught smoking, the feeling that lies behind this mockery comes to the surface:

> Jack made no attempt to defend himself: he knew it was of no use. He silently put aside the things he had been using, went into the room where he had left his tool-bag and coat, removed his apron and white jacket, folded them up and put them into his tool-bag along with the tools he had been using—a chisel-knife and a shavehook—put on his coat, and, with the tool-bag slung over his shoulder, went away from the house.[27]

The quiet dignity accorded to Linden in these few words is all the more striking when one considers that it comes only a few lines after Owen's explosive conclusion that the workers '*were* dirt'. A similar concern is shown in the long and careful descriptions of the work the philanthropists do, in Owen's immersion in his decoration of the front room of the Cave, and, pre-eminently, in the attempts that some of them make to defeat the soul-destroying system. Newman, for example, has a family dependent on him, and knows he can be sacked at any moment, but when Hunter creeps upon him unobserved:

> He was at his old tricks. The woodwork of the cupboard he was doing was in a rather damaged condition, and he was facing up the dents with white-lead putty before painting it. He knew quite well that Hunter objected to any but very large holes or cracks being stopped, and yet somehow or other he could not scamp the work to the extent that he was ordered to: and so, almost by stealth, he was in the habit of doing it—not properly—but as well as he dared. He even went to the length of occasionally buying a few sheets of glasspaper with his own money. . . .[28]

The measure of respect accorded the philanthropists here—and much the larger part of the novel is in fact devoted to the philanthropists at work—is also present in what we do see of them outside their working hours. Because Tressell feels that their everyday lives are important, he makes no attempt to dramatise or sensationalise those stretches of domestic life that he does depict. And, countering his scorn for what he feels is their imbecilic worship of the system, he again indicates something of the dignity and inherent possibilities within them despite their degrading environment. Thus Easton is eventually reconciled with his wife, Ruth,[29] while Philpot for all his infuriating philosophy of 'There ain't no use in the likes of us trubblin our 'eds or quarrellin about politics',[30] is shown throughout the book quietly and unobtrusively helping his fellowmen, culminating in his elaborate subterfuge for aiding Mary Linden without the aid appearing as charity.

What must not be forgotten, of course, is that these scenes involving Philpot, Newman, Owen, Easton and his wife are in addition all specific answers to the kind of criticism we have seen contained in *The Case Against Socialism*. In reply to those who insisted that Socialism would mean a reign of brutish lust (and perhaps also in reply to such 'free love' advocates as H. G. Wells), Tressell stresses the naturalness of marriage and implies that it is the Capitalist system which is, if anything, brutalising it. To those who worshipped at the altar of *laissez-faire* and charity, Tressell points out the results of such a policy and how people instinctively recoil from charity. To those who thought that Socialism would mean slavery and/or botched work, Tressell suggests that the British workman of his time is in a state far worse than that of a slave and that any good work being done is in spite of, rather than because of the system. These arguments are, however, all couched in human, positive terms, so that today when such anti-Socialist sentiments are heard far less frequently, the scenes refuting them have not lost any of their strength.

From Tressell's conception of the workmen—a mingled scorn and hatred for their misguided philanthropy and at the same time a concern for them as human beings and for their potential—emerges, furthermore, much of the artistic tension of the book. For there is a tension throughout *The Ragged Trousered Philanthropists*, a tension in one sense between what is and what might be. But this 'what might be'—an important element in the book's success as propaganda—is not expressed in any impossibly utopian terms, as it had so often been in previous Socialist books. Rather, it is expressed in Tressell's or Owen's attitudes, in the workmen's actions, in Owen's moments of explosive rage—particularly in his passionate confrontation with Rushton towards the end of the book—and in the glimpses we get of the future Socialist Commonwealth; glimpses punctuated, it is important to note, by the ribald and disbelieving cries of the workmen. The world is nearly always with us. Philpot is killed by the '65' ladder, Linden dies in a workhouse, and Owen has the constant reminder of his blood-flecked phlegm. The world stays with us even in the following extract, as the workmen who are leaving Mugsborough to go on their annual expedition find

> themselves journeying along a sunlit, winding road, bordered with hedges of hawthorn, holly and briar, past rich, brown fields of standing corn, shimmering with gleams of gold, past apple-orchards where bending boughs were heavily loaded with mellow fruits exhaling fragrant odours, through the cool shades of lofty avenues of venerable oaks, whose overarched and interlacing branches formed a roof of green, gilt and illuminated with quivering spots and shafts of sunlight that filtered through the trembling leaves. . . .[31]

They seem momentarily, in fact, to be in some future land of cockaigne, but a few lines later, the confining world closes in once more: 'From time to time the men in the brakes made half-hearted attempts at singing, but it never came to much, because most of them were too hungry and miserable'.[32]

At moments, it is true, this tension is in danger of breaking down, particularly towards the middle of the book, when the long period of unemployment gives rise to some of Tressell's most monotonous denunciations. It is only in the final chapter, however, with the appearance of Barrington, that one could say that it does break down completely. Barrington is one of the few characters not properly absorbed into *The Ragged Trousered Philanthropists*. He is mentioned on the fifth page, has several more silent appearances, and then appears in his full glory at the 'Beano', giving his conception of Socialism. Finally—and this is what is most out of place—he emerges as a rich *deus ex machina* to give presents to the children, money and hope to Owen, and a promise to return again with a Socialist van.[33] This section, in fact, with its almost dreamlike atmosphere, satisfies everything but our intellect.

If the revelation of Barrington's wealth is a rather unhappily intrusive element from some earlier English novels, Tressell's humour—which is part of a tradition including Fielding, Swift, Shaw, Wells, Blatchford, and, pre-eminently, Dickens—is most certainly not. It is, indeed, another highly important and constant feature of *The Ragged Trousered Philanthropists*, ranging from the farce of the Reverend Belcher oscillating around the Sunday School and literally blowing up on the station platform at Monte Carlo, to the Swiftian savagery of Owen when he suggests that were the Capitalists able to bottle up all the air in gasometers and sell it they would do so:

> And when you are all dragging out a miserable existence, gasping for breath or dying for want of air, if one of your number suggests smashing a hole in the side of one of the gasometers, you will all fall upon him in the name of law and order, and after doing your best to tear him limb from limb, you'll drag him, covered with blood, in triumph to the nearest Police Station and deliver him up to 'justice' in the hope of being given a few half-pounds of air for your trouble.[34]

But it is undoubtedly in speech that Tressell's humour is seen at its best: in the conversation of the workers, in the glorious dialogue between Sweater and his friends at the Cave, and in such vignettes as the following, where a newly converted but still ragged Philanthropist has his moment of glory at an open-air evangelist meeting—conducted, ironically enough, by 'Nimrod' Hunter, the painters' merciless foreman:

> 'My dear frens, I thank Gord tonight that I can stand 'ere tonight, hout in the hopen hair and tell hall you dear people tonight of hall wot's been done for *me*. Ho my dear frens hi ham so glad tonight as I can stand 'ere tonight and say as hall my sins is hunder the blood tonight. . . . If you'll honly do as I done and just acknowledge yourself a lost sinner –'
> 'Yes! that's the honly way!' shouted Nimrod.
> 'Amen,' cried all the other believers.
> '—If you'll honly come to 'im tonight hin the same way as I done you'll see that wot 'E's done for me 'E can do for you. Ho my dear frens, don't go on puttin' it orf from day to day like a door turnin' on its 'inges, don't put it orf to some more convenient time because you may never 'ave another chance. 'Im that bein' orfen reproved 'ardeneth 'is neck shall be suddenly cut orf and that without remedy.'[35]

After Tressell, this tradition of Socialism—or, indeed, social concern—and humour seems to die out in the novel.[36] It is momentarily revived by Grassic Gibbon in *A Scots Quair*, but apart from him, seriousness and Socialism seem inseparable in the thirties.

It was noted above that the Reverend Belcher literally disintegrates on a station platform, and the two workmen discussing the incident do not sound particularly surprised. Nor, in the context of Mugsborough, does Owen's picture of the workmen paying for their air sound particularly farfetched. For though in some respects Mugsborough's world is an absorbingly realistic one, there is at the same time an element of an altogether different nature. The reality of the workmen, the fidelity to detail have already been discussed, and, in his book on Tressell, F. C. Ball further elaborates this point by persistently stressing the factual basis of most of the events recorded in *The Ragged Trousered Philanthropists* and the actual existence of the places described. But, as Jack Beeching has pointed out, even in this matter of location there is an important omission. While Mugsborough is recognisably Hastings of about 1908 to a native of the place, in one important particular it differs from its model. There is no sea, 'a treacherous, noisy, seductive and dramatic element in our lives—the salt fields which charged no rent and gave shrimps, prawns, dabs and whitebait, not to mention excitement. The country and the sea interpenetrate Hastings; yet with instinctive artistry Tressell suppresses them, and gives his book a generalised locale, which is distinctive enough and yet universally valid. Mugsborough is your town as well as mine'.[37] While it is not quite true that the country is entirely suppressed—the section on the expedition has already been mentioned—the point is still a sound one: Mugsborough is any town.

Perhaps it would be even closer to the truth, however, to say that Mugsborough is Tressell's town, springing energetically from the force of his scorn, his passion and his Socialist convictions. For so intense is his emotional and intellectual commitment to his beliefs that he makes us accept completely not only a world of flesh-and-blood workmen, but a world where these same workmen read a paper called the *Daily Obscurer*, are chivvied and driven by a man called Hunter, nurse in their midst a hypocritical Christian called Slyme, fawn and cringe at the feet of a man called Sweater, sell their furniture to Didlum, see their old buried by Snatchum, allow themselves to be governed by a band of Forty Thieves, and send their children to worship with a Reverend Belcher who will eventually explode on the station platform at Monte Carlo. All this aspect of the book, as has already been suggested, owes a strong and important debt to Dickens,[38] but the point to be made here is that this element in no way detracts from our absorption in Tressell's world. Rather, surely, does it strongly add to it, for, as he soon makes us see, as far as the workmen are concerned their daily paper *is* a Daily Obscurer, they are mugs, and they are worshipping a gang whose chief characteristics as felt by them are that of a Didlum or a Sweater. Tressell makes no claim to have a collective vision— that vision which in the thirties more often than not turned out to be a severe case of astigmatism—and to prise Sweater and the others from the world of Mugsborough and judge them by objective standards is clearly absurd. They are not intended to be faithfully accurate representations of the middle class of 1908, but almost allegorical embodiments of the system which Tressell felt was crushing the life out of his fellowmen.

Irving Howe has said of Ignazio Silone's novel *Fontamara* that it 'is the one important work of modern fiction that fully absorbs the Marxist outlook on the level of myth or legend; one of the few works of modern fiction in which the Marxist categories seem organic and "natural", not in the sense that they are part of the peasant heritage or arise spontaneously in the peasant imagination, but in the sense that the whole weight of the peasant experience, at least as it takes form in this book, requires an acceptance of these categories'.[39] With a slight change of wording—from 'Marxist' to 'Socialist', and from 'peasant' to 'worker'—this judgement could be applied with equal relevance and force to *The Ragged Trousered Philanthropists*. For has not Tressell's book, more than any British novel before or since, absorbed its author's Socialism on the level of myth or legend, and does not the whole weight of the workers' experience, as it takes form in the novel, require an acceptance of these categories? It is true that, unlike Silone, Tressell is not content with the weight of this experience, and explains at great—and sometimes, it must be said, repetitious—length his 'categories' and how to make a better world: one justification for this, however, is the simple fact that Tressell wanted people to join some sort of Socialist Party, whereas Silone, who had left the Communist Party three years before he wrote *Fontamara*, was clear about his anti-Fascism, but not about anything else. A possible result of *Fontamara*, with its climactic massacre, might be, as George Woodcock has suggested,[40] to turn people away from direct political action: Tressell's sense of urgency and conviction was too great for him to leave the issue in doubt.

4 Love, Utopianism, and some Revolution

I

The hope expressed in *The Ragged Trousered Philanthropists* was given some encouragement four years after the book's publication when, in February 1918, the Labour Party, now over three million strong, adopted as part of its new Constitution a clause which for the first time explicitly committed the Party to a Socialist basis: 'To secure for the producers by hand and brain the full fruits of their industry, and the most equitable distribution thereof that may be possible, upon the basis of the common ownership of the means of production and the best obtainable system of popular administration and control of each industry or service'.[1] Later in the same year a policy statement gave a more detailed account of the extent of this Socialism: by Parliamentary means it demanded the progressive taxation of larger incomes, the nationalisation of large sections of industry, and a massive extension of the social services.[2] With this basis, and helped by the growing effects of the postwar slump in Britain, the Labour Party gradually increased its representation until by the end of 1923 it had gained enough seats, not to hold an overall majority, but sufficient, with the support of the Liberals, to form Britain's first short-lived Labour Government.

The Revolutionary Socialists, meanwhile, remained a small, if for a brief period buoyant, minority. An upsurge of industrial strikes in the years immediately preceding 1914 had died down with the onset of the war: but there had remained pockets of industrial agitation, particularly on the Clydeside and in Wales. Prominent among the leaders of this agitation were members of the Socialist Labour Party and the British Socialist Party (formerly the SDF). It was the members of these Marxist groups together with individuals from such organisations as the Workers' Socialist Federation and the National Guilds Movement that, inspired by the success of the Bolsheviks in Russia, merged in the years 1920 and 1921 to form the Communist Party of Great Britain. It was a merger that initially appeared to promise well. Indeed, in the first heady flush of enthusiasm everything seemed possible; a delegate to the Foundation Congress of the Party was by no means alone in his opinion that there was no time to convert the electorate to any extent as 'the revolution was too near for that'.[3] But this optimistic view could soon no longer be justified. Many of the intellectuals such as Ellen Wilkinson, Francis Meynell and Raymond Postgate, who had been associated with the Party in the initial fervour, were shortly to leave it, either unable to stomach the rigid centralised discipline which the Communist International insisted on, or disgruntled by the seemingly anti-intellectual moves made by the Party. Nor was the Party able to make much headway in its ambitions of becoming a mass movement: its requests for affiliation with the Labour Party were persistently rejected and its permeation of the trade unions was basically unsuccessful. Its membership, after rising to 10 730 just after the General Strike of 1926, had declined to 3200 at the end of the decade, several hundred less than its original foundation membership[4]; those who remained were engaged in bitter dissension.

But the very existence of the Communist Party and indeed the existence of the USSR, provided Labour's opponents with an almost irresistible temptation; a temptation made greater by the fact that the Labour Party, while maintaining hostility to the British Communists, pressed for friendly relations with the USSR. Just as earlier these opponents had labelled the Labour Party as Socialist, and had tried to obscure the difference between evolutionary and revolutionary Socialism, so they now tried to foist on the public the myth, either of Communist – Labour unity, or, worse, of the Labour Party as a dupe of the Communists. The publication of the Zinoviev 'Red Letter'[5] just four days before the 1924 election, seemed but a fitting climax to these efforts, an example of which may be noted in one Conservative election poster which contained—in reference to the Labour Government's efforts to provide a loan for the Russians—the cautionary rhyme, 'Bolshevik, Bolshevik, where have you been? Over to England where the Reds are still green'.[6] Philip Gibbs was in fact voicing a fairly middle-of-the-road attitude when he wrote, after the rejection of the Labour Government at the 1924 polls, that there was the 'uneasy suspicion that behind the Labour Party, and in it, there were sinister influences foreign in origin, anti-British in character, revolutionary in purpose'.[7]

There appeared, too, in this period, as in the years 1907 – 11, a flood of anti-Socialist or anti-revolutionary novels. It is true that some of them were written by Labour Party members themselves—such as James Welsh's *The Morlocks* (1924) or Martin Hussingtree's *Konyetz* (1924)—to express their own hostility to the revolutionary credo, but others sought less innocently to foster the image of the Labour Party as having 'Wild Men' in the background. Thus H. Hessell Tiltman's novel *Poverty Lane* (1926), which seems to start as a novel sympathetic to the Labour Party, in fact ends with an attack on the Communist influence and violence in the Party, and the complete disillusionment of the wealthy hero, Jerry Prentice. 'It seems to me [he tells his supporters] that if labour has no other argument than organised rowdyism the wise man will vote for any other party who [sic] knows how to keep mobs within bounds.'[8]

With this kind of opposition it was, then, hardly surprising that spokesmen for the Labour Party frequently felt it necessary to disassociate the Party from Communist methods, and even to state, as in the election manifesto of 1922, that 'Labour's programme is the best bulwark against violent upheaval and class wars'.[9] Nor is it to be wondered at that it is this problem of revolution and the relationship between the classes that is one of the dominant themes of the few fictional expressions of Socialist propaganda during this period.

II

With the exception of Theodora Wilson Wilson's *The Last Dividend* (1921)—which is a series of soporific lectures on Christian Socialism rather than a novel,[10] and need not detain us here—all the Socialist novels dealing with contemporary life were written by people who achieved some prominence in the Labour movement: Mary Agnes Hamilton, James C. Welsh, and Ellen Wilkinson. The first-named was in fact still in the rank and file when *Follow My Leader* was published in 1921: not until eight years later did she become Labour MP for Blackburn, and, following this, a Governor of the BBC. Another middle-class affirmation of faith,[11] her novel reworks the device of the heroine coming simultaneously to Romance and Socialism—a conclusion which always has the faintly uneasy ring of trying to make the best of both worlds. *Follow My Leader* in point of fact gives an effective picture not so much of the heroine, Joan Heriot, torn between two creeds, as of her being torn between two dominating men: her father, John Heriot, a Conservative MP, and a former employee of his, Sandy Colquhoun, a Labour leader. Miss Hamilton is at pains to establish that the Socialism she believes in involves no violence and can in fact cut across class-barriers. Joan is repelled when she hears a militant left-winger, Lewis, speak: 'The force there was in Lewis was a terrible thing: the attraction of hate, a principle active and infectious, was in it; and he was using it to play upon all the dumb, uncomprehending bitterness there was in these suffering and disappointed men and women'.[12] Sandy, on the other hand, explicitly rejects violence, and it is to him that she is gradually drawn throughout the novel. When she finally makes the decision to embrace Socialism, and Sandy, the latter feels this need not entail a complete break with her father. 'I like him . . . We've got to fit men like him into our world, somehow; they make it go . . . It's like machinery. It runs us—but we could run it . . .'[13] Her father is similarly philosophical: 'After all, it will shut up the Liberals, to have a Socialist son-in-law. And daughter too, no doubt'.[14]

A similar rejection of immoderation and violence is found in James C. Welsh's two books on Labour leaders, *The Underworld* (1920) and *Norman Dale, MP* (1928). A former Scottish miner who became a Labour MP,[15]

Welsh forms a somewhat tenuous link between Tressell and the proletarian novelists of the thirties. Tenuous because—without involving oneself in Marxist ideology, or agreeing with the rather meaningless accusation later made by the Russian magazine *International Literature* that he was a 'social fascist'[16]—there is a clear difference in tone, apart from ideas, between Welsh and Tressell and the later proletarian writers. He comes, it is true, to the same conclusion that it is with one's own class that one must remain: but the overall impression left by his books—an impression doubtless fostered by his penchant for melodrama and his lachrymose style—is slightly Pollyana-ish rather than Socialist.

His first novel, *The Underworld*, initially recounts with vivid detail and some force the rise to manhood of a Scottish miner, Robert Sinclair, whose father is killed beside him on his first day at the mine. Robert feels the inadequacy of the social structure, but it is not until Keir Hardie visits the town shortly after the formation of the Labour Representation Committee, that he is drawn towards the possible solution, Socialism. The men are spellbound by Hardie: 'This was not the politics of the vulgar kind, of which the newspapers had told; on the contrary, every man in the hall felt that these were the politics to which every reasonable man subscribed. They were the politics of the fireside, of sweetness and light, of justice and truth, of humanity and God.'[17]

From this point onwards Robert devotes his time to the working-class movement, and is soon recognised as one of its coming forces. Exactly what he does believe is, however, not made clear, except that he is sure that his class 'needed serving—needed love. It passed on blindly, wounding itself as it staggered against its barriers, bruising its heart and soul in the darkness, and never learning its lessons. Saviours in all ages had lifted the darkness a bit, and given knowledge, and sometimes it had profited for a while till false prophets arose to mislead'.[18] An accident cuts short Robert's career before we can learn more: he is trapped with the men he goes down to save and dies. Welsh's final message seems more a call for trade unionism than anything else: ' . . . men who have wives, men who have mothers, men who have sweethearts and sisters and daughters, stand firm together; and preserve your women folk from these tragedies, if you would justify your manhood in the world of men'.[19]

If *The Underworld* left Welsh's views in some doubt, his next novel, *The Morlocks* (1924),[20] dealing with the failure of a revolutionary uprising in Britain, at least made clear one negative aspect: his complete rejection of violence. Three years later in *Norman Dale, MP* he returned to the more positive aspect of his beliefs. Packed with melodramatic incident, the novel has the same Scottish mining background as *The Underworld*, and a similar young hero who this time lives with his mother and a girl called Corrie whom he finds abandoned in the rushes at the beginning of the story. Although originally intending to become a colliery manager, Norman finds himself drawn into trade union activities, and soon fully involved in

the Union and other Labour causes. He decides to start a Socialist Sunday
School in the village, but it will not be a gospel of hatred that he will
preach. 'I want to encourage them to think about life and its beauty. I
want them to be able to recognise its nobility . . . I want to establish a
school that will see life as love, as beauty, as happiness, as service. That's
my creed, and that's what I conceive as Socialism.'[21] The local hardline
leftist, Snike, who is always calling for new leaders and a 'scientific
organisation', and is always just as promptly howled down, not unnaturally hoots with disgust when he hears that: 'Teach them the real
working-class economics an' industrial history. Gae them Marx's theory of
the material conception of history. Teach them to hate the ———— like hell,
an' tae prepare tae hing them frae every lamp-post in the streets'.[22] Later,
Snike's exuberantly expressed views are quite thoroughly discredited when
it emerges that he has been secretly in league with the pit-manager to get
himself the best work.

After the war—during which his stature is increased by the firm stand
he takes against conscription—Dale is elected as Labour MP for his area.
Feeling nothing but respect for his opponent, the Hon. John Fraser, and
sadness 'that modern life and conditions had made them opponents in a
system which neither of them could be blamed for',[23] he tries to crash the
class-barriers by forming a friendship with him, but growing protest from
some of his followers forces him to abandon the attempt. In London he has
the same problems, as society women deluge him with invitations.
Eventually he succumbs to the amorous advances of a Lady Darbury, and
this time it takes the combined shock of a rebuke from the Party leader and
a mine disaster in his home town to recall him to his senses. When Lady
Darbury finally dies in a car crash, racing to bring the injured Norman
some oxygen, he realises that his heart has all the time belonged to Corrie,
and, implicitly, to his own class. He concludes, as he avows his love to
Corrie on the lawn in front of her house:

> Here we stand at the end of one day, but there is the promise of beauty
> and fullness and happiness for to-morrow. There is joy in a life of service
> for a Cause that can never die.'
> The lark ceased singing, and with a glad little dive swooped down
> upon the soft earth and the silence deepened with the gathering
> gloaming.[24]

The ultimate blurring of conviction in Welsh's novels—that arises, as
has been indicated, as much from his sentimental style as from the fuzziness
of his message—is present, though less glaringly so, in Ellen Wilkinson's
novel centred on the General Strike of 1926, *Clash* (1929). It is an
appropriate novel with which to conclude this group of books, for Ellen
Wilkinson not only became one of the most prominent left-wing MPs of the
thirties, but was also for a time associated with the Communist Party in the

early part of the twenties. She provides, in fact, far more than Welsh, a suitable link between these more moderate expressions of Socialism and the revolutionary Socialism of the thirties. Though she, like Welsh, rejects the Communists, it is a rejection motivated not by any hatred of their policy but on the grounds that they have irresponsibly gone too far ahead of the vast mass of the working class. As one of her characters—with her evident approval—says: 'I've been through the mining districts lately. I would lead a revolution to-morrow if I thought there was the faintest chance of getting one. Our people are far too patient, unfortunately'.[25]

Miss Wilkinson once claimed in an interview with Ethel Mannin that, 'it's no use my pretending that I am more interested in A's falling in love with B and the possible reactions of C, than in politics, because I'm not. There isn't really anything I care as much about as politics, and there's no use in pretending there is!'[26] However, although *Clash* is essentially about a political event, she does manage fairly successfully to interweave some human stories among the bustling details of the Strike and its aftermath. The heroine, Joan Craig, a Socialist trade-union organiser who has come to London to watch the pre-strike negotiations, becomes involved in the lives of several men and women: Mary Maud Meadowes, a rich spinster; Anthony Dacre, a well-off journalist who is emotionally in sympathy with the strikers; and Gerald Blain, who is very close to being a Communist. Joan, like the author, has come from a working-class background, and is filled with a passionate desire to see her class given its rightful place. She has no doubts at all about the selfish inadequacy of the middle and upper classes *en masse*: 'They wanted inequality. They could not conceive a society without someone to bow before and others to cringe to them. The Socialist ideal of a commonwealth of equals "simple in their private lives and splendid in their public ways" made no appeal to the class that governed England in 1926'.[27] On the other hand, she finds it impossible to dislike them individually, and the situation is further complicated when she finds herself falling in love with Anthony Dacre. Like Norman Dale, she has to make the choice of sticking to her own class, or mingling with the rich, and very probably blunting the edges of her Socialism: the choice is, however, presented at greater length and with rather more subtlety. She wavers for some time, but eventually some thoughtless remarks about the miners by some silly upper-class girls decide the issue for her. As she tells Gerald Blain: 'It's difficult when you get to the fine shades between class and class, but the big broad issue is there. It's the issue that this century will be occupied in fighting out. We don't want to face it, but it's there'.[28]

As the decision runs counter to her expressed character—she is essentially tolerant and good-natured—one naturally has some doubts as to how long it will remain in force; but for all this, and the somewhat clumsily drawn-out description of her feelings for Anthony Dacre, the book remains an interesting and exuberant account of left-wing problems and attitudes in the twenties. The next decade was, after all, to see some far more violent clashes between character and ideology.

Whatever the particular merits of *Clash*, it is still true to say of this book, as of the other books just discussed, that its interest is for us primarily historic rather than aesthetic. Quite apart from the more obvious artistic shortcomings that have been referred to, there is a pervading unintended uneasiness about these novels, weakening and softening them at the core. One is drawn, in fact, to the unavoidable conclusion that the Labour Party's own somewhat uncomfortable position is reflected in them to their detriment. Welsh and Miss Hamilton communicate so well their anxiety to be disassociated from any revolutionary policy, that they often seem to be on the verge of disavowing their own Socialist beliefs, while Ellen Wilkinson's wistful references to revolution hardly help to make her own attitudes very much clearer. Certainly there is no trace of the passionate conviction of Tressell.

Nor is this to be found in the few utopias of the period, although H. G. Wells's contribution, *Men Like Gods* (1923), remains as always readable and fascinating. It is his only fictional work of the decade in which he unambiguously expresses his hope for Socialism, to which, he comments, 'vision was returning . . . and the dreary spectacle of a proletarian dictatorship gave way once more to Utopia, to the demand for a world fairly and righteously at peace, its resources husbanded and exploited for the common good . . .'.[29] The 'Utopia' in which the writer Mr Barnstaple and several other representative 'earthlings' find themselves has, as Wells suggested in *New Worlds for Old*, evolved after centuries of education and legislation; although existing in a parallel time dimension with earth, it is in fact several thousand years ahead of it in progress. On this Utopia god-like men and women live a life of anarchic Communism, a life in which all government, competition, and private property have been eliminated, and in which the factories, cities, and ugliness of twentieth century earth have been eradicated. Indeed, as J. Kagarlitski has pointed out,[30] Wells comes here as close to Morris as he was ever to come. The essential difference, of course, is that Wells's utopia is based upon science; the men are like gods because the dull part of the race has been weeded out eugenically, and instead of the free and easy educational process of the people of Nowhere, there is a constant search for new scientific discoveries. 'I had never thought before [reflects Mr Barnstaple] that socialism could exalt and ennoble the individual and individualism degrade him, but now I see plainly that here the thing is proved.'[31]

Whether it is proved to the reader's satisfaction is another matter. There is admittedly a far greater interplay of people here than in either *The World Set Free* or *In the Days of the Comet*: the earthlings are all, within the limitations of their roles, reasonably differentiated characters—even though the working class is, with the exception of two feebly whining chauffeurs, conspicuously absent. What remain elusive, however, are the Utopians themselves. So far removed from and ahead of the earthlings are they that there can be little satisfactory contact, and indeed the only Utopian of whom we are given more than fleeting glimpses is Lychnis, a negative side of Utopia, one of their failures. Of their ennobling sense of common aim and purpose we have once more to take Wells's word.

This problem of giving life to Utopia was not only not overcome but seemingly ignored in a very feebly written Utopia which appeared at the beginning of the twenties, *A Dream City* (1920). Like Wells, the anonymous author of this pedestrian Christian Socialist Utopia apparently has little brief for the existing Socialist parties: they serve, in his opinion, only to inflame class hatreds.[32] Ironically, however, his dream-envisaged state of 'Delectaland' is in fact founded upon social catastrophe. It appears that shortly after the Great War, when all the countries concerned were in a state of internal discontent, the disintegrating forces of the opposing factions suddenly 'broke forth in their fury, and, like a volcanic eruption, scattered all barriers, and sent forth a scorching stream of class-hatred and bitterness, until mankind, bankrupt of hope, as of material resources, was brought to the very brink of despair'.[33] Fortuitously there appeared at this time a Mr Veritas, who during the War had discovered a book which spoke of a king whose laws were founded on love, purity, temperance, and justice. Mr Veritas and his friends decided to try to set up a Socialist Commonwealth founded on his laws, and so, while the destruction of the world was proceeding around them, they were busily setting up an everexpanding chain of Communities to this end. 'In course of time, through sheer weight of numbers and personal worth, Veritas's party dominated the country and formed a Government elected to power by universal adult suffrage.'[34] Pneuma, the Viceroy of the absent King, presided over this Parliament, and the book was adopted as the basis of the laws of Delectaland.

On the somewhat dubious assumption that the reader is still with him, the author then gives what is essentially a by now familiar picture, but in the form of a straight tract and unenlivened by their imaginative powers, of a Bellamy–Wells Utopia. Wages—which are equal—are paid by a stampbook, all the essential services are free, armies and navies have disappeared, and class-differences have been eliminated. The threadbare nature of his inventiveness is best illustrated by the awe with which he unveils a tap—which has a switch to provide hot water. The only intriguing features of this State are that the Government is essentially by plebiscite, pubs have closed down, and the bookshops have been stripped of all that is 'calculated to feed an unnatural or immoral appetite or to pander to the evil passions in men'.[35]

III

There remains only one question to be answered. What of the rev-

olutionary Socialists in this watershed period? As yet they had found no
completely committed voice. However, apart from Ellen Wilkinson's
yearning references, there had been some incipient signs. A rather cynical
book published in 1922, for example—H. R. Barbor's *Against the Red Sky*—
had dealt with a revolutionary uprising in England, and the establishment
of a Workers' Republic, without however showing any great enthusiasm
either for or against the idea. The hero, who ends the book in an important
position in the Republic, has decided that *plus ça change, plus c'est la même
chose*: 'He had no enthusiasm now; now no sacred fire burned within him.
Of course, he kept on doing the things that came to hand. He found them
interesting, absorbing even. But it was not as it had been'.[36] Another novel
published in 1928 by F. le Gros Clark, who was later associated with the
Communist Party, had come to a slightly more revolutionary conclusion,
but still expressed in a vague way. In this book, *Apparition*, the hero finds
himself turning more and more to Socialism, until he can say, with a
somewhat lukewarm interest, that 'I suppose it will come, I suppose the
Revolution will come. . . . Whatever comes, I shall have to participate in
it, eat it and drink it, and nourish myself on it and grant it recognition.
That is so. If I find myself next week mingled in some revolutionary pie, it
will not give me any surprise; I shall only smile sadly—it is the world today.'[37] His involvement was sufficient for a reviewer in the Communist
Sunday Worker to seize upon the book with some delight. 'Here at least . . .
is a writer who has put the fact of social conflict at the heart of his theme.
This is his first work—we hope he will report progress.'[38] Progress—in the
form of a completely committed revolutionary stance—was not to come
for several more years.

5 At Last, the British are Coming

If the Communists had ended the twenties a disunited and politically insignificant group they could at least derive some immediate ideological comfort from the opening events of the thirties. For the depression from which Britain had been suffering since 1918, now exacerbated by the spreading world slump, was reaching what seemed to be virtually revolutionary proportions. By June 1930, with the official unemployment figures running to a total of 1 761 000 it was becoming obvious that the Labour Government—elected the previous year with the increasingly conservative Ramsay MacDonald at its head—had no panaceas, Socialist or otherwise. Rejecting Sir Oswald Mosley's unorthodox plans for economic recovery, and ignoring the dissident cries of the Party's Socialist conscience, the restive ILP, they could in fact only watch helplessly as the crisis deepened. By June 1931, the unemployment stood at 2 707 000,[1] and, unable to get his cabinet to agree to unemployment benefit reductions, MacDonald accepted their resignations, and then shuffled several paces to the right to form a new, predominantly Conservative 'National' Government. In the elections held later that year the 'National' Government romped home with a staggering 497 seats; the Labour Party found itself left with only 46, the now separate ILP with 5, while the Communist Party and Mosley's New Party—the latter hurriedly formed to propagate his economic plans—were also-rans.

Mosley wasted no time in founding yet one more Party, the British Union of Fascists, his autocratic answer to what he called the 'national combination of "the united muttons"'. 'Surely nobody', he declared, 'can imagine that the British, as a race, are free. . . . Many unemployed, the remainder living in the shadow of unemployment, low wages, long hours of exhausting labour, bad houses, shrinking social amenities, the uncertainty of industrial collapse and universal confusion: these are the lot of the average man to-day. What humbug, then, to talk of liberty: *The beginning of liberty is the end of economic chaos*.'[2] The reasoning is persuasive, and was to be echoed many times in the months and years that followed, as the stolid and seemingly reactionary National Government retained its immovable grip on the reins of power. The end result, of course, was not always to swell

Mosley's barracks in King's Road; just as convincingly could the argument justify the Communist dictatorship of the proletariat.

As conditions worsened, in fact, there must have been many Communists who hastily imagined—despite their resounding failure at the polls—that the millenium was not too far around the corner. For the immediate consequence of the National Government's assumption of office seemed to be an increase of economic chaos, with unemployment surging dizzyingly to the heights of 2955000 by January 1933.[3] Although thereafter it fell steadily, there remained the depressed areas, those new kinds of social hell where a blanket employment mocked the national averages. In these areas—industrial Scotland, South Wales, West Cumberland, the Tyne – Tees area in Northern England[4]—lived thousands of families who were, Margaret and G. D. H. Cole wrote in 1937, 'being starved, if not to death, at any rate into ill health'.[5] If the reaction of most was to withdraw into a sullen state of lethargy, it was hardly surprising that some, at least, began turning to Communism as their solution; nor was it surprising that a number of members of the middle-class, especially those in the universities, found their social conscience—prodded by the hunger marchers from these areas—awakening as the misery dragged on.[6]

There was also room for Communist optimism in the sporadic outbreaks of violence that inevitably accompanied this economic misery. To one Communist observer, indeed, accounts of the scattered clashes that took place between police and demonstrators in 1931 and 1932, satisfyingly read, 'with a change here and there in local colour, like a twenty- or thirty-year old account of the smashing up of a demonstration of Russian workers by Cossacks'.[7] Just as promising seemed the violence that flared around the activities of the British Union of Fascists, as, gaining in strength[8] and more and more scurrilously anti-semitic, they marched provocatively through Jewish districts in the East End of London. The triumph of Hitler in 1933, and the increasing stories of Fascist brutality filtering back from Italy and Germany, made this menace seem even more real and imminent. The Communist Party, whose supporters were prominent in resisting these encroachments, was soon drawing into its ranks many people of anti-Fascist feelings, working class and intellectuals; and particularly young Jews, who were easily convinced that Soviet Russia with a Jewish Foreign Minister,[9] had solved its own Jewish problem. Inclined too in sympathy were those intellectuals who had travelled abroad and had actually seen Fascist brutality at first hand.

But this intellectual interest in Communism—and proportionately the intellectuals formed the largest number of the new adherents—did not necessarily spring solely from an awakening of the conscience or from anti-Fascist feelings. As Neal Wood has pointed out, in the spring of 1934 out of a total 'black-coat' force of about two million, including the professional and clerical occupations, between 300000 and 400000 were unemployed.[10] Many a promising young graduate came down from the university and was forced, not generally into unemployment, but to take a position as teacher or tutor, which seemed inferior to his qualifications. Writers such as Edward Upward could see possibilities of the poetic life only under a triumph of Communism: 'There would be a world in which everyone would have freedom for self-fulfilment, would be expected, would have the prime social duty to become whatever he was born to be . . . The poetic life was the finest life. . . . There was only one way towards it, and that was the way of constant political effort, of Communist struggle for a struggleless world in which poetic living would at last become actual.'[11]

Strengthening all these feelings, and contrasting vividly with the stories from Italy and Germany, the chaos in Britain, came stories of the new Russia, which related how the first Five Year Plan was working, unemployment was destroyed, and culture was flourishing. Its obvious lack of political democracy was easily justified by the same arguments that Mosley used, and any other doubts were stifled by the excuse that it was a period of transition. Visits by eminent people such as G. B. Shaw in 1931, and books such as John Strachey's *The Coming Struggle for Power*[12] and the Webbs' *Soviet Communism: A New Civilization?* (1935),[13] further helped to spread this interest in the Soviet Union and Communism. If it was at times a relationship of extreme delicacy and artificiality—the writer Ethel Mannin has recorded how she refrained from mentioning the agonising bout of dysentery she had in the USSR for fear it might be interpreted as criticism of that country[14]—it was one entered into with great fervour while it lasted. For many, in fact, the Soviet Union and Communism provided a belief, a faith in a faithless world: '. . . the look of infinite sweetness and kindliness on the face of dead Lenin . . .', wrote the novelist Naomi Mitchison, 'had the same effect on me as a glance at a crucifix might have on others'.[15] George Orwell's comment that worship of the USSR was simply the 'patriotism of the deracinated'[16] was an over-simplification; but like most of his simplifications it did contain a germ of truth.

A further impetus to the Party's fortunes, and particularly to the radicalisation of the intellectuals, came with the start of the Spanish Civil War in 1936. The aid given by Stalin to the legal Spanish Government, the prominent activity by the British Communist Party on behalf of the International Brigade, all stood in startling contrast to the neutrality of the British Labour Party—which officially refused to join in any 'United Front' with the Communists. Many left-wing Liberals, feeling that the fate of such ideals as Democracy and Freedom stood in the balance in Spain, thus found themselves moving far more to the militant left than their actual convictions warranted. The death of Communist Party members in Spain only helped to increase this movement: '. . . indeed for the Communists, as for the early Christians, the blood of the martyrs was the seed of the church'.[17] The Party's membership—still, it should be noted, a staggeringly low 7700 at the beginning of 1936—gained almost 4000 recruits in the first year of the war,[18] although thereafter it slowed down.[19]

II

It was against this background—of mingled inertia and burgeoning faith—that at long last a revolutionary literary movement had begun making its cautious appearance in Britain. The adjective is carefully chosen, for despite the apparent auspiciousness of the occasion, there was certainly no overnight cascade of books dedicated to the revolutionary cause. Indeed, to many Communists, waiting impatiently and vainly for a full deluge, and glancing uneasily at the flood of revolutionary literature in the United States, the sluggishness of this movement—especially that of the novel—remained a source of dissatisfaction throughout the thirties. '. . . . There are many workers who write', said Bob Ellis at the Second World Conference of Revolutionary Writers at Kharkov in November 1930. 'There are also people who write about the proletariat, but we have no proletarian writers. . . .' 'It must be recognized', agreed the other British delegate, Harold Heslop (and it is significant that the British delegation was the smallest, bar Italy's, of all major Western countries) 'that proletarian art in Great Britain is in a very backward condition— and is in fact hardly begun'.[20] Nor did the next two years radically change this picture: the first issues of the Russian-based magazine *International Literature*, though devoting much space to lauding (and chastising) *New Masses* and other American left-wing magazines, could find little more to comment on in Britain during this time than the predominance of 'social – fascist' writers, such as Stacey Hyde and James Welsh.[21] Even events as promising as the appearance of the short-lived magazine of revolutionary fiction, *Storm*,[22] in 1933, the publication of A. P. Roley's proletarian novel *Revolt* in the same year, and the growth of the 'revolutionary' poetic movement,[23] received but a limited welcome; Britain was still felt to be badly lagging. The following year in *Viewpoint*—a magazine of militant Communism soon to be absorbed into *Left Review*—D. A. Willis had the same sorry story to tell: 'Almost without exception the leading English novelists of to-day turn aside from the sight of starving humanity. . . .'[24] *Left Review* was started at the end of 1934 in an attempt to encourage the growth of proletarian art, and by the next year was well established, but the complaints did not cease. In 1935 C. Day Lewis was writing of the predominance of the 'talented, average, vaguely revolutionary young writer', and the lack of the 'complete revolutionary',[25] while in 1936, in *International Literature*, Andrew J. Stelger gave some significant figures for books published in the last six months of 1934. Of the twelve English authors translated into Russian, only three of them were modern (two of them being Shaw and Wells), whereas of America's authors nine were modern and only three were classics.[26] At last, 'The British Are Coming', exclaimed Granville Hicks, in the December 1936, *New Masses*, pointing out that some revolutionary fiction writers were finally making their appearance,[27] but two years later in the same magazine C. Day Lewis was still complaining about the number of novelists who were writing 'as though there was no war on'.[28]

From the point of view of quantity alone—and quantity is all that this chapter is concerned with—this anxiety and dissatisfaction was understandable enough. For while Britain's total of thirty or so revolutionary novels sounds formidable when compared with the meagre number of pre-thirties Socialist books, it would seem to be anything but that when compared with, say, the seventy proletarian novels published in America from 1930 to 1939.[29] For a decade in which more was said and written about the relationship of politics and art than ever before, in which writers were constantly urged to use their pens as weapons in the class war, a perhaps surprisingly overwhelming number continued stubbornly to go their own unpolitical way, or at best refrained from implying or drawing any revolutionary conclusions. C. Day Lewis's choice of writers to be sympathetically mentioned in the *New Masses* article referred to above is particularly illuminating: Christopher Isherwood, Arthur Calder-Marshall, and Jack Lindsay (these have 'taken the impression of their times'); a 'number of rising proletarian novelists': Ralph Bates, Simon Blumenfeld, John Sommerfield, James Hanley, V. S. Pritchett, and Leslie Halward; and finally, two 'Communist writers', Rex Warner and Edward Upward. Of these, Hanley professed indifference to all political parties and ideologies;[30] Pritchett and Halward rarely allowed their political sympathies to seep through; Arthur Calder-Marshall in his anxiety to be objective[31] was rudely dismissed by his fellow-leftists; while Isherwood— admittedly something more than a camera—was less intent on making a choice between the warring ideologies in Berlin than in capturing the eccentricity of his characters. And these were all writers specially singled out for mention in a radical magazine.

The point to be made is that alongside the fairly small body of unashamedly revolutionary fiction, and those few books which made clear their continued faith in Parliamentary Socialism of the Labour Party variety, there was a much larger body of literature of social concern or social protest which either disdained politics altogether, or else treated the subject with varying degrees of objectivity, leaving the reader free to draw his own conclusions. And, of course, looming over all this, there was the even more formidable body of literature which cannot by any stretch of the imagination be called social protest. When one considers that in 1937— one of the peak years of extreme left-wing activity—there were 1817 new novels published,[32] of which perhaps only six can be said to be expressing unequivocal revolutionary sympathies, the smallness of the movement is even more apparent.

The message of these figures would certainly seem, then, to support the contemporary Communist dissatisfaction. But one may at this point legitimately ask whether they were perhaps expecting too much. Indeed, a closer examination of some of the factors that help to explain this smallness will also show that if the movement was of limited size it was, all things considered, certainly not humiliatingly so. In the first place, one has to take account of the dimensions of the Communist movement itself. That there was, as has been said, a significant increase in the Party's ranks throughout the thirties, and particularly a significant increase in the number of intellectuals, is undeniable, but it also remains true that viewed in the context of the British political scene, and compared with the gains of overseas parties, this increase was still embarrassingly unspectacular. Winning only one parliamentary seat during the decade—that of Willie Gallacher in 1935—the Party failed completely to break through to the large mass of the working class, or even, for that matter, to a considerable proportion of the intellectuals. It is not within the scope of this study to examine the reasons for this fully, but one can say with confidence that among the reasons are the comparatively unrevolutionary tradition of British politics over the previous two hundred and fifty years, the absorbing presence of the British Labour Party, and the important fact that for all the sporadic violence and the very real misery, statistics coldly tell us that Britain suffered least of all the industrial nations at the time of the Depression. The violence was confined to a few scattered outbursts, the misery limited to manageable proportions. Sullen discontent, rather than revolutionary gestures, remained the dominant feeling of the thirties. The large mass of British voters, in fact, remained solidly unrevolutionary, plumping either for the ruling right-wing 'National' Government, or for the battered, but still formidable, Labour Party—which cherished no theories about literature and politics.[33] One must not exaggerate the difference between the British and American Parties—the American Communists, after all, remained a minority group within their own sphere—and nor is it meant to be suggested for one moment that paid-up Party members are the final reflection of a Party's influence, but the fact that the Communist Party of Great Britain's 2555 members at the beginning of the thirties had reached only 15570 by 1938,[34] whereas the American Party had increased from 7000 to a claimed 75000 in these eight years,[35] is at least some indication of their *comparable* importance. It was not for nothing that a Russian Central Committee member, Manuilsky, complained in March 1939, that the British Party was one 'of the most backward sections of the Comintern'.[36]

What this situation meant in more specifically literary terms was that the American Party, because of the far more widespread, violent, and totally involving nature of the American Depression,[37] attracted to it from the start a far larger proportion of the intellectual ranks of the middle class. And, even more significantly, it meant that the American revolutionary novel received an initial snowballing impetus—again in the main existing because of the very shattering nature of the Depression—from a succession of distinguished fellow-travellers and a proliferating network of literary clubs and magazines: an impetus that was almost totally lacking in Britain.

At the beginning of the decade, indeed, the American Party could already point to such famous writers as John Dos Passos and Theodore Dreiser as sympathisers, and many others were soon to join the list. The Party also had committed in sympathy to it both a literary magazine, *New Masses*, 'which was self-consciously prepared to act its role as a catalytic agent for the combination of literature and revolution',[38] and an organization, the John Reed Club, to 'clarify the principles and purposes of revolutionary art and literature, to propagate them, to practise them'.[39] Together the magazine and the Club sent six delegates to the Kharkov Conference of Revolutionary Writers in 1930, and by 1934 there were thirty such clubs in America, many of them with their own publications which were training grounds for potential proletarian novelists.[40] The British Party, on the other hand, as we have seen, started the decade with no established writers openly sympathetic to it. It was, it is true, within two or three years to have the somewhat doubtful support of a number of rebellious young poets, such as W. H. Auden, C. Day Lewis, and Stephen Spender, but certainly no novelist of any distinction emerged until Grassic Gibbon's completion of *A Scots Quair* in 1934. Nor—and the two factors are inextricably interwoven—did the Party have any adequate literary machine for some years.[41] It managed to scrape together enough financial support to start a daily newspaper in 1930, the *Daily Worker*, but its intellectual supporters were not able to set up any properly literary organ—if one excepts the short-lived *Storm* and *Viewpoint*—until late 1934, and by the time this, the *Left Review*, was properly established, the wave of enthusiasm for the proletarian novel was half over. Victor Gollancz's *Left Book Club* was established in 1936, and was soon able to provide the Communists and other Socialists with a captive audience reaching 50000,[42] it is true, but as its actual book choices were almost exclusively confined to non-fiction, it was still hardly of any great direct help to the aspiring revolutionary novelist. Much more helpful was the best of all left-wing magazines, John Lehmann's *New Writing*,[43] which gave encouragement to such middle-class writers as Edward Upward and Rex Warner, and such working-class writers as George Garrett and Leslie Halward. But even this magazine's usefulness to the revolutionary literary movement in Britain had its limitations, for although Lehmann vowed to exclude all writers of 'reactionary or Fascist sentiments',[44] he certainly did not confine his material to the politically orientated, and, moreover, he gave up much of the space to foreign contributors.

As if this lack of plentiful 'training-grounds' and of any real conscious-ness that they were part of an inexorably advancing movement were not enough discouragement, there is the subsidiary point that the Spanish

Civil War—which saw the height of *intellectual* left-wing involvement—
lent itself far more to the immediacy of poetry than to the length of the
novel. It was necessary, in the urgency of the moment, to say things
quickly; poems were needed like bullets. It was also possible for the poet at
home to write of his generalised support of the war without getting
involved in too many awkward matters of detail. As Julian Symons says of
'Spain' by W. H. Auden—who did actually spend two months in Spain
while the Civil War was raging[45]—'it is a poem, one is bound to say, which
might have been written by a man who had never set foot in Spain',[46] and
so on a much lower level of achievement the bloodthirsty generalisations
embodied in such poems as Jack Lindsay's 'On Guard for Spain'[47] also
passed muster amongst a number of people at the time.[48]

Other difficulties, cited by the potential revolutionary novelists themselves, were in part aggravated by the peculiar British situation, in part
shared by their American colleagues. A few found political activities
severely restricting their output: Ralph Fox, for example, apparently had
many literary projects, but little time to complete them,[49] Charlotte
Haldane abandoned novel writing altogether,[50] while Edward Upward's
long silence during the thirties indicated difficulties confirmed in the
ending of *Journey to the Border* (1938).[51] There was a very real fear, too—
and with some justification when one considers the size of the Communist
movement—that the completely revolutionary posture would lose them
their audience altogether. As C. Day Lewis expressed it: 'The middle
classes . . . [the young Marxist writer's] main financial support, are not
likely to go on supporting him once they perceive that his work is
undermining their own security of mind and estate'.[52] Clearly, if a writer
has something to say he will consider it worth saying to an audience of one,
but nonetheless it must have been dampening to have 'the feeling that the
people who had money didn't want to read what one wanted to
write . . .'.[53]

Many a potential working-class writer might well have retorted that it
was lucky 'one' had the leisure or ability to write at all; and, indeed, their
educational and material limitations were again frequently a very real
handicap. The most common difficulty, however, was that usually cited by
the middle-class writer: his lack of knowledge of his heroes and of the
conditions in which they lived. It was a difficulty shared in part by the
American novelist, although the far less rigid class-structure and the more
universally involving depression and violence made the difficulty less
intense. To many a British writer the problem of vitalising a creed which
worshipped the proletariat—when one knew neither the proletariat nor
the social conditions under which they suffered—seemed at times
overwhelming. Unable or unwilling in most cases to take the complete step
and cross over into the ranks of the workers, to 'work, eat and sleep with
them',[54] they teetered uneasily, searching for a compromise.

We were like those neurotics who cannot cross a road; one step from the security of the pavement into the road and we retreated. And on the pavement, we argued, was the material of our art. All that we knew was the middle-class society which we denounced; we couldn't leave it, any more than the scarabaeus can leave its ball of ordure. So in the fear of losing the old material of our art, we never acquired new material.[55]

But of course this problem was in truth but one aspect of the old problem of the incorporation of ideology into art, and as such was shared by all writers, irrespective of their background. It was the problem faced by the pre-thirties Socialist writers, too, but now with a creed comprising far more wide-ranging, revolutionary, and at the same time more dogmatic articles of belief, it had clearly acquired new dimensions. If, for example, Richard Whiteing's failure to exhibit any real concern for or knowledge of the working classes vitiated the final effect of his novel, at least he was under no obligation to convey the idea that they as a class held the key to the future; nor even in the final resort is this Robert Tressell's aim. Exactly how the revolutionary writers set about their task—of translating into human terms a set of dogmatic beliefs (with little more at hand to most of them than the intractable material of a basically unrevolutionary Britain)—will be examined in the following chapters; if few of them succeed, the difficulties facing them should not be forgotten.

6 A Decent Working-Class Upbringing

I

The writer emerging from a stratum outside the middle and upper classes was no nineteen-thirties phenomenon, but he certainly figured more prominently in British literature, and particularly in prose writing, than hitherto. This new prominence is reflected in the revolutionary novel, where just under half of the books were written by those whose upbringing and backgrounds—while varying from the farms of Scotland (James Barke) to the East End of London (Simon Blumenfeld)—were all demonstrably different from the traditional conception of the British bourgeois intellectual.

It has already been implied that these writers with their presumably greater awareness of social hardship, and, more importantly, in the case of those from the towns, their knowledge of proletarian life and conditions, were blessed with an advantage denied to most of their middle-class colleagues. What remains to be seen is whether they had the ability or skill to capitalise their experiences and breathe some life and conviction into their beliefs.

II

One group of these writers came up with an appealingly simple solution to the artistic problems facing them: drawing in part upon their own very individual experiences, in part upon sensational stories of detection and love, they heightened and dramatised the lives of their worker-heroes with liberal layers of romance and suspense, and then dosed the whole, when they remembered, with the political message. Perhaps the most extreme, the most disastrous example of this can be found in a book which appeared towards the beginning of the thirties, A. P. Roley's *Revolt* (1933). A verbal cartoon strip rather than a novel, *Revolt* has for its background the creation of the British Communist Party in 1920, and the industrial problems in the following two years. Undistinguished in style, construction, or characterisation, it is nonetheless a useful compendium of many of the faults that were to dog later attempts at proletarian fiction—with its failure to integrate the personal with the political, its dour, heavy-handed humour, its insistence that all things bourgeois were bad, and finally its signal failure to convince the reader of the necessity and validity of the political message.

Its hero is an ex-soldier, Jud Bacon, who in 1919 finds work at the docks and then as a passenger-porter in a Northern town. Appointed a delegate to the local Trades and Labour Council, he eagerly reads some Communist tracts lent to him by another delegate, Newsome. No sooner has he been converted, however, than Newsome leaves him to go to London to help in the formation of the British Communist Party. Jud now virtually steps into another story, finding himself first involved with an Irish girl called Kitty, and then trapped by Donovan, a Government agent, into being caught carrying what he believes are guns for the Irish revolutionaries. To his bewilderment he is accused of having taken part in a robbery and is placed on trial, where the foreman, 'As a staunch waver of the Union Jack . . . was determined to see justice, the right kind, of course, meted out to this Irish-cum-Bolshevik agitating disturber of the peace . . . Mr Forsdyke had, to assist him in this matter of "Justice", amongst others, Messrs Jones, Smith, Brown, and Robinson, all worthy, pot-bellied representatives of that triumph of modern democracy, the British Bourgeoisie . . .'[1]

Emerging from nine months' imprisonment, Jud finds that he has first to justify his anarchistic actions before a Communist Court: a court composed this time of 'simple men and women from the same ranks of life as himself'.[2] He is exonerated, given a job as an unemployment organiser, and rewarded by the author with Kitty. He is soon involved in tragedy, however. A large demonstration of unemployed men that he has organised is clubbed down by the police as it is about to enter the Art Museum: '"An' you know, Hilda, my poor arm got tired with banging them about, an' I split my baton on somebody's shoulder. But, by Jesus! it was a wonderful day." Police-constable Witherton stretched his legs out full length on the couch, and sipped noisily at his cup of tea. Police-constable Witherton was tired, he had helped to oppose the terrible menace of Red revolution inside the Art Museum, and was a hero.'[3] In the ensuing confusion Kitty is run over by a taxi, and, before concluding a deathbed marriage with Jud, tells him that she had previously been Donovan's mistress.

It is now 1922, and Jud is delegated to lead one group of hunger-marchers to London. The book again bursts at the seams as Irish terrorists cross the pages, pursuing and ultimately murdering Donovan. Jud is implicated, and Newsome, sadly telling him that he is in danger of becoming an anarchist, arranges his escape. The book closes as Jud, vowing that he will carry on the work, boards a ship under a covering identity. It is only with an effort of will that one remembers that the hero is in fact a Communist, dedicated to the overthrow of this society.

In his naive, essentially humourless caricatures of the bourgeoisie and its representatives, Roley arouses irritation rather than laughter—and so it is with too many of the left-wing books of the thirties. Satire is used with notable success only by Grassic Gibbon in *A Scots Quair*; and even here in the third volume he shows a predilection for punching holes in cardboard dummies. While hardly agreeing with Harry Kemp and Laura Riding that 'One of the chief disadvantages of being a Communist must be that you miss many good jokes',[4] intended successful humour is undoubtedly at a premium in these books: too often their authors substituted abuse for satire, or ventured into a deprecating humour with an embarrassing air of 'you see we are human after all'. They were not helped, it is true, by the attitude of their colleagues: when the ex-weaver and Communist Councillor William Holt made light fun of the first Communist meeting attended by the hero of his novel *Backwaters* (1934), E. Woolley in the *Daily Worker* pointed out primly: 'The featuring of the Communist Party is not good, as Holt, while correctly satirising the language which the weavers cannot understand, tends too much to belittle the Party. A Party member reading this part will note it, but the reader who has not been in association with our Party will probably draw the wrong conclusions'.[5]

This 'reader' would have probably drawn far worse conclusions from other parts of *Backwaters*: for Holt, apart from this scene and a few other deft touches of humour, almost completely ignores the opportunity for social satire as his semi-picaresque hero moves from one class to another. Relying, indeed, on the same uneasy mixture of adventure and romance with political trimmings as *Revolt* (and initially apparently leaning heavily on *Tono-Bungay* for plot), *Backwaters* details the wanderings of one Joseph Stone, a frustrated warehouse assistant who has dreams: '"I've got an appetite here somewhere" (he thumped his breast) "and all I get is food for here" (he thumped his stomach), "like an animal"'.[6] After being presented by an alcoholic analyst with a formula for hardening leather, he soon finds himself, assisted by a less scrupulous businessman, in control of a large and flourishing business. He abandons his working-class girlfriend, Mary Simpson, and marries Thelma, a stockbroker's daughter. A paper-thin caricature of an upper-class girl, she ends their honeymoon abruptly because, as she says: 'I like to live and go about in English society . . . Not necessarily in England because often English society goes out of England; but Deauville, Estoril, Wiesbaden, somewhere where one feels in touch with things. Civilisation. Hearing the very latest. Seeing the best and smartest in dress'.[7]

Wealth, married life, and the tactics necessary for survival in the business world soon pall, and Joseph, after settling all his fortune on his wife, departs for the sawmills and lumber-camps of Canada. But he still finds himself restless and dissatisfied, and so he returns once more to England, to the arms of Mary Simpson—who has, unknown to him, meanwhile borne his child—and to the mills of the north. Despite an initial unsatisfactory contact with the Communists, when he fails to understand a word of their jargon, he buries himself in the Marxist classics and in a short while: 'The philosophy of Marx had taken hold of Joseph's imagination. The idea of the teeming millions of the world's working people, the property-less multitudes of the earth, the proletariat, breaking through the bonds of bourgeois society and building a new world of production for use instead of profit, appealed to him'.[8] Unfortunately it fails to appeal to the other workers, and although Joe has initial success in persuading some girls to go on strike, the strike soon collapses. Depressed and unemployed as he is, the book ends on a note of optimism, as Joe tells his wife that 'It is our problem, and it is we working people who must solve it'.[9]

In Holt's descriptions of the sawmills of Canada and the looms of Yorkshire, his writing comes to life: he is drawing direct from the experiences he later described in his autobiography *I Haven't Unpacked* (1939). But the book as a whole is mechanical and contrived, and the Marxism almost an afterthought. Indeed, like that of the hero of *Revolt*, Joseph's conversion is completely unconvincing, and he remains at the end very much a maverick, with no suggestion of Party discipline being imposed upon him.[10] Fundamentally *Backwaters* is, as has already been said, another attempt to hang a few rags of ideology onto a body of romance and adventure, and the same applies—for all their greater number of Marxist slogans—to Jim Phelan's *Ten-a-Penny People* (1938) and Simon Blumenfeld's *Jew Boy* (1935). *Ten-a-Penny People*, for example, written with a crude vitality reminiscent of some of the 'tough' American proletarian novels, is clotted with class-hatred and Communist slogans, but so absorbing are its intricate romances and its involved cases of mystery and murder that one tends not to treat the political implications too seriously. Set mainly in the Manchester shipbuilding firm of Gannet and Swon, it tears along at a breakneck pace, featuring numerous Communists, Fascist bosses, a traitorous trade-unionist, three romances, violent clashes between police and strikers, an attempted suicide, nine deaths, and finally as a climax the trial for murder of an innocent man, Tom Rogan, the Communist hero of the book. 'Fascism knows the Tom Rogans are its death—and Fascism from here to Kobe wants Tom killed',[11] comments his wife, and as they look at the jury, their fears are realised: 'Dull, heavy, stout of face for the most part, the majority of the men bore the stamp of prosperity, the hallmarks of ownership. Even in the first minutes of the trial, there was an expression of calm certitude on more than one face as they looked at the man who menaced property'.[12] But Tom's brother, Dick, who closely resembles him, falsely claims at the last minute that he is the guilty one, and, rather than serve a life-sentence he is facing for robbery-and-assault, is happy to go to the gallows in Tom's place. The Communist leader is freed to carry on the good work, there is an upsurge of bright hopes, and the book ends with a series of staccato conversations registering the moral:

' . . . Seen about Tom Rogan?'

'Yes. Bloody fine. You used to work at Gannet and Swon's, didn't you.'

'Um. Learnt me a bit about the Labour movement, *and* the Fascist movement, up there.'

'From Rogan and the boys, eh?'

'No, from Gannet and Swon.'

'Ha, ha, ha. So long, Lenox. See you in the big days. The big days, eh. . . .'[13]

Phelan—a former Irish tramp, IRA member, and reprieved murderer[14]—would certainly seem to be trying to carry out with a vengeance part of the spirit of Edward Upward's advice to the Marxist writer: '. . . a good book is one that is true not merely to a temporarily existing situation but also to the future conditions which are developing within that situation'.[15] For *Ten-a-Penny*'s numerous Communist workers and its equation of the bosses with Fascism was indeed a futuristic—and optimistic—look at Lancashire: the true situation was that Lancashire, and Manchester particularly, strenuously resisted Communist penetration, probably, according to Henry Pelling, 'owing to the strength of Catholic and Orange sympathies among the workers. Indeed, if any totalitarian creed stood a chance of adoption by the Lancashire workers, it was likely to be Fascism'.[16]

Utopianism—and sheer bad writing—apart, ultimately all the books so far discussed are failures because their political message tends to be lost in a welter of generally improbable incident, and one is inclined not to take what the authors are saying too seriously. It reflects perhaps a confusion in their own minds. This is especially noticeable in the exuberant but at times preposterously melodramatic *Jew Boy*, a novel set in the Jewish tailoring district of the East End of London. The author, Simon Blumenfeld, a tailor's presser himself, was one of a number of talented angry young Jewish writers then emerging from the East End. The poverty around them, combined with the sight of Mosley's rampaging hooligans, made the adoption of Communism or some form of Socialism inevitable. But if Blumenfeld's own views were clear, he certainly does not communicate this clarity to his naive, rebellious young hero, whose beliefs seem now a reaction against antisemitism:

. . . all that bigotry would crumble away when workers ruled the land. Jews wouldn't be lumped together as financiers and bolsheviks. Nor would they be pointed out like tame zoological specimens by tolerantly superior Anglo-Saxons. . . . Under the rule of the proletariat Jews would have the same rights as other workers. In Russia, anti-semitism was a crime[17];

now a rationalisation of his own frustrations, as when, envying his friend Dave's ability to pick up women, he moralises that,

> He had to be steadfast, a class-conscious proletarian, but it was hard.... And the only way to restore the balance was a mistress . . . though here economics came in. Always in the way. Another major defect of the damned system![18]

and now a hypocritical conscience-appeasing gesture:

> Some people had nothing better to do with themselves. They were not concerned with the fight for bread. Slaves existed to struggle for them, and they had nothing better to think about other than the pleasures of the flesh . . . But maybe some of those poor devils couldn't help themselves either. Perhaps the very same forces that drove these girls on the streets were responsible for twisting their desires. . . . Back of everything, always, he came up with a bump against that solid wall, economics. What was the use of scratching on the surface? Take away the root cause of all the trouble, and most other difficulties would adjust themselves[19]

(he muses, before being seduced by a prostitute).

It will be shown later, however, that confusion of motives is certainly not confined to these books. It occurs in many of the radical novels of the thirties; in some cases the confusion is consciously exploited for artistic ends, in others it remains unconscious, usually marring the validity of the message.

III

Three other writers whose origins were in the working class, Harold Heslop, James Barke, and John Sommerfield, made more strenuous— though not necessarily more successful—attempts to integrate ideology within the body of their work, by constructing some kind of artistic pattern from their beliefs. The first of these writers, Harold Heslop, a former miner, proclaimed his allegiance to the world revolutionary movement in 1930 at the Kharkov Writers' Conference, but his only revolutionary novel, *Last Cage Down*, did not appear until 1935. His previous books, written in a prose style as rough-hewn as a coal face, had shown a somewhat confused attitude to politics. *Goaf* (his first work,[20] but not published in Britain till 1934) and *The Gate of a Strange Field* (1929) both deal with miners and politics in the north of England (the 'gate' of the latter book was the 1926 General Strike[21]) but are so full of bitterness towards the present Labour Party and Trade Union politics that little of a constructive nature emerges, beyond a vague nostalgia for the past, purer values of the Labour Movement.[22] *Journey Beyond* (1930) deserts the world of mining and politics, and describes the depression tribulations of Russell Brent, an ex-bookshop assistant, who learns nothing beyond, as his wife expresses it: 'I suppose we're all for ourselves in this world?'.[23]

On the surface anyway, *Last Cage Down*—while written in little more sophisticated a style—seems to leave all this mainly negative revolt behind, and comes down squarely and firmly on the side of the Communists. Heslop takes as his pattern the disastrous personal and public effects of the actions of an individualistic mining leader, Joe Cameron, contrasting them with the constructive Marxist-orientated tactics of a Communist leader, Joe Frost. While the personal vendetta of Cameron against Tate, the colliery agent, leads to the former's imprisonment on a charge of threatened assault, his mother's eviction from their home and his replacement as Secretary of the local Miners' Union by a boss's 'yes-man', Joe Frost is quietly hovering in the background, urging that Cameron forget his personal quarrel and think of the men, organising a soup-kitchen for the striking miners and regaling them with descriptions of his visits to the USSR:

> They *saw* a host of men and women pouring out their simple toil upon a gigantic construction, which, when completed, was going to change the entire nature of the Ukraine. They saw men and women performing a useful job of work without the weary haggling after so may extra farthings a shift. They scrambled about the huge structure of steel and concrete watching men trampling great masses of concrete into the mould, building socialism with simple tools—feet, hands, concrete and steel.[24]

When Cameron emerges from prison and sees the disastrous results of all his actions, he realises how right Joe Frost has been all along in urging him to think of the mass rather than the individual, and as an unemployed man, sees the reason for the Communists' insistence upon the organisation of the unemployed. '. . . *for the unemployed were that part which capitalism could not go on governing in the old way*. . . . To organise the unemployed meant to come to grips with capitalism, and that would never have done because capitalism had stuffed the whole Labour Movement into its coat pocket and marched off with it.'[25] Frustratingly powerless, denied leadership in the union, he is unable to stop the opening of a new unsafe coal seam, and it is ironically his brother who is the first to die when the roof of the seam collapses. As a final harsh blow the mine is closed, just one 'part of this great crisis-wracked system'.[26] The book ends on a note of grim resolve, as the miners realise that all that is left to do is to go on fighting the boss.

For all the note of conviction, one feels two aspects of Heslop's beliefs struggling throughout this book. One side sees satisfaction only in the mass struggle of the proletariat, while the other, fighting incongruously and apparently unconsciously through on many occasions, is far more interested in men as men, divorced from political beliefs and actions. One feels with Heslop—as indeed one feels with all the writers so far discussed—that he would probably be happier in an apolitical world, that he has virtually imposed a political burden upon himself. This dichotomy is seen in *The Gate of a Strange Field* when the hero, Joe Tarrant, is in London as a delegate to the meeting which decides to call a General Strike. Joe Tarrant, Heslop tells us, is 'thrilled as never before' by the prospect of a General Strike, but his actions confusingly indicate he is far more interested in renewing acquaintances with his long-separated wife.[27] In *Last Cage Down* Jim Cameron is meant to represent the disastrous effect of anarchistic action, but in fact the character runs away with his creator, and as an individual rebel, morosely brooding on the death of his father and irritated at Joe Frost's call for organisation and leadership, is a far more powerful and more interesting character than the tamed rebel he becomes.[28] Possibly realising this, Heslop belatedly tries to turn Joe Frost into a hero, but he is a poor substitute, and the latter part of the book limps disappointingly. Similarly, the villain, Tate, is meant to be a representative of the boss class, but he emerges more as the archetypal villain, interested in evil for its own sake: '. . . he was an evil person. His mind was evil. It smelled. Words became putrid when he uttered them. . . . He was one of those people who oozed out of the abscess of society'.[29] His ancestry seems to owe more to *The Red Barn* than to the *Communist Manifesto*.

There is a somewhat more developed use of contrasts in the books by the two other authors mentioned—*Major Operation* (1936) by the Scottish novelist James Barke,[30] and *May Day* (1936) by John Sommerfield—although here the contrast is between the proletariat and the bourgeoisie, rather than between the Communist and the individualist. Set in Glasgow, Barke's novel describes the descent into bankruptcy of a middle-class businessman, his conversion by a Communist unemployment leader, Jock Mackelvie, his temporary weakening from his new faith, and then his final hardened resolve as he heroically and fatally throws himself in front of a police-horse to protect Mackelvie. The contrasting scenes between proletariat and bourgeoisie in the first half of the book, the bourgeois' initial contact with the proletariat in the common ward of the City Hospital and the symbolic and actual major operation[31] from which he emerges a new man was a potentially interesting pattern, but the writing is too slipshod, the characterisation (especially of MacKelvie) too improbable, and the ideology too naively and aggressively obtrusive for this potential to be realised. One longs for a devil's advocate, especially during the hospital scenes, as Anderson the businessman wilts before MacKelvie's trite arguments and finally admits: 'If you're a Red, then I'm a Red. Not such a good Red as you, MacKelvie: I can never hope to be that. But with all my strength, mental and physical, I'm with you'.[32] His mentor,

Jock MacKelvie, the apotheosis of proletarian virtue—morally pure, but sexually attractive; a giant, physically and mentally, among men—intrudes later, as we shall see shortly, in Barke's *Land of the Leal* (1939) and gives a similar air of unreality to the ending of that book. There is an indication, however, that Barke was well aware of the idealised nature of his hero, when he comments after Anderson's conversion:

> Anderson had clarity on many things. But for and of the working-class, in the lump and in the raw, as they were manifest in South Partick, Anderson had no great faith. . . . From considering them abstractly, as a theoretical proletariat—the advance guard of history—to seeing them as men and women standing around corners, living in squalid tenements, drinking in mean and horrible public houses, going to football matches and dog racing . . . this brought confusion and an element of despair to Anderson.[33]

In *May Day*, the other book contrasting the workers and the bourgeoisie, the working-class characters are rather less idealised. It is only by implication, by contrast with the bourgeoisie, that they seem to possess most of the virtues. And this is true of the majority of the books that have as major characters members of the proletariat. There are few Ernest Everhards; it is usually the intrusion of the bourgeoisie or their representatives—who are seen as thoughtless, vicious, or corrupt—that makes the fallibilities of the working class seem very unimportant. What is notable, however, is that the latter's general level of militancy would hardly seem to be typical of the period—and it is perhaps to make this aspect more plausible that John Sommerfield has set his novel of Communist agitation in London (his only novel of the thirties[34]) 'a few years' in the future.

May Day concentrates on two things: capitalism (represented here by the giant firm of AIE) moving into its final phase, as it engulfs more and more of the smaller firms and assumes more openly the characteristics of Fascism; and the concomitant growing militancy of the workers. Imposing a collective (but certainly not objective) vision on the three days up to and including May Day, Sommerfield moves swiftly and quite excitingly from character to character, class to class, in small contrasting scenes, until the final climactic episode when the workers hold a successful but violence-torn demonstration in the centre of London. Apart from the growing momentum of the Communist agitation and preparation for May Day, other events and characters bind the book and give it whatever unity it possesses. James Seton, for example, returning after a long absence in Spain, spends the three days searching for his brother, John, who works at Langfier's factory. After resolving to return to Communist activities, he finally catches sight of John at the May Day demonstration, but is crushed to death by a police-horse as he runs to meet him. John, too, we see glimpses of throughout the book, and learn of his growing conviction that the Communists have truth on their side. Ivy Cutford, a young Communist factory worker at Langfier's, very lonely in her squalid little room with its picture of Lenin and its *Daily Worker* calendar, has her moment of triumph, when, following an accident, she seizes the moment to propose that Langfier's form a factory committee. In contrasting scenes we are shown such bourgeois characters as Sir Edwin Langfier, still clinging on to his ownership of Langfier's, but worried about the rapacious designs of AIE and its cynical attitude towards the workmen. The latter are never far from the background of his thoughts, 'their half-visioned faces pale, dumb, and resentful, hating him for their hard work and little wages, seeing his imagined greed in every accident, the cause of every one of those factory-maimed and broken lives. They worked under an invisible whiplash, and thought him the giver of their pain'.[35] But while Langfier is presented with some sympathy this is certainly no sign of objectivity on Sommerfield's part, for it is soon quite obvious that he is deliberately reserving his attack for the representatives of the 'fascist' stage of capitalism, the members of AIE, and in particular for their delegate to Langfier's board, Dartry, who is shown as vicious, cynical, lecherous, and nearly impotent to boot. Nor do any other of the workers' enemies fare much better.

One's complaint, however, is not with the weighted attack, but with the manner of attack: for once more facile abuse is all too often substituted for satire. Clearly with so many characters—and there are dozens more than those mentioned—given equal prominence, one cannot expect very fully rounded portraitures; but one can legitimately expect more subtle comments on people's habits than, for example, Sommerfield's on middle-class tea: 'not the strong and cheerful drink of common people, but a pale, an ethereal Chinese distillation at six bob the pound',[36] or more probing summations than his dismissal of a Labour MP as a 'quite stupid . . . opinionated old man who got four hundred a year to help rule the country'.[37] But then Sommerfield's whole attitude to his characters is somewhat dubious. Consider for example his self-betraying comment on some female factory workers: 'These silly girls with their synthetic Hollywood dreams, their pathetic silk stockings and lipsticks, their foolish strivings to escape from the cramped monotony of their lives, are the raw material of history'.[38] This kind of remark occurs far too often in this well-constructed and readable book, reminding us sharply that these people are not people but simply ideological chessmen, and all Sommerfield's manipulative skill is unable to turn them into anything else. He has in this sense gone to the other extreme from *Last Cage Down*.

IV

In all the books so far discussed in this chapter there has been little attempt to convince the reader of the inevitability of Socialism, of its historic necessity. Characters are either Communists when the book opens, or become so after a short testing period, with very little real weight behind their decision: certainly the reader is left with almost no consciousness of Socialism as being part of the dialectic of history. It was partly in an attempt to show something of this historical weight that three writers— Lewis Jones, James Barke, and Grassic Gibbon—chose, not to return wholly to the past, but at least to extend the time-period of their novels, to show some of the economic, political, and social processes at work behind the thirties.

Lewis Jones's declared aim in *Cwmardy* (1937) and *We Live* (1939) was to 'novelise' a period of working-class history from about 1890 to 1936, as it was seen from the Welsh mining valley of Cwmardy. 'Cwmardy' is a thin disguise for the Rhondda, one of the most depressed far-left areas in Britain during the thirties,[39] and a scene throughout this century of some of the most bitter working-class struggles. Indeed most of the events that Jones describes can in fact be found in the trade union histories of the period— although he does take liberties with time, place, and on occasions, he is not averse to embellishing the facts. In the foreword to *Cwmardy*, Jones—who was first a miner, and then a Communist organiser in this area[40]—insists that the work is 'really collective, in the sense that my fellow workers had to fight the battles I try to picture, and also in the sense that I have shamefully exploited many comrades for incidents, anecdotes, typing, correcting and the multifarious details connected with writing'.[41] This should not be taken to mean that the books have any of the machine-made qualities of some recent American epics: on the contrary, though extremely amateurish in style and construction, both books do have an awkward passion and sincerity—especially in the descriptions of the accidents and the working conditions in the mines.

Cwmardy deals with the boyhood of Len Roberts, his first horrifying days in the mine, and his growing feeling of revolt against this sytem. When a more educated friend lends him some books on Parliamentary Socialism, he is ripe for conversion. He takes an increasing interest in mining politics, an interest which is particularly fostered by the Miners' Strike of 1910. This long-drawn-out strike, in which the miners find themselves savagely battling first the police and then the troops called in to quell the disturbance (so savagely, in fact, that Len's father thinks he is back in the Boer War, and salutes the miners' leader, Ezra, before coming to his senses), rises to a bloody climax with the shooting of eleven miners: 'In the long, deathly silence that followed the volleys one of the shot men rolled with weak, funny squirms, over on his side. His fingers tore into the roadway as, with infinite slowness, he twisted his head and looked at the dumbstruck mass of people. A geyser of hot blood squirted from his neck and sent thin veins of steam into the still air'.[42] With the coming of the War, Len's feelings are clarified, as he reflects that, only a short while

before, the soldiers had been just as intent on killing the miners as they are
now the Germans. The book ends with a conversation between Len, Ezra,
and his daughter Mary, in which the Russian Revolution and the success of
their prewar strikes are cited as examples of what the workers can do if only
they take their destiny in their hands.

We Live takes up the story from 1921; Len is now married to Mary, and
has just joined the Communist Party. A large strike sees only the
Communists holding out, as Ezra, the Parliamentary Socialist—who, it
should be noted, is treated sympathetically—leads the men back to work.
This, and the protracted miners' struggle after the General Strike,
persuades Mary that Communism is the only solution. Both she and her
husband now become actively engaged on behalf of the Party: Mary as a
local Communist Councillor and Len as an unemployment organiser.
Their lives are truly 'Party lives': as they discuss their failure to have
children, 'Len caught her arm and pressed it to his body. "Never mind,
comrade," he consoled, both himself and her. "If we can't create anything
with our bodies, we can with our minds and the work we do for the
Party"'.[43] When the Spanish Civil War starts, Len is chosen by the Party
to go out to Spain. His last message tells Mary that 'Fascism may kill us . . .
but it can never kill what we die for. No, never! Our very death is creation,
our destruction new life and energy and action. . . . Sleep happy in the
knowledge that our lives have been class lives, and our love something
buried so deep in the Party that it can never die'.[44] He is in fact shortly
afterwards killed on the battlefield, but Mary chooses to go on fighting at
home. We last see her in a workers' procession greeting the returning
Spanish Brigade, and the book ends with the strains of the Red Flag.

This tenuous plot does little to hide the true heroes of *Cwmardy* and *We
Live*—the miners; and it is their work and their violent strikes that
dominate the books and give them whatever unity they possess. Jones had
few, if any, of the novelist's gifts: his style is overstrained and littered with
dead metaphors—with lightning that 'cynically' blinds men's eyes, with
thunder that 'wantonly' joins 'in the game' crackling 'unholy
laughter'[45]—his humour is all too often simply embarrassing, and his
conversations are frequently hopelessly staged and artificial. But for all that
his books do have the merit of showing the militancy of Communism
arising inevitably out of the miners' lives, out of what Ezra sums up in a
bleak moment as their 'poverty, struggle, and death'.[46]

Much the same aim—in a different *milieu*—presumably inspired
James Barke in his second revolutionary novel of the decade, *The Land of the
Leal* (1939). Set first in the Scottish farming country in the 1870s, and later
moving to the slums of Glasgow, Barke's novel has many superficial
resemblances, in structure and subject matter rather than in quality, to
Grassic Gibbon's *A Scots Quair*. Indeed logic might well have dictated a
consideration of the latter work at this stage, were it not for the fact that
Gibbon's peasant background puts him outside of the class struggle, and,

far more importantly, his very considerable achievement can only be properly judged in the light of all the revolutionary novels. A discussion of his work will, therefore, be deferred until the end of this survey of the thirties.

It should be stressed at the outset that *The Land of the Leal*, for all its faults, is a far better novel than *Major Operation*, probably because Barke is dealing for the most part with the working-class farming people of his own childhood.[47] It is essentially the story of two characters: Jean, the daughter of the foreman of a local farm; and David, the son of Andrew Ramsay, stonedyke mason. From his father, from his love of Robert Burns, and from the evidence of his own harsh experiences, David acquires a radicalism which flares but intermittently. At this stage his instinctive antagonism for the 'gentry' is presented in a muted fashion by the author; for example, at the funeral of Sam MacKitteroch, a local schoolmaster, we are told that 'Sir Thomas MacCready who was held up in his carriage by the cortège was indignant when he found out how socially unimportant the corpse was'.[48] Having trained as a dairyman (the occupation of Barke's own father), David marries Jean, and the two of them move from farm to farm, their existence hard and comfortless, their surroundings affording them ample evidence of the ease with which the workers, deprived of security and education, can slip into lives of drunkenness and lechery. Only once does David's radicalism flare into practice, when he tries to organise a small futile strike of farmworkers. Jean, who was 'content to let the rich in some mysterious way govern and dominate',[49] lashes him mercilessly for this revolt, and David, realising that 'He was tied to the drudgery of life, chained by circumstances and his own limitations to work without respite',[50] allows his radicalism to flare no more.

Neither the Boer War nor the First World War have initially much direct effect on the main characters, apart from the fact that David, shocked by Russia's abandonment of her allies in 1917, comes to regard Communism 'as loathsome and corrupt political poison'.[51] After the war, however, the estate they are working on is sold up, and they are forced to move to Glasgow. Here it is that Socialism is first discussed at any length, and although David and Jean are both antagonistic towards it, their son Andrew is soon converted. David, indeed, is unsure whether life has any meaning at all: 'And for what did man live? For a few moments of physical happiness between the cradle and the grave! All activity was as dust in the end. The grass would grow on the Galloway fields when man was no longer there to husband the soil'.[52] Perplexed, only just scraping a living, and seeing no rest this side of the grave, he is finally killed in a car accident. Over his deathbed Andrew and the other son, Tom, argue the validity of religion. Barke's strident doctrinaire side is coming more and more to the fore. He comments: 'It was true that Tom had studied nothing of the materialist philosophy, relying merely upon the pathetic refutations of the idealist apologists. It is true that his approach to the Ultimate Reality was obscured by a mist of mysticism and the self-hallucination of obscurantist poetic word-imagery and thought-concept. But there was no question of his sincerity.'[53]

It is now 1938, and Andrew, whose initial hopes have been shattered by the ineffectualness of the Labour Government and the collapse of the General Strike, finds his old political enthusiasm returning. Hearing Jock MacKelvie, the unemployment leader, speaking on Spain, he volunteers to join the International Brigade. MacKelvie, after gratuitously rebuking him for leaving his union, says he will try to arrange this. Andrew feels exultant: 'He felt that all his life had moved towards the making of this momentous decision. . . . But not only his own life. Now the life of his father and mother might be fulfilled. They had toiled and laboured from the Galloway fields to the city itself—from one century into another. How often had he thought of the senselessness and futility of their days!'[54] The point has been made, but Barke feels the necessity to grind it further in. To Tom, Andrew crudely states the situation: 'The old folks lived a life of slavery—I'm not. They didn't understand: I do. And when I get out there and get a gun in my hands I'm going to wipe off a few scores on their behalf'.[55]

The book crumbles as Barke further riddles it with his harsh and naively expressed dogmatism. After the news of Andrew's death in Spain, Jock MacKelvie—who should have stayed firmly pinned in the glass cage of *Major Operation*—meets up with Tom. The latter, now calling himself a Christian Socialist, but inexplicably speaking at times like a Marxist tract, asks MacKelvie for advice about his 'petty bourgeois' wife. Pompously and arrogantly MacKelvie tells him that 'A decent working-class upbringing is the greatest asset a man can have. I come across a lot of intellectual and bourgeois types. Pretty fine types some of them. But taking them by and large, they're vain, petted and ridiculously childish. They've got to be treated like spoiled children'.[56] Barke tries to retrieve the situation as he gives the last few pages to Jean, daydreaming of her final rest in the land of the leal (a final scene corresponding in some ways to Chris's in *A Scots Quair*, although Jean is allowed no explicit apolitical message), but the damage has been done.

However—although again I would make no claims on behalf of Barke's still somewhat slipshod literary style—for a while it seems he has partially solved the propagandist's problem: the natural and artistic development of the political message. Communism comes in response to the oft-repeated question mark posed by the figures of Jean and David: 'What is the point of our lives? What is the point of our slave-driven existence?' The pity of it is that in his final, almost hysterical eagerness to deliver his message, he drums home with irritating harshness many of the points he has already made with some charity and artistry earlier in the book. Perhaps part of the reason for this is his consciousness of the smaller stature of Andrew and Tom beside their parents, who, dominating the larger part of the book, have inevitably a greater authority. Certainly it springs from some fear that his message will be overlooked. One is reminded—here and elsewhere—that this was the age of repetitious harangues.

v

At one point in Harold Heslop's *Last Cage Down* the name of Dimitroff is invoked by Joe Tarrant in an effort to encourage the miners to struggle more earnestly. The invocation brings a moment of absolute silence:

> It was a moment when the great heroism of one of the noblest creatures in the world stood amongst them, a moment filled with the sweet poignancy which is the workers' share of the joy of the earth. In far-away Leipsig, amongst the howling wolves of the world's worst form of fascism, a barbarous, cruelly anti-semitic hideousness, a pogrom in itself, stood one, a worker, fearless of the headsman's blade poised above his upturned face, defying even the outrageous trumpeting of a maddened Goering. . . .
> Bill Hanson spoke. 'Now that's what I call a man,' he said. . . .
> 'Aye! If we had a few like him on the T.U.C.,' began another, and then he stopped. The spectacle was too wonderful.[57]

If the juxtaposition of Dimitroff and the TUC seems a somewhat bizarre one from our cosy viewpoint in the seventies, it certainly should not blind us to the fact that there was violence and savagery in Heslop's Britain, and that some of the clashes that took place in 1931 and 1935, for example, only just fell short of the uglier disturbances that took place overseas. But the fact remains that the violence had its limitations, and Heslop's book can only end—given the contemporary British situation—in no more re-volutionary a gesture than the decision to 'go on fighting the boss'. *Last Cage Down* was probably completed before the almost universal celebration of King George and Queen Mary's Jubilee in May 1935, and certainly before the ending of the Jarrow Crusade in 1936, when the 200 marchers from blighted Jarrow docilely ate tea and cakes in the House of Commons cafeteria, but Heslop must have been aware—and to some extent communicates this awareness to his book—that revolutionary ideas were anathema to the large majority of the English population.

There was one revolutionary writer of the thirties, however, who was in a peculiarly privileged position to bypass this stubborn reality: he had no need, like Heslop, to invoke more overt class-clashes; nor, like Som-merfield, to pitch his novel into the future; nor, like Phelan, blissfully to anticipate events. For the country which he knew intimately by living and working within it was one from which revolution sprang organically throughout the thirties. The country was Spain and the writer was Ralph Bates.

Born in 1899 into a northern working-class family, apprenticed to a factory at sixteen, Bates had left England for Spain in 1923 and settled in a small fishing village there. Soon he became a professional revolutionary, involved both in the Spanish revolution of 1931, as an organiser of the Spanish dockers, and in the Civil War as a political Commissar in the International Brigade.[58] In addition to these activities he found time to write numerous short stories and poems, a book on Schubert, and two much-praised revolutionary novels, *Lean Men* (1934) and *The Olive Field* (1936). Although both these books are set in Spain, they were at the time an accepted and welcomed part of the English revolutionary literary movement—welcomed to such an extent, indeed, that for a while Bates bid fair to becoming an English André Malraux.[59]

The first of these novels, *Lean Men*, is centred on the abdication of Alfonso XIII in 1931. Francis Charing—an English revolutionary whose love of Spain, of music and of ironwork make it a safe asumption that his character is modelled in the main on Bates himself—is sent out from London by the Comintern to build up a Communist Party in Barcelona. Soon his work meets with some success, and in the few months before Alfonso's abdication he has established amongst the dockers a 'Centre for Free Studies' which he hopes will act as a cover for the eventual establishment of a Communist Party. At this Centre, apart from discussing political matters, they listen to lectures and hear music recitals; they even nourish a workers' poet, Alonso Martinez. Clearly for Bates the Centre partly serves as an illustration of 'what life would eventually be like in a society from which poverty, violence, the ceaseless battle of classes and war had been eliminated, where the spirit might drink as deeply as it wished of knowledge, of art, of music and all things lovely that haunt the tormented spirit of man'.[60]

But Charing's life has its complications. Quite apart from the inherent danger of his position, he also faces other problems: the choice he must eventually make between the two mistresses he has left behind in London, Elizabeth and Lydia; the distracting allurements of sex in Spain; and, at times, doubts about his very faith. An act of anarchism which he wrongly believes has been perpetrated by his followers, leads him to wonder: 'Were the masses worth this effort? This abandonment of comfort, this constant self-denial of peace and natural enjoyment? The things he had learned to love with a profound passion that astonished even himself were music and literature, music before all else . . . And he had sacrificed all that loveliness for the sake of a movement that had collapsed into the excrement of gutters'.[61]

When the elections unwisely held by the Alfonso régime result in an overwhelming Republican victory, and the establishment of a Republican Government, Charing's life is soon even further complicated. Not only is

there great dissatisfaction with the Government, but also intense antagonism between the various left-wing groups and even a split amongst
Charing's followers, some of whom, in opposition to him, want immediate
action. A letter from the International, seemingly dissatisfied with his
tactics, recalls him to Moscow; he decides after much thought that 'For a
revolutionary there was only one thing to do: to keep his place in the battle
proceeding below. It would perhaps mean expulsion from the Party: well,
membership might be regained, but defection from the ranks during the
spiritual agony of a nation would be an affront to conscience too serious to
live down'.[62]

At last, violence does break out, predominantly inspired by the
Anarchists. In the confusion that follows many of Charing's friends and
colleagues are shot. A guard seems to stand between him and safety, but
Charing, who despite his constant exposure to danger has not lost his sense
of the importance of life and death, allows his conscience to persuade him
not to shoot. A few minutes later, the guard's attention is distracted, and he
does make good his escape. He feels he will return again some time. 'A brief
respite, that was all, a little while of love and beauty, Elizabeth, music and
rest, and then he would return. They would expect him. . . . They would
build up the Party, fight again soon, perhaps be defeated, no matter, the
workers would lose every battle but the last.'[63]

There is much to be praised in *Lean Men*. There are some tense and
exciting descriptions of the revolutionaries in action, and there are, apart
from the more complex figure of Charing himself, some fine portraits in
cameo, notably that of Don Gumersind Trepat, the master smithy whose
love of iron and hatred of steel is all-consuming. There is, too, some attempt
to show the force and strength of Catholicism, in the figures of the
revolutionaries Masera and Gerard, both of whom find at crucial moments
that their Communist beliefs are but a veneer over their more deeply
embedded Catholic faith. If this conflict is presented somewhat
superficially—Charing's comment that 'almost the whole of the Church's
apologetic philosophy appears vulnerable to me'[64] is hardly justified by
anything in the text—it is at least there. There is, finally, despite Bates's
somewhat utopian tendency to attribute to his Spanish dockers an
incredible degree of culture and enlightenment, much of the colour and
atmosphere of Spain, in the streets, the nightclubs, and in the occasional
scenes of horrendous poverty.

But overall there remains a sense of confusion. This is undoubtedly
partly owing to the very chaotic nature of the period Bates is writing about.
It is partly owing, too, to his own lack of narrative skill: there are many
disjointed, unrelated episodes and awkwardly contrived elements of
suspense. But more significantly the blame lies with the central and
dominating figure of Charing. He has, as we have seen, some fullness and
complexity, but in the final judgement too much of his motivation remains
unclear and muddled. In the first place the women he has left behind never

emerge with any clarity from his thoughts, and his final decision to marry Elizabeth leaves the reader unimpressed and unmoved. More importantly his attitude towards the revolution is not explored consistently or deeply enough for him ever to become a really believable revolutionary figure. His motives—a love of Spain and its people, a loyalty to international Communism, a sense of order, a feeling for the oppressed, a love of excitement and danger—are at times finely expressed, but constantly conflicting, revealing fundamental discrepancies of which Bates seems hardly aware. In the adventure, for example, that he plunges into very soon after his arrival in Barcelona—the escorting of a Republican leader across the border—he reveals primarily a sense of exhilaration in the sheer danger and unconventional nature of what he is doing. As he and his companions crouch in the darkness watching a train go past,

> A shiver ran down his back, not of cold, for the excitement had thrilled the cold from his body, but of *awareness*, the shiver that he always felt upon encountering a line of great poetry, or in moments of profound music, like those hushed and mysterious chords of awful expectation which are whispered as before a storm in the Trios of the Eroica and the Seventh in A. It was the passing of that lighted train which shook him so. There were human beings, living within the framework of their secure little plans, leaving friends to go home, travelling upon humdrum and practical matters of business, from whose lives the outer terrors of peril and great emotion had been fenced away by conformity and submission, as the darkness of the night lay beyond the steamed windows of the carriages. The orderliness and comfort of the normal world rattled by as they crouched among the cactus, and in that sharp contrast was a significance that only poetry or the sad majesty of music could express.[65]

Earlier, it is true, he had found some practical justification for this excursion, in that it 'would place large numbers of people in debt to him',[66] but he can find no such justification in the escapade that he plunges into a little later, that of helping some strolling players recover their money— 'The best way to excuse it to himself, he decided, was to call it a piece of boyish high spirits, an exaggerated prank'.[67] And yet, only a few pages later, when some members of the Centre want to take the law into their hands, and assassinate a former police gunman, Charing righteously tells them: 'If we strike back we demean ourselves, we become anarchists, tormentors of our class spirituality'.[68] He talks much of the need for order and for a sound and disciplined Party, but when it comes to the point and he is ordered back to Moscow by his superiors, it is the workmen of Spain, 'the rebellious, the loyal men, lean with poverty and consuming thought'[69] who take first place in his decision, and there is little indication that the decision is a particularly hard one to make. Nor is the vexing question of whether such a sensitive and, on occasions, highly moral, man could ever operate in this kind of situation successfully, ever cleared up to the reader's satisfaction. Charing is plunged into agonies of remorse when he shoots a man in self-defence, he finds some nude dancers sexually stimulating but fundamentally degrading, and he firmly refuses to take advantage of a young Communist's proffered virginity, but it never appears to cross his or Bates's mind that much of his own life is based upon deceit and political expediency; that he makes friends with the Republicans only so that he may later use them; that he enlists the support of the State when it suits him; and that his actions are leading towards a bloodbath that he must know will equal any that he has seen so far. Too much of his faith in the final resort is taken for granted, and the conviction of the whole of this intelligently written book inevitably suffers.

Although Bates's second novel, *The Olive Field*, which appeared two years later, is again impaired by a structural weakness, and, as will be seen, a similar failure of the imaginative nerve, it is nonetheless a more solid work, which both makes a greater attempt to understand and portray other faiths, and also more clearly shows Bates's profound love and knowledge of Spain and the Spanish people.

In this book, which opens in 1932 shortly after the establishment of the Republic described in *Lean Men,* the tenuous links with England have been altogether discarded: instead its characters are all representatives of the predominantly rural area of Andalusia, and in particular of the small olive-producing town of Los Olivares. To the inhabitants of this town, the Republic presents different aspects. To Don Fadrique, the owner of the olive fields, it is 'like a knife turning in his mind', [70] an ominous warning of things to come, when death and destruction shall overtake himself and his property. To the rector of Los Olivares, Father Martinez, the Republic is the evil embodiment of the anti-clerical feelings which he sees daily growing stronger. To the massive Don Argote, the virile and domineering manager of the fields, the Republic represents the loss of his political power and the necessity to milk the estate at an even more rapid rate. To the anarchists, particularly Mudarra and Joaquin Caro, and to the Communist Town Secretary, Justin Robledo, the Republic is weak and vacillating, and for all the talk of governmental expropriation of land, life under it seems just as harsh and pitiless as before.

But all—even Don Fadrique at moments—are united in their passion for the olive fields, in their instinctive love of the land. In a very real sense they are rooted in their environment. Caro, for example, approaches his work with love and delicacy, regarding a healthy tree with 'a pleasure he could not have described, for it was not within the power of the olive-workers' terms to describe it'[71]; even as he is on his way to fulfil a dangerous anarchist mission, he has time to stop and examine with disgust a badly cut grove. Don Argote, inspired originally by mercenary motives which flower out into a real passion for the olive, buys books and treatises relating to it in many languages, and as he dies, mistakenly shot by a Civil Guard, images of the tree mingle with the blood and distorted figure of his killer. Father Martinez also is involved with and loves the olives, and for all the growing anti-clericalism, the ceremony involving his benediction of the groves is faithfully observed. Even Don Fadrique, his mind occupied with his dead wife, his passion for music, and his buying of valuable books against the day when he may have to flee, starts thinking of the trees. Momentarily he realises that all he has bought, his planned escape, is as nothing compared with them. 'Even his crowning fortune, the discovery . . . of the missing lute books of Narvaez now seemed cold and insignificant. A little bundle of leather and inked paper, a few phrases of curious and beautiful language, a day of exquisite music against this enduring, accusing army of trees in which was the gravity of God himself.'[72]

But when the workers gather for the olive field harvest, not even this relationship, this 'deeper-than-joy which man feels as the friut of his trees are gathered',[73] can still their discontent when they find that their wages will be lower than in living memory. A spontaneous anarchist uprising takes place, and in a 'wave of exaltation'[74] the 'expropriators' rush from tree to tree, stripping all the fruit, ripe and unripe alike. However, as Justin Robledo has continually prophesied—and it is significant to note that he, one of the only articulate spokesmen for Communism, is pictured as anything but a paragon of virtue—without a Party, without a State to back them up, the anarchists must fail; the revolt dribbles out ineffectually as the workers find that they cannot get the fruit pressed. The ringleaders, who include Mudarra, are subsequently arrested, and in a final brutal attempt to crush dissension, a peaceful delegation of men, women, and children protesting about the arrests is massacred by the Civil Guard. The people of Los Olivares make one silent ominous protest before the Guard barracks house, but after this they

> made no judgments. At the burial of the dead a voice had cried, 'Death to the Civil Guards', and a hiss of condemnation put immediate end to the irreverence; and all that grinding and in-boring silence in the cemetery became a monstrous force to thrust down trivial anger. All that day, as the black, round-backed procession had moved out of the Sevilla Gate to the cemetery above the Huerta, and as the rioters' coffins had been slid into their white-painted pigeon holes in the cemetery wall, it had seemed as if the townspeople, or a mystical entity that included all the past, the present and the future of Los Olivares had willed this. That day the quick passionless singing of the Dies Irae had disclosed its real and quelling horror that escapes recognition at a private and trivial death; when it is but a little black flag fluttering in a sleet wind. It was a chant of sacrifice, a cold chant of enforced submission before the god of death, for all the gods of life, declared the silence around the chant and its own passionless singing, died long ago.[75]

Gradually, however, Los Olivares arises out of its stupor, although not to the life it has known before. For one of the men affected in an indirect way by the massacre is Don Fadrique; as he goes through the possessions of the dead Argote—shot by mistake in the massacre—he learns of the latter's all-consuming passion for the olive tree, and realises that it would be 'disrespect, irreverence'[76] to employ another man in his place. When he shortly leaves, taking with him his money and books, the olive fields, bereft of owner and manager, are allowed to deteriorate. It is this, and the death of his tubercular brother, that persuades Joaquin Caro, now a Communist, that it is time to leave with his family and fiancée to seek a better living in the Asturias mining area. His only regret is that he must leave the fields in this bad state: 'If the trees were abandoned they would put off their own seemly dress and sink back into wildness, the swollen fruit, rich with oil, which man had taught them to bear would shrink into bitter and wooden berries, the thorn and the matted herb would invade and filch all the nourishment and the trees would tinder and die. . . .'.[77]

It is, in fact, in this last quarter of the book, with the scene shifting wholly from Andalusia to the Asturias, that *The Olive Field* itself falters and nearly dies. For the motive behind this sudden and wrenching move is soon only too crudely obvious. The '34 miners' revolt is nearing, and Bates wants Caro and his old friend Mudarra to play prominent parts in it. This they do, Caro as an organiser, and Mudarra as an officer. As the revolt, unsupported by the rest of the country, is drawing to a bloody conclusion, Mudarra, fighting heroically, is captured and hideously tortured to death. Caro tries to persuade the remaining miners to escape: 'They would not; everyone spoke the same thought, "Everything is lost, we never had anything to live for but the Revolution". . . . "One can only die once.". . . "There is no reason in life—this is as reasonable as anything" '.[78] But these are mere words, with no artistic conviction behind them; after the deeply rooted lives of the Andalusians, the revolutionary scenes here, for all their superficial excitement, are rootless, even comic-book stuff, with the animals on one side, the angels on the other. Characters such as the 'Dynamiter' spring up out of nowhere, play their mock-heroic role— ('"The revolution is dead", the Dynamiter answered, and pulled two cartridges of explosive from his waist and examined the fuses. Then he replaced them in his belt, their fuses inclined to the left that they might be easily withdrawn. He patted them gently with a strange smile upon his face and whispered "Yours'll be the last song in this show, dearies."'[79])—and then disappear. There is no sense of involvement; instead we feel disorientated and cheated. It is partly because he too feels a sense of disorientation that Caro, still working for the revolution, decides at the end of the book to return to Andalusia, to the 'solemn olivars beneath the tiger hills of Jabalón'.[80] Life for him is nothing without the olive trees.

Historically, of course, Bates is quite accurate: the people of Andalusia did not arise, and this was primarily why the revolt of the Asturias failed.

Justin Robledo's earlier warning, that the feeble expropriation plans of the Republic would accomplish nothing but the silencing of the country-workers, who would then watch the town-workers 'fight like hell and be smashed to pieces',[81] has been fulfilled. But instead of following this Andalusian passivity to the bitter end, Bates, as we have seen, leaves the olive fields, leaves the solidity and reality he has so painstakingly created, and switches with an almost indecent haste to the Asturias—solely to make the point that for some men at least revolution is the only solution. This final message cannot in consequence be seen as anything other than an intrusion, a sign of a failure of the imaginative nerve which nearly undermines all the careful work that has gone before.

The qualifying word is 'nearly'. If Bates has a limited structural skill, and if, far more importantly, few of his characters linger in the memory, he has in these two interesting and intelligent books contributed something of more than minor distinction to the revolutionary novel. What now remains to be judged, before we can make any overall assessment, is the contribution of his middle-class colleagues, and, finally, that of Grassic Gibbon.

7 The Middle-Class Dilemma

'We're Writing a Book', announced the British novelist Naomi Mitchison in the September 1936 *New Masses*. She went on to tell her presumably bemused readers that she was in fact writing her latest novel under the guidance of a 'Proletarian Committee' assembled for her by a skilled factory worker. '. . . I put it to him as a craftsman that I, as a craftsman, was in difficulties; and he offered to get together a group who would help me and not be shy of me. . . . I read the book aloud and whenever I go badly wrong on details they interrupt and we wrangle about it; if they think I've left something out I can very often put it in there and then . . .'[1]

Miss Mitchison's experiment in collective writing was not a new one— she herself admits that she borrowed the idea from a Russian poet who read his poems aloud to the factory workers in the dinner hour—but it is an indication of the anxiety and solemnity with which many of the left-wing middle-class writers approached their self-appointed task. One can hardly blame them for either of these feelings. If Ralph Bates, for example, for all his experience of revolutionary conditions and revolutionary workers, was not able to effect that final perfect fusion of belief and action, then how was the average middle-class writer to fare, often bereft of first-hand knowledge not only of revolutionary workers but of any workers—or for that matter of the facts of social hardship and privation? He or she could , like Naomi Mitchison, form a Proletarian Committee, or as Storm Jameson suggested, go on periodic, document-gathering excursions into the workers' territory,[2] but whether such measures would spawn anything of real value is another matter. The novel that Miss Mitchison is discussing was never published:[3] but some guidance is afforded by her previous novel, *We Have Been Warned* (1935), which did have the aid of a kind of embryo proletarian committee. The astonishing attitudes and conceptions revealed in this work—which make it read at times more like a contribution to *Punch* than what it is, a painfully honest examination of her own attitudes—make it seem highly unlikely that a fully fledged committee would have helped matters. A book poised uneasily between revolutionary Communism and Labour Party Socialism, *We Have Been Warned* relates how the middle-class heroine, Dione Galton, befriends Donald MacLean, a young Communist workman. When MacLean tells her that he has killed a distant relative of hers, a newspaper proprietor who had been attacking the Communists in his paper, she offers to help him escape by taking him on a planned trip to Russia. Her husband, a Labour Party candidate, is similarly understanding, and agrees to the arrangement. It is soon apparent, once they are on board ship, that Donald is virginal: when Dione wears a swimming costume he can 'scarcely look at her at first; it was like those capitalist papers with the photographs of actresses and that'.[4] Dione is anxious to help him, but is unsure exactly how. 'What does a Socialist woman do?'[5] Eventually she resolves the problem by promising to give her body to him in Russia. '"Mustn't Socialist people be kind to one another? Mustn't we share everything? It's wrong, isn't it, Donald, to be one thing in politics and another in living? I'm trying now to live the same way that I think. How could I leave you all oppressed and bound as you were? . . . I think I am being a good Communist to you, comrade", she said, and rubbed her cheek lightly over his.'[6] But the promise is made more with fear than with pleasure: it is obvious that for Dione a merging with the proletariat also involves a physical violation. It is in fact with some relief that she finds her sacrifice is no longer necessary, for in Moscow Donald meets a Russian woman factory worker who is only too anxious to put her comradely principles into practice.

When Dione returns to England, however, the problem arises again. She meets Idris Pritchard, another Communist, and this time, 'wanting so much to dispel the hate and envy in his mind, feeling intensely and painfully his needing all that but having to live in this dreadful, poky room, with nothing to look at but those two pictures of shouting Lenin and silly old Marx',[7] she allows him to make love to her. When it is all over, at first she feels nothing but disgust, but then looking round the sordid room, she thinks: 'No wonder Idris Pritchard was like he had shown himself to be. No wonder. Poor Idris. Poor people in this house. In other houses like it. Oh, poor dears, poor dears, how could one blame them for anything!'[8]

Although the whole of *We Have Been Warned* is quite absurd in its silly solemnity—and staggeringly so when one considers the intelligence displayed in Miss Mitchison's historical novels—it is worth noting how often in less silly books the merging with the proletariat is seen in primarily physical terms. It is seen in this way, for example, in Ethel Mannin's *The Pure Flame* (1936), where the middle-class heroine, Elspeth Rodney, brings together the tubercular working-class hero, Harry Winchell, and her niece Chloe. She hopes to take them both to Russia, 'that country of the young, where everything we who are the minority here are working for has come true',[9] but Harry dies before the relationship can be consummated. It is seen at times too in the novels of Jack Lindsay and Sylvia Townsend Warner. Another aspect of the same theme—the hero fighting cathartically with the working-class—is present in Rex Warner's *The Wild Goose Chase* (1937) and in Randall Swingler's *No Escape* (1937). (Even Grassic

Gibbon's Ewan Tavendale, it will be seen, establishes himself in the workers' eyes by proving himself their equal in strength.) While this concept can, of course, be seen simply as an attempt to personify a political abstraction, one cannot avoid the feeling at times that their attitudes are as ambiguous as Miss Mitchison's. Only the fact that the workers are usually off the stage too quickly, perhaps, saves us from finding out.

The majority of the middle-class writers, in fact, unlike Miss Mitchison, steered clear of giving the contemporary proletariat any major role in their novels. This, however, immediately plunged them into, if anything, even worse difficulties. For if the world of the British working classes of the thirties was predominantly an unrevolutionary one, then even more so was the world of the British middle classes. In their layer of society, Fascism and the class-war were generally but evanescent shadows, more a future threat than any present reality, and tangible reasons for resorting to the barricades were rare. The writer's problem in this case was either to capture and corner these shadows, somehow give them flesh, and relate them to the world working-class movement of which he professed to be a part—or else to approach the problem from a completely different angle.

II

Of those novels that did deal directly with contemporary or near-contemporary middle-class Britain, Alec Brown's massive *Daughters of Albion* (1935) was certainly the most earnestly intentioned. Indeed, Brown—a graduate of Cambridge and a former lecturer at Belgrade University[10]—espoused the Communist cause with such enthusiasm in the thirties that at times he seemed to be trying to become more working-class than the working class. In his contribution to a debate on the purpose of *Left Review*, for example, apart from warning that potential middle-class converts should be watched with a 'Robespierrian suspicion',[11] he urged that a 'propaganda committee' be formed to work towards 'the pro-letarianisation of our outlook' and 'the proletarianisation of our actual language'. He went on to suggest that Revolutionary writers have a slogan: 'LITERARY ENGLISH FROM CAXTON TO US IS AN ARTIFICIAL JARGON OF THE RULING CLASS; WRITTEN ENGLISH BEGINS WITH US'.[12] The style of *Daughters of Albion* is, apparently, just such an attempt at this 'proletarianisation'; an attempt, as he says in the Author's Note, 'to write a normal English based solidly on spoken English'.[13] The result is hardly outstandingly successful. His innovations seem to consist, in fact, of an indiscriminate omission of capital letters, apostrophes, and hyphens, such contractions as 'alright', and such onomatopoeic eccentricities as 'she turned to the lamp on the low table beside her narrow bed and puff! puff! puff! blew it out'.[14]

Nor, with the best will in the world, can one find very much kinder words to say for the whole of *Daughters of Albion*, despite its vast length. It sets out—with side-diversions to hit at everything bourgeois that moves—to illustrate the Marxist thesis that the bourgeois family is based on 'capital, on private gain. In its completely developed form this family exists only among the bourgeoisie. But this state of things finds its comple-ment . . . in public prostitution'. The Etchams, Roger and Violet, are the heads of just such a bourgeois family. Roger, outwardly proclaiming the sanctity of marriage and the family, maintains a series of mistresses in town, an arrangement in which Violet cynically acquiesces so that she may retain her position as a respectable well-to-do mother. Their offspring are, Brown tells us, the inevitable result of such a marriage. Charlotte marries a philanderer, but holds the marriage together for the sake of appearances. The thoughtlessly sensual Muriel marries a slumming parson, and then proceeds to lecture their mainly on-the-dole parish on the necessity of sexual restraint. The oldest of the five daughters, Cynthia, a farmer, patronisingly tries to educate one of her farmhands, but he rejects her middle-class culture. No more successful in her life is Irene, who, after falling in love with a young Yugoslav, finds it impossible to face up to the thrusting capitalist stage of the dialectic in Yugoslavia, for this country, she feels, should remain a picturesque haven for the rich. Eventually she becomes a prostitute, thus bringing Roger and Violet's 'kind of lying life to a logical perfection'.[15] The one hopeful member of the family, Mary, is a Communist sympathiser who falls in love with another Communist, Jimmy Wingfield, unfortunately already married. Even she, Brown suggests, is marred by her upbringing, for, rather than upset her parents by sleeping with Wingfield and thus dragging the Etcham name through the divorce courts, she wants Wingfield to gain his divorce by sleeping with a prostitute. Eventually, much to her father's hurt resentment, Wingfield persuades her that such reasoning is outmoded.

If Brown had been content with the one positive picture of Mary and Jimmy Wingfield, the novel would most certainly have been more successful. The book ends on no false rousing revolutionary note, and the picture of Roger—his family scattered and disunited, his sexual life more and more openly sordid—complacently putting up decorations for Christmas: '. . . while such a fundamental custom as christmas lives on, I dont think there's really any call for worry . . .'[16] is a reasonably effective one. Unfortunately, however, partly consumed it would seem by the fear that the lack of revolutionary gestures—natural enough in a typical middle-class family of the thirties—will be seen as a condonation of middle-class society, Brown has very early on buried most of the satirical possibilities beneath the stifling weight of a pompous and often long-winded didacticism. There *are* touches of humour in this book, such as the congregation which is 'replete with worship, swollen to the point of discomfort, like so many camels distended with water, ready to pass the desert of another week to the emotional oasis of the next Sunday',[17] but to reach them one has to wade through tedious masses of verbiage, reminiscent of Tressell at his very worst. Every scene, every incident, and nearly every action, however unimportant, is given its deadening commentary, to emphasise the fact that this is 'a society which has nothing more in itself to create, no interest in creation'.[18] Even an innocent grocer's boy, trying to help out, is handicapped by 'that inability to give lucid directions to a traveller, resulting from a system of education which ignores system',[19] while the mention of gas meters spurs Brown to point out that 'the gas in penny meters, used by the poor, costs more than the gas used through ordinary meters by the better-off'.[20] But only a longer extract, from Brown in full swing, can perhaps give the real flavour of his pedantry:

> Some of the committee came in their own little saloons, Hillmans and Morrises, a Riley and a Ford, and three of them in taxis; whereas some of them came most of the way on foot. It is quite jolly walking in the rain, if you're well coated and well shod and well fed. They of course *were* well coated and well shod and well fed. The little cars they came in were thirty to fifty pound a year cars. The others who walked could have afforded them but just did not want to. The taxidrivers employed received respectively, one shilling, three shillings, and four and ninepence for their fares. . . .
>
> The unemployed without exception came on foot, all the way in the rain. They were neither well shod nor well coated nor well fed.
>
> The illustrious visitor came in a pair of Daimler limousines.
>
> Here we might insert an observation from the point of view of health. There is no doubt but that walking within measure is good for us, and that nothing makes a city dweller more out of condition than constant use of cars, trams, trains and taxis. At the same time too much walking, like too much of anything, is bad. These men did nothing but walk. They did many miles a day looking for work. Activity which has become monotonous, and is in addition hopeless, as the walking of these men, is exceptionally exhausting. Their hopeless five miles equals more than thirty hiker's miles.[21]

Brown was by nature a long-winded writer—as his earlier and later books show[22]—but the self-consciously imposed task of becoming a complete 'proletarian', the frantic flagellant urge to shake off all middle-class taint, has here helped to turn the fault into a nightmare.

Closely allied to Brown's attempt to show the decay of middle-class society, were those novels which concentrated rather on the progress of the middle-class intellectual to the Communist commitment. The problem remained no less great: how was one to bring to life the issues leading the hero to participation in a mass working-class movement, issues which were frequently emotional or intellectual, but rarely tangible? The old devices—the hero slumming temporarily, the simultaneous romance-conversion—had clearly been worked to death: how then was the revolutionary movement to be more than a *deus ex machina*, an inorganic panacea?

It was at the actual point of conversion that these novels most often foundered. It was at this point, for example, that Ethel Mannin's first politically orientated novel, *Cactus* (1935), became most blatantly strained.[23] After holding apolitical pacifist feelings throughout most of the novel, the middle-class heroine, Elspeth Rodney, in the course of a few paragraphs suddenly adopts violently revolutionary views. The realisation that her shares have multiplied a thousandfold as a result of the Great War makes her reflect that 'Perhaps *this* is what they are killing each other for—behind it all a nationalistic and individualistic lust for money, a capitalist racket? A corrupt system made it possible, and only a corrupt system could allow it to be. . . . Whether Germany triumphed or the Allied Powers, so long as the system remained it would be all one to the workers. . . .'.[24] Despite the fact that she continues to abstain from any kind of political activity, and despite her failure to make any contact with any worker in the course of the book, we find her at the end once more emphasising her common cause with the workers: 'Soon out of the rich warm soil of Spain will come revolt, from the Basque country and Catalonia . . . and possibly as in America, as in Austria, the workers will go down for the count, and the troops fire on the people, one mass of workers in uniform against another mass in uniform and without. But soldiers and workers have been in council for their common good before, and will be again, for that is the history of mankind, which is the history of revolt'.[25] In the context of the book, such sentiments can only sound completely abstract and artificial.

Rather more convincing and coherent—but still floundering at the moment of conversion—is *No Escape* (1937), a novel by the final editor of *Left Review*, Randall Swingler. *No Escape* is set in the days before the First World War, and in a small village far removed from industrial disputes and trade unions. But Swingler's thesis is that there is no escape from the large issues, however tranquil the surroundings may seem, and in fact his small village is a microcosm of the class-war raging in more ferocious ways outside. The Earls, who own most of the village, live in a state of deadness, Mr Earl being 'an almost entirely actionless man'.[26] But they are still capable of sudden bursts of power, and their eviction of the Haggy family from their cottage arouses in the village the slumbering sense of the class-struggle, 'the antagonism which no goodwill, no straining after friendship, could ever resolve'.[27] In the midst of these forces is Rolf Taverner, the son of the vicar, aware that much is wrong with the state of the world, and that 'Everywhere, it's money, money, money, and an ugly monotonous job to get it . . .'.[28] When the villagers, in their fury over the eviction of the Haggies, attack him as a scapegoat, he realises that the attack is justified, 'was always justified by a general guilt which was unavoidably upon him'.[29] But his unease is assuaged for a time in the arms of Sonia, the Earls' adopted daughter, and together they flee to Paris to escape the prison of the village. The war now threatening seems of no consequence to them. 'What had they to do with war and killing, who had only just started to savour the real satisfaction of living?'[30] Eventually, however, they find this refuge palls, and they return to England, and Rolf to his job in the bank.

When the war does finally come, Rolf still ignores it, just as he ignores politics, thinking as he does that the only outlet for his dissatisfaction can be found in widening his own community 'on the basis of love and honesty and trust'.[31] But his unease grows, as he sees more and more men joining up. At last, when some workmen sneeringly tell him that he will not have to fight, because 'It's chaps like us that have to do the bloody fighting',[32] he realises that as there is no escape for them, there is virtually no escape for him.

Up to this point, if a little slow in pace and irritatingly mystical in his attitude to the class-struggle,[33] Swingler has with reasonable success related his hero's sense of dissatisfaction to the wider social issues. But when Rolf goes off to the war his attitude is still predominantly anarchic: 'Perhaps what we are fighting for really does represent something, some struggle against meanness in the common living. . . . Perhaps the world, our civilised world, has reached a dead end, and must now submit to the immersion in the flood of death, so that something cleaner and more courageous may be resurrected on the other side'.[34] He comes back, barely six pages later, a transformed man. 'It was right to go. There is work to be done. But what I didn't realise . . . there is a real enemy. We are fighting the wrong enemy now. We are fighting ourselves, as it were, while the real criminals sit well out of harm's way and suck the blood. But one day the ordinary man will see how he's been fooled . . . and then we shall have a different kind of war. . . .'[35] Again the leap: again the stumbling performance.

We see Rolf only once more. As Swingler was later to do, he refuses a commission in the army, and is caught distributing copies of the *Communist Manifesto* to his fellow soldiers. He dies in the next attack. Sonia at home has meanwhile understood the point he was making, and dedicates herself to the struggle: 'A new war, a war against the system that made wars'.[36] In a final somewhat forced, symbolic flourish, the book closes on her labour pains and the new life that is struggling under the hard winter soil. 'Sonia felt the strength hardening in the darkness of the earth, a new shape of life, already forming, tightening, organising itself, underground, which must at length break through the barriers inhibiting it, destroying the old and dead pattern of life, and pushing forth into light, into consciousness. . . .'[37]

One final novel involving middle-class conversion will be considered here: C. Day Lewis's *Starting Point* (1937). Like Brown and Swingler, Lewis was a middle-class Communist who involved himself actively and strenuously in the affairs of the Party, a member from 1935 to 1938, and a frequent platform speaker and writer in the cause. However, although he was among the first of the so-called Revolutionary Poets, his views about what should be expected from the revolutionary writer were distinctly unmilitant. He was always adamant that the committed writer should not simply sloganise the Party line and produce mere polemic. As he wrote in 1935: 'The tendency of much proletarian art is to use individuals as lay-figures expressive of political ideas instead of depicting them as living agents and instruments of political forces . . . the imaginative writer who simply uses characters to express a political philosophy will find that he has produced, not a novel or a play, but an illustrated text-book.'[38] This is, of course, a fair and valid point, but all the same the words hardly anticipate the predominantly lyrical nature of Lewis's first novel, *The Friendly Tree* (1936), a lyricism which caught a number of left-wing reviewers by surprise. Indeed, despite A. L. Morton's profession to see in it a special English revolutionary method, a method that 'may be a long way round, but . . . that must arrive in the end',[39] it is clear now that *The Friendly Tree* shows two impulses—the lyrical and social—struggling within Lewis, and presages the virtual defeat—as far as his writing is concerned—of the latter after 1938. For the hero, Stephen Hallam, a professed Communist, mouths his revolutionary convictions at the most inopportune moments, without any real conviction, and with little relevance to the novel, which is basically a lyrical love-story written in a post-Virginia Woolf style. The occasional statements that seem to indicate a more serious purpose, as for example when Richard, Stephen's friend, tells his sweetheart, Anna, 'You and Steve are the children of the future. When the Red Dawn comes you two will blossom out, and I shall fade conveniently away . . .'.[40] seem quite pointless intrusions. There is in fact little in the novel to gainsay Anna's thoughts when Stephen starts talking about the collective farms: 'Anna was only vaguely interested. She could not see what all this had to do with her, with her and Steve'.[41] For all the haphazard political issues raised, there is a strong apolitical feeling in this novel.

In the following year, however, in *Starting Point*, Lewis tried to grapple more directly with his political opinions, by making the central issue the decision whether or not to join the Communist Party. This novel traces the interconnected lives of four friends—Anthony Neal, Theodore Follett, John Henderson, and Henry Voyce—over a period of about ten years, from 1926, when they are still at Oxford, to about 1936. Theodore is a sadistically inclined writer, whose life is dominated by the oedipal feelings he has towards his promiscuous mother. Both in his novels and in his life he carefully refrains from having anything to do with contemporary issues. When he finds his mother plunged into an affair with Henry Voyce, he shoots her and then himself in a moment of insane jealousy. The act is enough to send Henry—who as a result of the affair was losing some of his own feelings of inferiority and his latent fear of his homosexuality—back into his tortured self; he enters a monastery. The third member of the group, John Henderson, has rather more concern with social issues, and is in fact a Socialist at the outset; but even he finds that in a world in which the means of production are owned by people antagonistic to Socialism he has to make compromises with his beliefs.

The most important of the four is Anthony Neal, who seems to be—from the evidence of C. Day Lewis's autobiography[42]—a composite picture of Lewis himself and of his friend Rex Warner. He is throughout searching for something to commit himself to, 'not to an ambition, not to one person, not necessarily to a Cause; but to the acceptance of some demand that sooner or later life would make upon him'.[43] His search then is seen from the beginning as a psychological problem: the emphasis is on his emotional deprivation, rather than on the injustice of society. He finds the beginning of the kind of involvement he is seeking in rugby and making love: but neither satisfies for long. 'Yet, somewhere in this direction, he was convinced, lay the thing he was so obscurely looking for; the influence that could bind individuals together into a community, however widely their temperaments and interests differed, not for an hour or two but for good.'[44]

When the General Strike comes, like Rex Warner[45] he joins the students who volunteer to take over the jobs of those striking: he feels that the Strike is bound to fail and it would be better for the Unions that it were over as quickly as possible. On this volunteer work he sees poverty for the first time, and feels the gap between himself and the working-class men and women: 'There was an elemental difference between them, he began to feel obscurely, like the difference of earth and water; they could touch, but never mingle'.[46] A chance encounter with a Communist makes him interested enough to start reading Marx, and he is soon convinced (though this, it is important to note, we are told only by implication) of the correctness of Marx's theories.

For a while, however, as agent of his father's farm, he tries to effect improvements individually, only to find, when the slump eventually forces his father to sell out, that he has in fact accomplished nothing:

> . . . his greatest error was the initial one of regarding his plans for improvement, his chosen way of life, not simply in the light of their social value, but as an instrument and setting for his own personality. Oh, granted he was quite sincere in his desire to help those people he had known from birth; but beneath that ideal was the self-seeking motive— self-seeking was the right word, he had hoped thus to find himself, his real purpose. . . . All he had accomplished was to learn that the individual could not battle alone against economic forces.[47]

But it is precisely this self-seeking motive, whose objective is not at all clear, that remains dominant. We remain confined, until the very last pages, in his basically introspective middle-class world, the social issues only hovering on its fringes.

Neal now becomes a teacher, still unsure of his purpose. Should he join the Communisty Party? The dilemma is still seen in subjective terms: '. . . how long shall I be satisfied with a Common Room, a unit which has no coherence outside the mere routine and technique of work?'[48] He feels that were he to join the Party while still a teacher, he would in the end betray either the Party, by not teaching Socialism, or the school, by doing so. Another middle-class Communist acquaintance, Percy Appleton, tells him that he is absurd in allowing such scruples to stand in his way. 'Who cares about your honour or your personal feelings? When will you understand that this isn't a game? You're mad if you think we can play at things, stick to the rules the other side have made to ensure their staying on top.'[49]

Finally Neal does conquer these scruples, and joins the Party. An epilogue a few years later sees him about to leave for Spain. He says to John: 'In a decent society, Theo and Henry could have been damned useful. Capitalism had no use for them. That's why we've got to get rid of it. It's twisted up too many lives already'.[50] At this point the book clearly will not bear the strain: there is little in the novel which has gone any way towards establishing that it is Capitalism which has twisted up the lives of Theo and Henry. One of the few implied links between them and Communist 'reality' in the course of the book is Appleton's single comment on a newspaper headline referring to the twin deaths of Theodore and his mother: 'My God, what tripe!'[51] A few lines later, Neal reveals the source of his own happiness:

> These men and women—the oppressed, the anonymous, the workers, —history had called them out of the ranks and given them her secret orders: they were the spies she sent forward into a hostile country, a land whose promise perhaps they alone could fully realise . . . Whether their hands were grained with coal-dust, marked with occupational scars, or pallid from the stagnant air of offices—it was these hands, Anthony believed, which would guide a new world struggling out of the womb. They would live and die and be forgotten: but their lives would be built into the deep foundations of the future. Of these he was one. With these he was one.[52]

From lovemaking and rugby to a mystical stream of workers, only one of whom has fleetingly crossed the pages before; it is a bizarre transition perhaps, but certainly not improbable, if one is to judge from the frequent love–hate references to the public school and university that Julian Symons has noted in the prose and poetry of the thirties.[53] But whether in the context of the novel it is an inevitable transition is another matter altogether. One is unable to shake off the feeling that Neal could have just as easily found his salvation in Buchmanism or in any other group spiritual combination. Lewis has in fact described something of the uneasiness, the restless dissatisfaction of the middle-class young man of the thirties, but he has been unable to make the solution to that dissatisfaction arise with any inevitability from the novel. What seems to be sought initially is some kind of psychopathic group release, a substitute psychiatrist's couch: but what we are finally presented with, virtually as a *fait accompli*, is a mass worker's movement, dedicated, again for no compelling reason that rises in the course of the novel, to create a new world.

III

In 1935 the volatile leader of the now revolutionary ILP, Fenner Brockway, took time off from his negotiations with the British Communist Party to write a somewhat crude melodrama called *Purple Plague*. This, his first and only excursion into fiction, admittedly did have certain muscularly promising elements. A purple plague is menacing the world, and Doctor Haden, one of the few men thought capable of finding a cure for it, is sailing in the English liner 'Angevin', working frantically in the ship's laboratory provided. A crisis comes when a victim of the plague is discovered on board: this means that the ship will have to stay in quarantine for ten years unless a cure is found. Having 'always felt that a liner mirrored class divisions exactly',[54] Brockway now has a revolution take place on the ship, with the sailors and tourist class forcibly setting up a Socialist Republic while Doctor Haden experiments on. Finally he manages to find a cure, just at the point when the social experiment on board is showing its obvious success. But Haden has himself caught the disease, and dies, leaving a message to the leader of the revolution 'to take the example of the ship to the world'.[55] If these elements were promising, however, the performance unfortunately was not, and this thriller – romance – allegory soon dies under the weight of its staged sentiments, postures, and language.

But Brockway had certainly not administered any death-blow to political allegory as such. Only two months after the publication of *Purple Plague* appeared the first of three rather more sophisticated allegories, written by middle-class writers who, partly inspired by the recently translated novels of Kafka, the Surrealist movement from the continent, and such eclectic English influences as Swift, Bunyan, Lewis Carroll, and the Auden – Isherwood social-fantasy plays, had turned to this form in an attempt to break away from the staleness of the conventional political attacks of the thirties. It is reasonable to assume, too, that the motives of these writers—Rex Warner, Edward Upward and Ruthven Todd— included the desire to avoid that kind of middle-class dilemma found in *Starting Point*, where the novel had resolved itself into the almost purely verbal, introspective problem of 'Shall I join the Communist Party?' For in allegorical form their doubts, their fears, their often abstract, theoretical views about the nature of society, and their anxieties and hopes for the future could be made concrete.[56]

It was with the future that Rex Warner, schoolteacher and son of a clergyman, was very much concerned when in 1937—in part of a collection of essays edited by C. Day Lewis on Socialism and the Cultural Revolution—he addressed himself to the general state of culture under Capitalism. 'On the one hand', he claimed, 'the material stagnation of capitalism brings it about that fewer and fewer scholars, scientists, and technicians are required for the process of production. On the other hand, being no longer able to represent itself as a progressive force, capitalism can no longer invite the support of the general ideals of culture and progress.'[57] It is true that in Britain so far 'no definite attack on culture as a whole has been made' but 'we must not suppose that it never will be made. Already such enactments as the Sedition Act are evidence of what may be coming'.[58] Already there is 'a general lowering of cultural standards. Capitalism can no longer make use of the best fruits of culture, and the result is an increasing output of second-rate work in literature, journalism and entertainment'.[59] The only way this situation can be remedied, and the progress of capitalism towards its 'final form' of Fascism be arrested, is through the actions of the organised working class: they have 'now become the guardians of culture'.[60] One need not be a trained Marxist to understand this, Warner concluded, one need only be an ordinarily decent person. It is true that trained Marxists are essential for a thorough understanding of the process, but 'If some people don't like the word "Marxism", we must be prepared to say "common sense".'[61]

Warner's allegorical novel, *The Wild Goose Chase*, which appeared later in the same year, is in many ways an amplification of this essay. For, while Warner obviously concerns himself with other issues than this, it is the contemporary state of culture that looms largest in his attack. Furthermore, his imaginary country over the Frontier is in large part a surrealist representation of a capitalist-imperialist state in just that final form of Fascism towards which Warner feared Britain was heading. Finally, his hero, George, despite his assertion at one point that his favourite books are 'Shakespeare . . . Karl Marx, *Tom Jones* and Isaiah',[62] is not initially a Marxist, which Warner at this stage would seem to have been, but an 'ordinarily decent person' led to the cause of the workers by morality and common sense. It is his pursuit of the Wild Goose—some vague symbol of human fulfilment and human justice—rather than any fully stated Marxist consciousness, that leads him to the recognition of the necessity of crossing the Frontier and ultimately allying himself with the peasants and the factory workers in their fight against Fascist rule.

It seems, though it was many years ago, only yesterday that we citizens of a seaside town, standing in ranks along the esplanade, watched, cheering at the same time with all the force of our lungs, the outset of the three brothers who, with the inconsiderate fine daring of youth, were prepared, each in his own way, to go far on bicycles, distinguishing our town by an attempt which even the brothers only dimly understood and which seemed to most of us who stood spectators vociferously cheering impracticable, to some even ridiculous. Young and vigorous they looked, different one from the other, as they wheeled into the square their diverse coloured bicycles, made by the same maker at different dates, and they seemed, by the expression of their faces, already in thought upon the moorland road which was to lead them to the frontier miles away, where very few of us had ever been, and those few shook their heads with a hint of dangers to be met, saying nothing but doubting much, as the rest of us doubted, whether the brothers ever were destined to achieve the purpose which they all, though very indistinctly, had in view.[63]

The stylised, classical prose, the weird dreamlike atmosphere of this opening paragraph of *The Wild Goose Chase* immediately establish the texture of the whole, which for the most part makes little attempt at surface realism or plausibility: the meaning—except for some stretches to be mentioned later—lies almost wholly in the allegory. Indeed, the three brothers—David, Rudolph, and George, roughly representative of the intellectual, the athlete, and the ordinary man—have not only little idea of the purpose of their journey, but almost no idea of where they are going, beyond the vague notion that they must cross the Frontier and pursue the Wild Goose.

George is the only one to return, half-crazed, to tell the story of his travels. It is him we follow as he journeys towards the Frontier, meeting Bob, a crooning asexual embodiment of popular Capitalist culture; Don Antonio, a morally and socially vacuous Philosopher; and finally Albert, the Christian, whose practical application of his beliefs has led to his acquiescence in the ruin and corruption of his wife. But worse is to come on the other side of the Frontier. Stopping at the first village he comes to, George finds that he is in a strange countryside which is part Alice's Wonderland, part pantomine, and part sheer nightmare. Imperialistically dominated and bled by the 'City', the village and others like it are ruled by comic-opera policemen armed with straw batons and hidden machine guns, whose cruelty is mitigated only by their preposterous inefficiency. But just as inefficient is the country opposition, a group of 'revolutionaries' whose melodramatics and confusion of evolution with revolution suggest aspects both of the British Communist Party and of the Labour Movement as a whole. Their mentors are at one moment the syrupy Reverend Hamlet with his belief that 'all this class-feeling is a terrible thing, when you come to think of it',[64] and at the next the would-be revolutionary Pushkov, whose false beard keeps falling off:

. . . the policemen roared with laughter at him. . . . 'Your beard, I think,' one of them said, offering it to him, but Pushkov hurried on, while the policeman followed him, still trying, with the utmost politeness, to persuade him to take it back. Finally Pushkov did stretch his hand out, but the policeman snatched the beard away, and, stuffing it into his pipe, lit it and began to smoke, while his comrades roared with laughter and clapped hands.[65]

George lingers at the village only long enough to make love to a farmer's daughter called Joan (during which scene the Wild Geese fly noisily overhead), and then journeys on. For despite his awakening sympathy for the peasants, he feels that the city is a stage through which he must pass: perhaps he will be able to help the peasants from there, and then later find the Geese on the other side. But, having gained admittance by answering the examination paper incorrectly, he finds he is doomed to disappointment. Vast and imposing from the outside with its covered roof and tall towers, the city is inside almost totally unreal and unnatural. To George 'the people who hurried shadowless to and fro' seem 'unreal figures, embodied but only just, and the buildings rectangular and gleaming . . . purposeless, as if made of sugar or of something else inappropriate for human architecture'.[66] Their god is a stuffed goose, and the centre of their culture is the school-cum-university 'convent', where the hermaphrodite students, presided over by a mysterious headmaster, spend their time in futile and often incredibly cruel studies.[67] At the heart of the convent itself is the Research Centre, where science and art pursued as ends in themselves have come, Warner implies, to their logical culmination:

> There was a poet who had invented a new language, but could neither pronounce a syllable of it nor attach any meaning to any of its words. There was an artist who spent his time rapidly arranging fir cones on the floor of his cell, and sweeping them together again with his hand when he was for an instant dissatisfied with their arrangement. A critic had discovered what literature ought to be; but he was unable to write. A philosopher had explained the world of sense; but he was blind and deaf, had lost his sense of touch, and had been, he informed them, since childhood unable to distinguish one odour from another.[68]

The specific political implications of Warner's attack on the City is made clearer when George is given the task of refereeing a rugby match between the Cons and the red-jerseyed Pros. The match, he finds, has been decided beforehand by the Government in the Con(servative)s' favour: the losers will enter the Research centre as specimens. In an episode in which pure nightmare is effectively mingled with burlesque, George makes desperate attempts to avert the result: finally, after the entire Pro side has been shot dead by machine-gun fire when it looked as if they might have a chance of drawing the game, George is himself bombarded with cushions:

> At first he hardly noticed. . . . but soon, so numerous had been the spectators, he found himself struggling towards the exits with soft feathers covered in pink silk about his knees. It was not long before the softness was waist high and George called for assistance, watching in angry despair the hordes dispersing. He was unnoticed and the cushions were about his throat, over his mouth, folding his eyes, and before the last throw he had become unconscious, softly inhumed, having wasted crying.[69]

Now certain of the basic evil of this state, Goeorge has several more bizarre adventures—during which he makes the Marxist discovery that the workers of the City, who are the only ones who can breed, are the worst treated—before finally making his escape and with relief turning his back on the City walls. He has now decided that 'Only an army, only the organized movement of the masses can shake that Government. . .'.[70] He stops briefly at the Free State of Lagonda—where Koresipoulis, a MacDonald-like advocate of the inevitability of gradualness, has been allowed by the Government, on condition that he betray his followers, to set up a Free State for Cats and Dogs—and then makes his way back to the village.

Here he gradually regains the confidence of the revolutionaries, and here, too, he wins the love of Joan after a long fight to the death with her husband. When three years have passed, the revolutionary army is ready, and they set out for the City. After battling through its superficially strong, but basically weak and neglected defences, and coping with a last line of priests toting gas-cylinders, they storm the City walls. Successful though the attack is, some of George's colleagues want to negotiate with the King, and he has to deal with their treachery, and chase the King—the spirit of this inhuman Government—from the City. At last a Government of the masses is established, a Government dedicated to 'comradeship, and to profane love, to hard work, honesty, the sight of the sun, reverence for those who have helped us, animals, flesh and blood'.[71] As these words are spoken by George, the portion of the City roof under which they are standing lifts off, and mile on mile of Wild Geese fly across the sky: 'Be the future as it might be, and no doubt that complete success was distant still, he knew that something not unworthy had been achieved already as he stood with the men and women, holding Joan's hand in his hand, and observed some of the Generals looking at him with an odd expression in their eyes, and their mouths smiling'.[72]

This account has necessarily omitted many of Warner's more fantastic surrealistic effects, but it should at least have conveyed the flavour of the whole. It should certainly have confirmed the point that any passion, any human involvement, any level of ordinary reality, has been quite deliberately expunged: the stylisation of the prose, the immediately established surrealistic atmosphere, and the representative qualities of most of the characters ensure this. Indeed, those episodes where the narrative does assume almost unchecked a semi-realistic level seem awkward intrusions: one inevitably asks, as in the chapters dealing with the gathering together of the revolutionary forces, what qualities of leadership has this cardboard Everyman shown that he should suddenly turn into a revolutionary figure; or, for that matter, how is this group of burlesque incompetents suddenly transformed into a disciplined force?

While recognising that this fact that Warner has chosen not to construct, as Frederick Karl puts it, a realistic 'persuasive surface of action',[73] is in itself a valid criticism to make of *The Wild Goose Chase*, one can still examine further and ask whether the allegorical effects are in themselves sufficiently powerful and pointed to enable the book to survive as an entity. This calls for some initial limiting definitions. What should be immediately stressed is that we are not dealing here, in any true sense, with Kafkaesque country. Certainly the opening situation and something of the dreamlike atmosphere would seem to owe a debt to Kafka. There is too at times the same haunting feeling that the hero is being played with by forces outside his control—particularly as George is frantically searching for the King of the City on his first visit there. It is also true that *The Wild Goose Chase* cannot be confined completely to a dogmatic pattern. Elements of Freudianism— such as George's dalliance with the King's mistress in an underground cavern towards the close of the story—are present, while the Wild Goose itself is a fairly effective symbol for the never-ending search for human justice *and* for human fulfilment. At the end of the book, even though the City Government has been overturned and the roof opened to the sky, all is certainly not over; there is the ominous expression in the eyes of the Generals to be considered, and, far more importantly, there is still the Wild Goose to be pursued. But much beyond this, one surely cannot go: the ever-widening ripples of meaning circling out from Kafka soon stop short in the case of Warner.

Some critics, however, while recognising this difference between the writers, that Warner is basically not dealing with 'hovering eternities', have still professed impatience at the determination to read political meanings in *The Wild Goose Chase*. B. Rajan, for example, felt that, quite apart from the political significance, the City 'merely stands in opposition to the village and the village (if we must have these equivalences) is nearest to Auden's village of the heart. . . . The city is mechanized, inflexible, determinist. . . . Nevertheless it must be conquered not denied. The opposition is stated not so that one of its terms can be deified, but in order to make possible the creation of a unity'.[74] Again one must concede that the closed-in City is a dramatic symbol in contrast to the village, from which flows love and life; and that there are strong elements here of the anti-scientific materialism that one finds, say, in Huxley's *Brave New World* (1932).[75] But whether they exist in their own right, and can properly be abstracted from the specific political connotations that Warner gives to them is another matter altogether.[76] It is true that by the time Warner came to write *The Aerodrome* (1941), the village had acquired another significance and can be seen as symbolic of the traditional, muddled values of English society, as opposed to the totalitarian order and discipline of the aerodrome. But at this earlier stage, Warner was posing a dichotomy which was, despite the presence of the Wild Goose, far more closely Marxist. The masses were for him the embodiments of life, of human values; capitalism, in its extreme form of Fascism, the embodiment of sterile, mechanical values; but he has not, surely, given these values an existence of their own. The 'creation of a unity' that Rajan refers to has as its only justification George's decision not to raze the town and its machinery, but to use them for the new way of life: if this seems a departure from Ruskin, it is certainly not from Marx.

What then, having to some extent defined its limitations, is the achievement of *The Wild Goose Chase*? Its overall construction, especially the concept of the Wild Goose itself, still remains striking and distinctive. Various of its episodes—the Football Match, the first days in the City, the parable of the Free State of Lagonda—also remain absorbing and effective to a degree. The impedimenta of school and university is here, certainly, but this time transformed into a new nightmarish significance. These are positive qualities, not to be denigrated. And yet, for all this undoubted strength, there is present at the same time far too much that is facile and hastily worked out. One has the feeling at moments, as he reiterates the same themes to no obvious purpose, that he has abandoned thought to paraphernalia or to the expression of private grudges. The weakness behind the apparent strength of Fascism, for example, is tediously returned to again and again in the episodes of the pilotless planes, the dud shells, the vulnerable giants, and the thinness of the city walls. There seems an almost obsessive personal preoccupation with clergymen—in the persons of the Prebendary, the Reverend Hamlet, the clergyman King, and finally in the long line of clergymen with their gas-cylinders hidden under their gowns. But possibly the most damaging criticism that can be made is that in many episodes a fractional surface froth has only to be blown away, and we might well be back in the pages of Barke or Roley. The dialogue between the Philosopher and George, for example, for all its aphorisms and epigrams, could have come straight out of the hospital scenes in *Major Operation*: the Philosopher places himself just as obviously open for attack as does Anderson, the businessman. The mindless, trigger-happy policemen—for all their straw batons—could come straight out of Roley's *Revolt*. The fight between George and Bill seems just as gratuitously muscular as anything in Phelan. Nor, finally, can one say that the virile workers, as opposed to the sterile hermaphrodites, are really very much superior to the most crude proletarian – bourgeois antithesis. For these reasons, then, one must conclude that for all the intelligence at work behind *The Wild Goose Chase*, and for all its strength in relation to many of the works we have been studying, it emerges as a book of potential rather than realisation, of scattered fragments rather than one successful, integrated whole.[77]

One publisher and editor who had much faith in Warner at the time was John Lehmann: it was in fact in Lehmann's *New Writing* that *The Wild Goose Chase* first saw print in the form of the self-explanatory episode, 'The Football Match'. Throughout the thirties Lehmann was on the lookout for new writers, first for the Hogarth Press and later for *New Writing*, and his autobiography, *The Whispering Gallery* (1955), provides an invaluable index to the literary cross-currents of the period. Warner was not the only left-wing writer, indeed, to benefit from his talent-spotting activities. In *The Whispering Gallery* he has recorded how in 1932 he 'heard with the tremor of excitement that an entomologist feels at the news of an unknown butterfly sighted in the depths of a forest, that behind Auden and Spender and Isherwood stood the even more legendary figure of an unknown writer . . .'.[78]

The 'legendary figure' was Edward Upward, schoolteacher and lifelong friend of Isherwood, a man who had espoused the Communist cause with as much enthusiasm as Alec Brown. He was to write one of the most uncompromising of all the Marxist critical essays of the thirties, his 'Sketch for a Marxist Interpretation of Literature'. '. . . no book written *at the present time*', he proclaimed in this essay, 'can be "good" unless it is written from a Marxist or near-Marxist viewpoint; . . . no modern book can be true to life unless it recognises, more or less clearly, both the decadence of present-day society and the inevitability of revolution'.[79] But this ideological certitude hardly resulted in the kind of literary flowering that would have justified the expectations of his admiring coterie: perhaps partially hampered by political activities, as the essay suggests, and partially by his efforts to relate his middle-class world to his new creed, Upward's literary output was to remain extremely small. Indeed, apart from this essay, and one or two short stories, his only published work of the decade was the novel *Journey to the Border*, one more attempt to employ the medium of allegory and surrealism to political ends.

As John Lehmann was early to point out,[80] the genesis of *Journey to the Border* can be found in a book published in the same year, Christopher Isherwood's semi-fictionalised autobiography, *Lions and Shadows*. In this work Isherwood describes how he and his friend 'Allen Chalmers' (Upward) began, while at Cambridge, to create a fantasy world, peopled partly by completely imaginary beings, partly by caricatures of those they saw around them in the real world. As this game evolved, and as such creations as 'Gunball' and 'Reynard Moxon' grew in their minds, they gave this world a name, Mortmere, and even contemplated writing a book about it.[81] By 1928, with the University behind him, Isherwood had tired of Mortmere—but 'Chalmers' had certainly not.

> Chalmers had created Gunball out of his own flesh and blood; he could never afford to abandon him altogether; if he did so, he was lost. He was to spend the next three years in desperate and bitter struggles . . . to find the formula which would transform our private fancies and amusing freaks and bogies into valid symbols of the ills of society and the toils and aspirations of our daily lives. For the formula did, after all, exist. And Chalmers did at last find it, at the end of a long and weary search . . . quite clearly set down, for everybody to read, in the pages of Lenin and of Marx.[82]

The main literary result of this 'long and weary search' was, as has been implied, Upward's *Journey to the Border*, in which Mortmere is wedded to Marx with some effective, some slightly absurd consequences. Unlike *The Wild Goose Chase*, the book opens normally enough, against the background of an English country house in which the solemn young hero is a brooding and reluctant tutor. Uncertain, introspective to a fault, he can see no way of breaking away from the clutches of his employer, Mr Parkin, a *nouveau riche* towards whom he feels a hatred compounded of snobbery, envy, personal animosity, and awareness of his role as a capitalist. Parkin is 'an ignorant snob who couldn't spell properly', 'a swine who had never doubted his power to impose his trivial swinish standards on everyone in the house. . . . Who poisoned the whole district. Who succeeded in making the farm labourers play up to his conception of them as simple rustic toadies. . . . Whose power extended even beyond the district, touched London, could buy up an expensively educated young man at any time to dance attendance on his boy'.[83] When asked to accompany Parkin and his friend MacCreath to the races, the tutor, instead of making a previously resolved gesture of defiance, tamely submits. As they drive there, he unhappily experiments with his sight and hearing, looking for a new 'technique'—much as Upward himself seems to have been looking so long for a new formula to express the realities of *his* world. The tutor hopes to cut off this world, first by deadening his sight and hearing altogether, and then by changing them, so that 'he would see and touch and hear differently, as he wanted to, happily'.[84]

The experiments bear fruit, until, indeed, the tutor has difficulty in distinguishing between what is real and what is the result of his new hallucinatory perception. The racecourse Marquee becomes fantastically inflated and richly decorated. A mysterious stranger in a blue raincoat assumes a malevolent threatening aspect. The tutor tries to enlist the aid of MacCreath; instead the latter inexplicably offers him a magnificent job, which half-attracts, half-repels him. A racecourse tout abuses him over the heads of his audience for his supposed Socialist sympathies: 'You're as keen to lay your hands on the goods of this world as the worst of us'.[85] An apparently harmless young man reveals he is a Fascist, and for a time holds the tutor in the spell of his brute strength.

Now thoroughly immersed in the hallucinations, the tutor enters the Marquee, where his mind wavers between outright rejection of the monied people there and the lure of their wealth and position. The accumulating hints that something momentous is about to happen now assume tangible proportions, as all the men present line up with their arms raised in the Fascist salute. Their leader, the Master of Foxhounds—who is also an important coalmine owner—tells them that a threatened revolution beginning on the racecourse has been brutally crushed. As the cheering that greets this statement reaches a shocking peak, the tutor feels panic and fear: 'War had been distant from him before; now it was rapidly approaching. It might break out at any moment—visibly, tangibly, in one form or another. . . . Darkness pressed in upon him once again, lifted him. Horror of the future alone supported him, kept his consciousness alive. He would be gassed, bayoneted in the groin, slowly burned, his eyeballs punctured by wire barbs'.[86] Terrified, fearing that the Fascists are pursuing him, he breaks out of the tent at a run. Wildly his mind now turns to the idea of an idyllic retreat: 'Don't consider the details. Imagine the cottage. He would arrive there. Then the life would begin—day after day after day. Innocent poetry. Walks, reading, contemplation'.[87] Just as wildly his mind turns to the idea of suicide, to complete nullity. He fears he is nearing insanity.

Up to this point the novel has its virtues. One can of course hardly overlook the awkward, tautological style, the clumsy manner in which the hallucinations develop, or the somewhat absurd bits of pure Mortmere, such as the mysterious threatening stranger, who seems like one of the 'enemy agents' that Isherwood and his friend encountered everywhere in Cambridge.[88] Nor can one overlook the at times excessive and apparently unconscious flights of solemn naivety: 'He had wasted in trivialities and dishonesties his one and only life, his life which might have been so full of, bright with, ardent for—what? Oh, wonders: love and knowledge and creation, history, science, poetry, interesting daily work, revolutionary politics, discipline, self-sacrifice, holidays, joy'.[89] But, granting this, the novel has presented in a fairly imaginative way the mental dilemma of one middle-class intellectual, secure and yet uncomfortable in his job, guiltily conscious of a disparity between his Socialist ideals and his actions, trying desperately to cope with the realities and very much aware of a confusion of motives. The hallucinatory episodes are virtually a dramatised version of the argument going on in his own mind, in which the attractions of wealth and easy living, the hypnotising strength and dread of Fascism, the hatred of Mr Parkin both as a philistine *and* as a Capitalist, the fear of war, the desire to live the poetic life and the desire to escape altogether, are battling and jostling side by side.

But suddenly, the mood, and virtually the technique changes. As the tutor walks away from the Marquee a little inner voice—in his left ear— explains that since leaving the house that morning he has been on the borderline of sanity and madness. There is only one way out from these unreal fantasies. He must go the way of the workers. Only in the workers' movement is there a 'future for anything except tyranny and death'.[90] '"But my upbringing, my education, my social origin—won't these tell against me?" ". . . Others from your social class have been accepted before you, have become loyal and exemplary fighters for the cause."'[91]

After these preliminary obeisances, it is perhaps hardly surprising that the only worker that makes his appearance on these pages comes to pieces in the author's middle-class hands. His inner Marxist voice—the doct-rinaire voice, as Samuel Hynes has commented, of the author of 'Sketch for a Marxist Interpretation of Literature'[92]— his inner Marxist voice having finished its explanations, the tutor strikes up a conversation with a nearby racegoer. The latter proceeds, with little prompting, to tell him why he is at the racecourse, what he does at the weekends, and where he works—at a factory: 'This was almost too interesting to be true'.[93] Without any sign of resentment at the question, the 'worker' tells him why there is no organised union at his factory. When 'almost didactically' the tutor tells him that this is a bad situation, again he shows no resentment. The tutor now feels humble. He 'was worthless compared with him'.[94]

Despite his resolution 'to cross over the frontier into effective action',[95] the tutor has two more slight relapses into his old hallucinatory state, when for a moment he imagines that a slight scuffle on the racecourse is the beginning of the workers' revolution, and when the sight of a clergyman sets his mind wandering along the religious solution. Then he pulls himself up sharply, and makes his decision. On a matter of principle he refuses to go back with Mr Parkin to his house, and says in fact that he will not be there at all that night. He will ask the local newsagent, who sells the *Daily Worker*, to put him in touch with the local workers' movement. 'His decision . . . would lead to difficulties. But he would at least have come down to earth, out of the cloud of his cowardly fantasies; would have begun to live. He had already begun. He had made a stand against Mr Parkin. Nothing, no subsequent danger, could cancel that.'[96]

The anticlimactic, even slightly comic, ending to this novel, an ending, as John Lehmann himself readily admitted, whose 'effect is extraordinarily lame',[97] is certainly not owing to its explicitly political conclusion. The novel, after all, has been explicitly political from the beginning. Nor can it be said to be solely or even mainly due to the absurdly solemn nature of its hero, and the almost schoolboyish fashion in which he defies Mr Parkin. The biggest contributory factor to this anticlimax is surely Upward's failure to show imaginatively why the way of the workers is the answer to all the tutor's problems. He seems, indeed, to be foiled by his own reasoning. Because he feels that these hallucinations are unreal 'cowardly fantasies', out of place in the proletarian movement, any retreat back to them would be for him a sign of sickness. But he replaces them with no imaginative alternative: the 'new thinking, the new feeling' promised by his Marxist self after an immersion in action presumably belongs to another novel.[98] Thus in these last forty pages is crammed the resolution of all his doubts and anxieties, neatly and facilely, and much of his earlier confusion of motives is entirely overlooked. It is true that he touches more closely the wider social ramifications than does, say, C. Day Lewis, but it is still primarily as a stated act of faith that we must accept his decision to join the Communist Party.

If neither of these middle-class allegories is in the end completely satisfying, even less so is the third example, *Over the Mountain* (1939) by the Scottish-born writer Ruthven Todd. Varying the frontier image by borrowing a mountain range from Auden and Isherwood's *The Ascent of F6* (1936), Todd has sited his hero, Michael, in a 'nameless' village at the foot of this range. Several men and even an expedition 'armed with hydraulic drills and all the latest house-breaking equipment'[99] have tried to climb it, but Michael, driven irresistibly by the thought of the unknown country on the other side, is the first to succeed. Before he gets to the summit, however, he is enveloped in a series of hallucinations, which culminate in the real discovery of the frozen body of Marlin, a previous person to attempt the climb. Then his compass goes haywire, his watch is ruined, his face is disfigured by frostbite, and, as he sets out down the other side of the mountain, he realises he has lost his memory. Finally he staggers into a house at its foot and falls asleep.

When he awakes he finds standing beside him a clergyman, Father Podmore, and an explorer, Colonel Roscoe. Although they seem to be vaguely familiar, 'Everything they said seemed to be slightly in excess, and they seemed to be caricatures of their types and professions'.[100] It is soon apparent—to the reader, not to the narrator—that he is somehow still in his own country, and that the mountain climb has disturbed his mental perceptions, so that, in a grotesque and fantastical way, he is seeing its social realities for the first time. Father Podmore, blessing everything in sight, spouts reactionary platitudes, while Colonel Roscoe, in reality head of the secret police, keeps his men happy by supplying them with sweets. The pantomine symbolism of Warner has become a kind of Fascist Noddy of Toytown as the policemen cry ecstatically: 'Oo-ee, we'll be able to buy aniseed balls and sherbert suckers. You are kind, dear, lovely Colonel Roscoe. We'll promise to be good boys now, and you won't never need to stop our Saturday pennies again. Oo-ee, how nice, how kind of pet, sweet Colonel Roscoe'.[101]

Michael has an equally violent reaction to all this: he suddenly discovers he has a social conscience, and is only too happy to make contact with the 'Reds'. His blown-up vision extends to them: they see all policemen as 'wall-eyed bastards'[102] and seem no less mindlessly violent than the police. But it is with them that Michael allies himself, a madman consorting 'with other madmen who shared the idea—the heresy—that all men were created equal'.[103] When he accompanies Roscoe to the latter's old school, he tells the ranks of regimented schoolboys that Roscoe and their headmaster 'are evil creatures that make oppression worse, the men who tread on the fallen'.[104] Finding the atmosphere at this point a trifle strained, he lashes out with Marlin's ice-axe, and escapes—only to find later that he is being hunted for the murder of Roscoe.

Todd now takes us to one caricatured party of idle rich, and then whirls us off into a series of muscular adventures reminiscent of Geoffrey Household's 'hunted' novels of the thirties—all irritatingly detached from the satirical purpose of the book. Finally Michael makes his way to the foot of the Peak, and begins his ascent. Again he is visited by a series of hallucinations of the 'oppressors' of this country; and again repudiates the values they stand for. Realising that he will not this time be able to reach the summit, he turns back, hoping that he will be able to find a hiding place from the police until he can later make a successful ascent. He stumbles into an inn and then regains his memory: he is back in his own country, and has never left it.

It is difficult to know what to make of all this. It is hard to avoid the conclusion that, despite the vague symbolism of the peak—which seems to be a multifaceted symbol of self-discovery, the inner reality, social justice, and perhaps (bearing in mind the icebound Marlin, who tells Michael that he will make a successful ascent one day) the Holy Grail—this is nothing more nor less in its essentials than a rather uninspired revamping of *The Wild Goose Chase*, 'a scarlet fantasia', as Derek Stanford expressed it, 'for the junior C.P.'[105] One can see that the 'land over the mountain' is a giant blown-up caricature of Europe of the thirties, and one can see the point that Todd is making that behind the platitudinous clergymen, the whisky-drinking Colonels in the Explorers Club, and the regimented public schools of Britain, there existed a potential Fascist state, and, finally, one recognises that the issues have been deliberately simplified as part of the satirical technique, but the plain fact is that the satire is too crude, too overblown, to have any impact. Michael's suddenly acquired social conscience is thrust upon us without any advance warning; the clergyman does little to deserve the derogatory epithets heaped upon him beyond making one or two mildly reactionary remarks; and the proletarian friends of Michael sound only slightly different in degree from the defective policemen. A little irony would not have gone astray.

Todd's novel illustrates very forcibly the perils of this kind of technique unless carefully controlled, but this and the other disparaging comments that have been made should certainly not blind us to the positive qualities of these three books. With varying degrees of success their authors have utilised the kind of experience found in *Starting Point* and to an extent broken away from the abstract presentation to which many middle-class writers must have felt themselves condemned.

IV

'The historical novel', asserted the Anglo-Australian writer, Jack Lindsay, in *New Masses* in 1937, 'is a form that has a limitless future as a fighting weapon and as a cultural instrument'.[106] The imaginative recreation of the revolutionary struggles of the past could, he claimed, have both an educative value in itself, and at the same time help to remind people of the inevitability and historical necessity of Communism. More importantly, he might have added, it could also provide one more solution for the British writer, and particularly for the middle-class writer, of that search for the elusive objective correlative of their beliefs. For in the past could be found so many more full-scale revolutionary situations than that prevailing in the Britain of the nineteen-thirties.

When Lindsay made this hopeful prediction there had in fact already appeared in Britain several examples of what may be loosely termed the revolutionary historical novel. Grassic Gibbon—under his real name of J. Leslie Mitchell—had written *Spartacus* (1933), a novel of tremendous physical impact which cast the slave-leader both as an earlier proletarian hero and as a proto-Christ figure. There is overwriting in this book, and Spartacus is forever hovering close to the level of comic-book superhero, more a proletarian inspiration than any conceivable real-life person. But then the real power of *Spartacus* is found not so much in its eponymous hero, or in any of his fellow-leaders, as in the compelling drive of the narrative, as the slave-host marches and counter-marches, gains victories and suffers defeats, and as finally the remnant meets its horrific end on six thousand crosses along the Appian Way.

Another writer to produce historical tales from a revolutionary viewpoint was Geoffrey Trease, whose books were underground reading in Nazi Austria during the thirties. They were intended for children, but as they were ardently recommended by Harry Pollitt to all workers everywhere,[107] they do at least deserve a mention here. In these two stories—*Comrades for the Charter* (1934) and *Bows Against the Barons* (1934—recently translated into Rumanian under the engaging title of *Umbrele din Pădurea Sherwood*[108])—the Chartists and Robin Hood reel off a stream of Communist slogans with a minimal regard for historical accuracy. 'Comrades!' shouts Robin as he leads his band into the last battle.' . . . To-day will be the first great victory of the people. Nothing can stop us. Forward then! All power to the workers! Down with the masters!' 'ALL POWER TO THE WORKERS!'[109]

Two other books which could be said to half-merge into this historical category were Robert Briffault's two novels, *Europa* (1936) and *Europa in*

Limbo (1937). These massive volumes recount with great gusto and little aesthetic care the adventures of an upper-class Englishman, Julian Bern, in the prewar capitals of Europe, in the war itself, in the Russian Revolution, and finally in his role as writer to an English radical magazine, *New World*. Real-life characters abound in its pages: Julian hears Karl Liebknecht speak, meets Lenin in Italy, waits for ten minutes for Henry James to end a sentence, and has a conversation with D. H. Lawrence, in which the latter talks about the radiations of vital fluid from the solar plexus. '"Good God, man," Julian had exclaimed, almost losing patience, "what will it profit your brothers, your two million brothers, who are fighting, bewildered, for their mere bread, for their existence, to have radiations of vital fluid from their solar plexuses?"'[110] They are hastily written books for mass consumption, but at the same time were clearly intended to help the revolutionary cause. Both are filled with an expressed hatred of anything bourgeois, and a confidence—once they have been freed from the enshackling education of the ruling classes—in the coming power of the workers. As the hero reflects towards the end of the second volume, while he is watching a demonstration in Paris in memory of the Commune: 'The space round the wall was full of workers, silent, calm. It was another France, this. They were another race, these French workers, large, good-natured, serious, another race from the wizened, bloated, French bourgeois, deformed outwardly to monkey-like, toad-like ugliness by corroding meanness, greed, vanity, fear, selfishness. Another France, another race. . . . This was the France which had made the Revolution, the Commune'.[111] Unfortunately for Briffault's intentions, however, this black-and-white partisanship is not enough to win the day. For, like so many other modern bestsellers which attack immorality while clearly revelling in it, the decadence of the bourgeoisie is recited with such lip-smacking prurience, such gratuitous detail, that the reader is finally left in some genuine doubt as to which side of the barricades Briffault is actually on.

Not much more successful was Sylvia Townsend Warner's attempt to express her revolutionary beliefs in the form of historical fiction. Her novel *Summer Will Show* (1936) relates the journey into revolution of the upper-class heroine, Sophia Willoughby. A thorough snob at the beginning, who sees the working class as not quite human, or at best, in a moment of hysteria, as a means of fathering her children, she goes to Paris just before the 1848 revolutions, hoping to find her errant husband. She finds him, but prefers his former mistress, Minna, a bohemian revolutionary. With almost no explanation offered as to why she should take this drastic course, she is soon living happily with Minna amongst the destitute of Paris, looking upon the upper classes as 'elegant and lifeless'.[112] Pirouetting even further to the left—although apparently more for the fun of it than for any Communist sympathies—she starts helping the fledgling Communists, collecting scrap lead for them to make into bullets. When fighting starts, she is in the thick of it, and only narrowly escapes death. Resolving that she cannot go back to her old life, she ends the novel reading 'obdurately attentive and by degrees absorbed'[113] the freshly printed *Communist Manifesto*. It is all great fun, a delightful piece of wish fulfilment—but utterly unconvincing.[114]

Whatever their relative merits, none of these novels—with the possible superficial exception of Briffault's—was written from a consistent Marxist viewpoint. They were all, rather, individual revolutionary gestures, emotionally sympathetic to Communism, but with almost no firm ideological basis. It was left to Lindsay, in fact—like Howard Fast in America[115]—properly to explore the possibilities of Marxist historical fiction.

It needs to be said at once that Lindsay occupies a rather special place among the left-wing novelists of the thirties, in that since that decade he has neither abandoned his Communist convictions nor stopped using his novels to express them. He was able to say as late as 1968 'I consider myself a revolutionary writer in the sense that I'm totally opposed to the existing society and want to see it changed root and branch. I've had my variations in stress, in theory, and so on; nevertheless, in all fundamentals I remain that'.[116] Although he has often been guilty of an extremely crude propaganda, he has maintained an individuality which make his books interesting even at their worst. As he says in his autobiography *Fanfrolico and After*: '. . . I found myself odd-man-out, a continuing outsider, whose work was rejected by the conservative or liberal as crudely committed to the proletarian cause, and was not much welcomed on the Left, which complained steadily over the years about all sorts of unorthodox elements, overcomplex and subtle, overpsychological, mystical, overlyrical, lewd, overnaturalistic or psychopathological, overconcerned with sex, et-cetera'.[117] He is certainly not a Party hack. His novels have never been published by the Communist publishing house, Lawrence and Wishart,[118] and it is interesting to note that he was among the signatories of a letter to the *New Statesman and Nation* in December 1956, which condemned the Soviet action in Hungary and the British Communist Executive's uncritical support of it.[119]

He had written a number of historical novels before 1936, but it was only from this year that he started writing in support of the Communist cause. (January, 1936, is the date when, as he puts it, he 'really reached bedrock. . .'.[120]) He made two preliminary skirmishes, the first with sixteenth-century Italian history (*Adam of a New World*, 1936) and the second with contemporary Cornwall (*End of Cornwall*, 1937). The latter, set in the Cornish port of Tregwidden, is as crudely partisan, and as basically improbable as *Jew Boy* or *Revolt*. The proletarian coal-deliverer hero, Roscorla, spends what little spare time he has frowning in concentration over a copy of the *Communist Manifesto*. Understanding slowly seeps in, until finally: 'He held the tattered pamphlet in his hand, holding reality."Marx and Engels,Marx and Engels." Around him he felt the new world coming into being, men standing up out of the earth, the men who made and fed the world arising to throw off the parasites, laughing, serious, invincible. He was part of this mighty move-ment . . .'.[121] He proposes successfully to the heroine, Bronwen, who is pregnant to another man. Elated, he shouts across the darkness to Gwennap pit where Wesley once preached to the miners: 'Hey there, Wesley. . . . I'll give you a text, Wesley. The workers have nothing to lose but their chains. Workers of the world unite! Workers of Cornwall, you're part of it. I'm a worker, that's my name and country. Look out, Wesley, and all you ghosts. Your day is done'.[122]

Interwoven with Roscorla's discovery of his proletarian significance, there is the story of the anti-trade unionist George Tangye, who murders his friend Sam Spargo in a fit of insanity, and that of Bob Rodda, a fisherman, forced to leave fishing because of the grinding pressure of the dealers. It is only when he becomes a tin-mining prospector, and faces the same economic pressures, that he realises that he, too, is part of the world working-class movement.

Lindsay's attempt in this book to mingle ideology with a romance and murder story is a failure, and there is an irritating partisan simplicity in the characterisation. The objects of his attack are nearly all humourless caricatures, while Roscorla, with his mystical ability to bring happiness to women, his utter goodness and selflessness, and his rather simpleminded persistence with the *Communist Manifesto*, is yet one more middle-class idealisation.

There is, however, as has been indicated, rather greater reward for the reader in Lindsay's historical fiction of this period. The first of these 'weapons in the class struggle', *Adam of a New World*, deals with the last years of Giordano Bruno, the sixteenth-century philosopher who was imprisoned and finally burnt at the stake by the Inquisition. Lindsay's intention is made clear on the dedication page: 'Dedicated to the many writers who have given their lives during the last few years in the fight against Fascist terrorism'. Bruno wants to 'go to Rome and save the Catholic Church from the rot that has set in. I shall use its organisation to create the necessary basis of world-brotherhood, and I shall transmute its theoretical basis from within, substituting co-operation and rationality for the present superstitious support of corruption, injustice, and greed'.[123] His pupil in Venice, Mocenigo, denounces him to the Venetian In-quisition for heresy. He is arrested and cross-examined at great length. During the cross-examination, he realises that his hopes of reforming the church from within are fruitless. He had hoped that the Inquisition judges would see his point of view and discuss matters in what he considers a rational way. 'Surely their attitude must be that superstitious hocus-pocus was needed to keep the common people in subjection, but for themselves they must have a higher standard of intelligence.'[124] But he decides that it is not a question of belief: 'They were merely the beasts of prey. They were cogs in the machine of murder, of greed, which once started off could not stop itself. Only a force from outside the machine could shatter it'.[125]

He is taken from the Venetian prison and placed in the Papal prison, making one unsuccessful attempt to escape on the way. He is now subjected to the Papal Inquisition, and in a scene reminding one as much of the Stalinist trials as of any Fascist parallel,[126] he tries to surrender to their demands, but finds himself unable to: 'He could not deny the new world already implanted in his flesh'.[127] After seven years of confinement, he is tortured and then burned at the stake. As he dies, he thinks: 'Yes, only from the people could come the will and the power to righteousness and brotherhood. The usurpers, the triumphant beasts of parasitic ownership, would never let go their grip unless they were compelled. . . . But some day the people would uproot the stake and scatter the murderous lords of the world. . .'.[128]

It will be obvious even from the short summary above that there is far too much of 1936 in *Adam of a New World*, and too little of the sixteenth century. It is true that in a sense 'all history is contemporary history',[129] and it is also true that many successful historical novels have been *romans-à-clef* in which contemporary characters appear—but there is an imaginative limit. In this particular novel Bruno is a clearly identified historical figure, whose actions and ideas are (at the outset, anyway) closely consonant with the real Bruno, and we should legitimately expect this to remain so. It was a valid and interesting idea to see the persecution of this Renaissance philosopher by the reactionary Inquisition as resembling in many ways the persecution of writers by the totalitarian régimes of the thirties, but where the novel pre-eminently fails is in Lindsay's attempt to wrest Bruno into the camp of the revolutionary proletariat—or at least transform him into a prophet of it. Bruno was essentially a spokesman— albeit unconsciously so—of the bourgeoisie, and Lindsay is spreading rather thinly his interpretation of Bruno's *The Expulsion of the Triumphant Beast* when he has the philosopher directly forecasting the triumph of the People against the world's rulers. He certainly fails by his own standards: '. . . Marxist fiction must in no way falsify the past. . .'.[130]

Another statement in the already mentioned *New Masses* article has a clear relevance to the trilogy of English novels which followed *Adam of a New World*: '. . . there is no task more important for the Communists in each country than to make clear that they stand for the true completion of the national destiny'.[131] In *1649: A Novel of a Year* (written in 1938: dealing with the Digger and Leveller movements), *Lost Birthright* (1939: the Wilkesite agitations) and *Men of Forty-Eight* (written in 1939: the Chartist and revolutionary uprisings in Europe)[132], Lindsay set out to vivify the historical traditions behind English Socialism and to show that it did indeed stand for the completion of the national destiny.[133] It is a limited aim: but in the first novel, *1649*, he transcends the limitation and gives to

Marxist ideology a life and conviction that few British novelists had so far been able to do. His characters are dominated by economic motives and class attitudes; but to a great extent he has made this convincing and truthful in the context of the world he has created.

The book opens with the execution of King Charles I; the Independent Puritans, dominating the army, the Council of States, and Parliament, are everywhere triumphant. The Levellers—a more radical group led by Lilburne, who wish to enact a more comprehensive programme of political reform—have temporarily allied themselves with the Independents. They are now waiting to see whether the latter will do anything about the Leveller-inspired 'Agreement of the People', which sets out their political aims. When the Independents instead arrest their leaders and make preparations to invade Catholic Ireland, certain Leveller-sympathising regiments mutiny. The mutiny—and later smaller ones—is put down. Some sort of triumph is achieved when Lilburne, after being found innocent at his treason trial, is released—but the Leveller movement, though still confident of eventual success, is splintering into ineffectual groups. At the same time as these events are taking place a very much smaller and more radical group of men led by Winstanley attempts to put into practice a form of agrarian Communism on the common lands outside London. This movement too is eventually crushed and broken.

Mingling fictional with historical characters, Lindsay has imposed a collective vision on these events: a vision which, though certainly ultimately a Marxist one, is not so in any simplistic, partisan sense. He is interested in showing, not only the importance of the Levellers and Diggers in the historical tradition of Socialism, but also the importance and strength and *necessity* of other impulses at this time, and in particular that of the individualist bourgeois commercial thrust. In the person of Ralph Lydcott, son of a well-to-do merchant taylor, he does show some of the strength of this other impulse. Ralph is at the beginning an enthusiastic Leveller and agnostic. When he comes into contact with his uncle, a bustling bourgeois merchant, filled with the vision of an expanding England (as distinct from his father, whose aims are limited to his personal salvation and profit), he is at first merely disconcerted: 'It was easy to stand up against the people who had views antagonistic to his own; what upset him about his uncle's pronouncements was that they seemed to come from an entirely alien universe of thought and action'.[134] Later, upset at the failure of a Leveller uprising, he decides to carry out a commission for his uncle. As he reads his uncle's letter of instructions he feels that 'beyond both guile and geniality there was a feeling of strength . . . an impression that the writer had sources of moral support which Ralph himself could not understand'.[135] He finds himself more and more immersed in business and less concerned about the fate of the Leveller movement. A chance meeting with an impressive evangelist, Stoat, further hastens the erosion of his politically radical beliefs. He marries the daughter of another merchant taylor, and finally, with no great sense of drama, burns his Leveller tracts and pamphlets. He starts attending church and the last we see of him he is discussing with his friend Arthur Boon the need to 'consolidate'. 'At the end of their discussions they emerged a little ashamed, but nevertheless much relieved.'[136] The bourgeois flowering has to come before the proletarian revolution: Lindsay makes the point without protruding too obviously the sharp elbow of ideology.

Ralph's friend, Roger Cotton, takes almost the opposite course. Fervently religious at the outset, seeking the perfect means of salvation by self-sacrifice, he is falsely imprisoned by his employer and comes to know by direct experience the real meaning of the poverty and beggary of London. The cry of Everard, the Digger, that 'We shall call on all men to join in the working of common lands, till all things are held in common',[137] seems to represent for him for the first time a cause 'he knew to be wholly worthy'.[138] At the same time Lindsay is honest enough to record his other mixed motives: '. . . Roger saw that only persecution could be now expected, and he thrilled with the painful excitement of the fate which he accepted'.[139] Through Roger, too, or rather through Roger's relationship with the prostitute, Nell, Lindsay symbolises the Marxist idea of the alienating influence of Capitalism upon personal relationships. The pity of it is that he drags this relationship past reader endurance, and also feels the need to make the symbolism explicit: '. . . in the conflict between him and Nell there was more than a personal disagreement. More every day now he felt that the conflict mirrored the dilemma of the suffering world'.[140] Eventually Roger recognises, after seeing the full power of the State brought to bear upon Lilburne, that though the Diggers' ideas are right, their unaided attempts to actualise them are bound to fail. Feeling the need to be 'at the heart of the struggle',[141] he returns to London, and joins in the Leveller activities.

Lindsay's world is an economic world. To a quite startling degree he convinces us of its reality: the small weavers in the north; the small smelting works; fishing in Yarmouth; the rudimentary ideas of trade unionism; the breaking down of the old craft system; the thrusting bourgeois impulse; the enclosures forcing the yeoman off the land into the newly burgeoning industries. It is partly because of his reluctance to make the simple partisan judgement that he convinces us: the landowner, Sir Henry Steyling, is seen not as a rapacious figure, intent on greater profits, but as a man imbued with a paternal attitude towards his tenants and facing bankruptcy unless he does enclose. 'I will not betray my tenants, he said, by the body of God I will not.'[142]

The book has its glaring faults. Lindsay overwrites frequently, and his phrases often have the slick meaninglessness of copywriter's English: 'The spring sky was bannered with the exaltation of the moment'[143]; 'The smoky tavern-room became bright with the light of swords—the swords of the soldiers of righteousness. Life overflowed in fullness, like wine gurgling from the flask'[144]; 'He seemed to be sinking into the ground, dripping in stupefied misery to the engulfing earth. His head was leaden-heavy, a ball of confused heat'.[145] He betrays his limitations when he extends his characters; his skill is more evident in his cameo portraits, such as those of Arthur Boon and Isaac Lydcott. But it is when his characters show a post-Marxist judgement that he is least convincing. The positive side of his message is clearly conveyed in his sympathy, for example, for the Diggers' Communism, and in the way in which Lilburne, with the power of the people behind him, is able to defeat the mechanism of the State; but he is overly anxious to make his point that the events of 1649 are part of a larger picture. Thus he gives to Ralph Lydcott and Lockyer, a Leveller soldier, a scarcely credible apocalyptic moment: '. . . the hugeness of the moment in which they were acting their part stole over them like a gigantic shadow, the wings of time . . . lifting them up into strange and rare regions; setting them on a giddy crag of vision from which they saw the mass movements of men suddenly coherent and understandable, a map of man, a landscape of time, perilous and engrossing, terrific as a burst of storm, yet clear as the printed page of a book'.[146] Again and again his characters seem to be approaching this wider understanding, as when Roger, for example, after seeing Lilburne and 'the scarlet judges', realises that the Diggers must fail: '. . . something else was needed before the preachings could be actualized'.[147] It is debatable, too, how far the Levellers can be yoked together with the Diggers; certainly Lilburne (and Lindsay recognises this) was an individualist, seeking personal liberties, and vehemently disowned the ideas of Winstanley.

With all these reservations *1649* remains an interesting, thoughtful, and to a large extent successful, attempt to concretise the abstractions of Marxist ideology. Regrettably, however, it also remains the peak of Lindsay's revolutionary writing in the thirties, for the two novels which followed it were infinitely less successful. The first of these, *Lost Birthright*, has for its background the Wilkesite battle for the liberty of the individual in the later part of the eighteenth century. Like *1649* it has one character, Harry Lydcott, moving towards involvement with the People and their agitation for their rights, and one character, John Butlin, coming to place his trust in the ever more thrusting bourgeois movement. It has little of the vitality and conviction of *1649*. The historical material is never properly integrated into the novel—primarily because there is no character fully involved with Wilkes. Lindsay's attempts to give his characters some consciousness of their historic role also strains our credulity even further. For example, the Jew Mendoza, building up the wealth of his bourgeois clients with astute stockmarket juggling, is sustained only by his vision of the future: 'There is something further, some structure of a different power emerging after all; I feel it at moments'.[148]

Men of Forty-Eight fails too, partly for the same reasons. Lindsay has tried to deal not only with the Chartist agitations in England, but also the uprisings in France and Austria, and as a result the novel tends to read in many places like a left-wing history textbook, with large chunks of unassimilated material. There is also a new shrill, hectoring tone, an inflated, melodramatic rhetoric which was to emerge even more strongly in Lindsay's books of the war years.[149] And if Lindsay has some justification for the now familiar Marxist consciousness, writing as he is about a year in which the *Communist Manifesto* first appeared, he has little justification for the way in which Boon, his main character, is talking in Marxist terms about the 'necessity of History' long before he has read a word of Marx. It is indeed with the central figure of Born that the trouble chiefly resides. The Chartist movement, unlike the movement of 1649, was essentially proletarian, and the upper middle-class Boon is never really a believable part of it. He talks in intellectual abstractions: 'What I feel about the working class is the beautiful fertility inherent in their fury; the infinite resources of release, peace, love, which I feel within their rejection of "freedom" as formulated by the possessing classes',[150] or is involved in a swashbuckling manner in the French street fighting, or else tries to make contact by making love to a village girl. Edith Sitwell found this novel 'profoundly impressive, and as moving as it is impressive',[151] but the reader is far more likely to be uneasily reminded of *We Have Been Warned*.

8 *A Scots Quair*

In the previous two chapters most of the revolutionary novels of the thirties have been examined or mentioned, and an attempt has been made to show why so few of them approached any degree of success. Of the least convincing novels by writers of working-class origin, such as Holt, Roley and Phelan, it was suggested that much of the trouble arose from their failure to convey the serious depths of their beliefs, thus leaving the reader in some confusion and perplexity as to how strongly these beliefs were held. Even a writer like Harold Heslop, who made more strenuous attempts to marry his ideological convictions with the events and actions of his story, ultimately mars his work with what appears to be an unconscious preference for the devil. With Sommerfield and Barke, on the other hand, the reverse appears to be true: their overzealously dogmatic embrace of their ideology led often to the creation of pawns rather than people. The distinction is certainly not absolute, of course: Holt's humourless caricatures, for example, are also in part a reflection of an overdogmatic simplification.

At the same time, however, it was implied—and as even the short accounts of the novels should have shown—that these books were also seriously flawed by their authors' lack of a mature creative and imaginative faculty. Holt's humourless police caricatures arise from a fundamentally naively developed imagination, while the incredible events in Phelan owe their genesis just as much to a lack of disciplined imaginative control as to a lack of disciplined political thought. James Barke's MacKelvie certainly stems in part from his dogmatism, but an examination of his other less Marxist novels of these years shows that he was basically a second-rate writer. Lewis Jones's more balanced political approach helped to make his novels more palatable, but they are still marred by his extremely ungainly style and stiff characterisation.

In the examination of the middle-class novelists, apart from similar points being made about ideological confusion, much stress was laid on the limitations of their experience. Clearly the latter was an important factor: Ralph Bates's own knowledge of revolutionary conditions and revolutionary workers undoubtedly played a large part in the success of *The Olive Field* as revolutionary propaganda. One has for confirmation of this only to turn to the fact that of the two more successful middle-class novels,

1649 and *The Wild Goose Chase*, one was set in a surrealistic world, and one in the historical past. But again this is by no means all that has to be said: the middle-class writers are on the whole better writers, but the flaws in their books can certainly not be solely ascribed to the limitations of their upbringing and experience—or for that matter to ideological confusion. Brown was a long-winded writer before he became a Marxist, Lindsay was employing an over-inflated rhetoric before 1936, and *The Wild Goose Chase* ultimately fails because Warner had not the imaginative powers equal to the task he set himself.

The final reasons for their failure, then, cannot be laid to the responsibility of any single, simple factor, but to a combination of the following: an imperfectly grasped, or imperfectly embraced ideology, resulting in superficiality or confusion; an overzealously embraced ideology, resulting in pawns, rather than people; and finally, the one constant factor, the lack, in varying degrees, of a mature creative and imaginative faculty.

None of the revolutionary books of the thirties, it seems to me, is unmarked by these flaws. There was one writer, however, often mentioned but not yet closely examined, who was able to escape their damning presence more than others. I have reserved discussion on this writer, Lewis Grassic Gibbon, not because in his work we may find a perfect blending of all the good points of the novels examined, nor because, in the Marxist sense, 'we find . . . in him the knowledge of how to move forward',[1] but quite simply because his work does seem to me to be superior to all the other revolutionary novels, and this superiority can be now more clearly established after we have considered the degree of success approached by the others.

II

Strictly speaking, Gibbon originated from outside of the class struggle, born and raised as he was in the peasant-farming country of the Scottish Mearns. Most of his books were written under his real name of J. Leslie Mitchell, and in the seven years before his death in 1935 he produced the astonishing number of seventeen full-length works.[2] But it is almost wholly on his trilogy *A Scots Quair*[3] that his reputation now rests. Indeed, it should be said at once that of all the revolutionary novels of the thirties, this impressive trilogy is the only work that remains in any real sense a living part of literature—reprinted year after year and having occasional critical attention paid to it. Sometimes one suspects, however, that the reason for the latter is that the revolutionary intent is glossed over and other intentions stressed at its expense.[4] It is important to remember that Gibbon was a revolutionary writer, stated quite firmly that he was one, and that all his books were 'explicit or implicit propaganda' against capitalism.[5] If his allegiance to Communism was rarely that of an orthodox party-liner, and was, moreover, coloured by his Diffusionist belief in a Golden Age of the past,[6] there is no doubt that there is throughout *A Scots Quair* a passionate hatred of the 'Masters' which leads inexorably in the last book to a passionate sympathy for Communism. How has this come to be seen as acceptable, while the other books of propaganda have been forgotten, or at best remembered as well-intentioned failures?

There is no doubt, as most critics have agreed, that the first volume, *Sunset Song*, is the most deeply satisfying, for here it is that Gibbon is dealing with the land and the people he knew most intimately. Set on the estate of Kinraddie in the country of the Mearns, it is the story of the sunset song of the crofters, the last of the peasant farmers, and at the same time the personal story of Chris Guthrie. The daughter of the crofter John Guthrie, Chris is initially torn between her love of the land and her love of learning. When her father dies, it is to the land she turns, and gives this decision symbolic weight by marrying Ewan Tavendale, a local ploughman. The marriage is shortlived, however, for in the latter stages of the Great War, wilting before the militaristic fervour of the district, Ewan enlists. He returns once, brutalised from his contact with the army and its barracks, and then leaves for the front, where he is later shot as a deserter. But the war is more than a personal disaster, for with its end, the Kinraddie estates are sold up, those who have profited from the war consolidating, enlarging, and mechanising their farms, spelling death to the old small holdings. In the last few pages of the book, Chris's new husband, the Reverend Robert Colquohoun, who helps the Ploughman's Union and talks as though 'Christ had meant Kinraddie',[7] delivers an elegy for the last of the crofters: '. . . lest we shame them, let us believe that the new oppressions and foolish greeds are no more than mists that pass. . . . Beyond . . . there shines a greater hope and a newer world, undreamt when these four died'.[8]

Much of the richness of *Sunset Song* (and, for that matter, of the whole of *A Scots Quair*) derives from the fact that the story is narrated, mainly by Chris, but partly by the changing often anonymous voices of the crofters, in a prose which has, in its lilt and flow, much of the rhythm, in its vocabulary, much of the pungency of Scots spoken speech. Avoiding the tangled thickets of bewilderment which so often plague dialect prose, Gibbon has by an unerring instinct only used those Scottish words which, though they may be directly untranslatable, vividly and often onomato-poeically suggest their own meaning. The result, whether Chris alone or the voice of the crofters is speaking, is extraordinarily evocative of the land and the people:

> Some said the North, up Aberdeen way, had had rain enough, with
> Dee in spate and bairns hooking stranded salmon down in the shallows,
> and that must be fine enough, but not a flick of the greeve weather had
> come over the hills, the roads you walked down to Kinraddie smithy or

up to the Denburn were fair blistering in the heat, thick with dust so that the motor-cars went shooming through them like kettles under steam.

And serve them right, they'd little care for anybody, the dirt that rode in motors, folk said; and one of them had nearly run over wee Wat Strachan a fortnight before and had skirled to a stop right bang in front of Peesie's Knapp. Wat had yowled like a cat with a jobe under its tail and Chae had gone striding out and taken the motorist man by the shoulder. And *What the hell do you think you're up to?* Chae had asked. And the motorist, he was a fair toff with leggings and a hat cocked over his eyes, he'd said *Keep your damn children off the road in future.* And Chae had said *Keep a civil tongue in your head* and had clouted the motorist man one in the ear and down he had flumped in the stour and Mistress Strachan, her that was old Netherhill's daughter, she'd gone tearing out skirling *Mighty, you brute, you've killed the man*! and Chae had just laughed and said *Damn the fears*! and off he'd gone.

But Mistress Strachan had helped the toff up to his feet and shook him and brushed him and apologised for Chae, real civil-like. And all the thanks she got was that Chae was summonsed for assault at Stonehaven and fined a pound, and came out of the courthouse saying there was no justice under capitalism, a revolution would soon sweep away its corrupted lackeys. And maybe it would, but faith! there was as little sign of a revolution, said Long Rob of the Mill, as there was of rain.[9]

The vein of humour running throughout this extract is also typical of the whole: for Gibbon—like Tressell—rarely equates seriousness with pomposity. Veering from the droll remarks of Long Rob to a humour reminiscent in its earthiness of one of the less scatalogical Burns folk-songs, his sense of the comic laces and enlivens the entire length of *A Scots Quair*. He is perhaps at his most engaging, however, when the communal 'speak'—which in the passage just quoted shares the narrative with Chris—is given its gossiping head. Constantly changing its viewpoint— sometimes so swiftly, indeed, that two voices sound in the same sentence: '. . . Mistress Gibbon herself came out to tell him that, kind and fine as she was, but he didn't like her, the English dirt'[10]—the 'speak' has one effect of tugging the reader into even closer intimacy with the people of Kinraddie. But in addition, through their vivid, humorous, and often self-revealing comments, the crofters highlight many of the author's own attitudes.

A good example of this process can be found in Gibbon's treatment of latter-day Christianity. Although as a rationalist he had little faith in religion or in its power to do good, Gibbon's real quarrel was with the hypocrisies masquerading in its name: a quarrel which bears most notable fruit in his characterisation of the Minister of the area, the silver-tongued but unprincipled Reverend Stuart Gibbon. The latter is seen with growing distaste through Chris's eyes, but he and the attitudes towards him are revealed in an altogether more delightful way by the 'speak'. When he first arrives in Kinraddie, for example, the whole Kirk is soon listening with relish to his sermon on the Song of Solomon: ' . . . it was fair tickling to hear about things like that read out from a pulpit, a woman's breasts and thighs and all the rest of the things, in that voice like the mooing of a holy bull; and to know it was decent Scripture with a higher meaning as well'.[11] There even remains a certain relish in the midst of the crofters' later shocked disapproval as they gossip about Gibbon's extramarital philanderings and general dissipation; his sermons, after all, remain as good as ever: ' . . . and feint the many could wag a pow like that in a Mearns pulpit'.[12] But sermons, Stuart Gibbon discovers in 1914 when he preaches on the meaning of war, are not quite all:

> . . . he said that God was sending the Germans for a curse and a plague on the world because of its sins, it had grown wicked and lustful, God's anger was loosed as in the days of Attila. . . .
> And just as he got there, up rose old Sinclair of the Netherhill, all the kirk watched him, and he put on his hat and he turned his back and went step-stepping slow down. the aisle, he wouldn't listen to this brute defending the German tinks and some friend that he called Attila. . . . the minister turned red and then white and he stuttered when he saw folk leaving; and his sermon quietened down, he finished off early and rattled off the blessing as though it was a cursing. Outside in the kirkyard some young folk gathered to clout him in the lug as he came from the kirk, but the elders were there and they edged them away, and Mr. Gibbon threaded the throngs like a futret with kittle, and made for the Manse, and padlocked the gate.[13]

Next week, however, he is back at the Kirk in as fine a voice as ever, this time armed with a new bloodthirsty patriotism : an apparently effortless switch which is reported by the 'speak' with only a hint of irony:

> . . . the minister said that the Kaiser was the Antichrist, and that until this foul evil had been swept from the earth there could be neither peace nor progress again. And he gave out a hymn then, *Onward, Christian Soldiers* it was, and his own great bull's voice led the singing, he had fair become a patriot and it seemed likely he thought the Germans real bad.[14]

Gibbon continues to stir up certain elements in Kinraddie with his pugnacious sermons, until he is posted to Edinburgh as a military chaplain, and then, finally, leaves Scotland to take up an appointment with a rich American church. The 'speak's' closing comment is far more openly hostile than hitherto, but still wavering somewhat in its sense of direction: 'Well, well, he'd done well for himself, it was plain to see; no doubt the Americans would like him fine, they could stand near anything out in America, their stomachs were awful tough with all the coarse things that they ate out of tins'.[15]

As has already been noted, the 'speak' is not the only medium through which Gibbon and some of the more dubious aspects of latter-day Christianity are viewed: but it does provide the author's attack with an extra dimension and bite—not only in that it affords other viewpoints, but more importantly in that it is a double-edged weapon, making fun of the foibles and prejudices of the crofters nearly as much as the hypocrisy of Gibbon. Hence the total picture has a depth and effectiveness which is almost completely lacking in the caricature of the Reverend MacShillock—seen through Grassic Gibbon's eyes only—in *Grey Granite*, and certainly lacking in the satirical excursions in the other revolutionary novels we have studied.

It will be obvious from what has been said that Gibbon, while admittedly sometimes lapsing into a nostalgic mawkishness—particularly in the idyll scenes between Chris and Ewan—is too much aware of the crofters' failings, as he is aware of the hardness of their lives, ever to present them as idealised beings. He may be deeply attached to them, and identify himself completely with their detestation of the 'gentry', but he is also quite capable of seeing them at times in anger through Chris's eyes as 'yokels and clowns everlasting, dull-brained and crude',[16] just as Chris is later to see Ewan's comrades as 'unwashed, their stink awful, their faces worm-white. . . . awful folk'.[17] This kind of approach is nowhere better illustrated than in the portrait of John Guthrie, proud and dour, embittered both by his hard life and by the constant poisoning struggle between his Calvinism and his sensuality. At the last, as he laid in his grave, Chris recalls 'wildly, in a long, broken flash of remembrance, all the fine things of him that the years had hidden from their sight, the fleetness of him and his justice, and the fight unwearying he'd fought with the land and its masters'[18]: but before this moment we have been spared little detail of his decline, from the time that he drives his wife to suicide because of her fear of another pregnancy, to the time that he is half-paralysed, lusting after his own daughter, in her terrified imagination coming down on her 'like a great frog struggling, squattering across the floor'.[19]

John Guthrie is certainly the most closely studied male character in *Sunset Song*—in the sense that we are given much insight into the inner man—but there are numerous other vivid and spirited portraits, for this volume is crowded, as is indeed the whole of *A Scots Quair*, with memorable people. Many, like the tragi-comic old Pooty, with his 'cow and bit donkey that was nearly as old as himself and faith! twice as good-looking',[20] are pure folk-story creations, appearing only in rare cameo incidents before merging back into the anonymity of the 'speak', while others like Chae Strachan, the Socialist whose dream it is to 'have all Tories nailed up in barrels full of spikes and rolled down the side of the Grampians'[21] are given more sustained treatment. The fact that Chae, one of the most sympathetically drawn characters in the book, is also a devout Christian, can help to put the satirical picture of the Reverend Gibbon into perspective; and so too can the fact that he is one of the first to volunteer for the war, believing passionately that the 'Germans had broken loose, fair devils, and were raping women and braining bairns all over Belgium. . . '.[22] When he comes back on leave, his peasant self predictably remarks that 'out there you hardly did fighting at all, you just lay about in those damned bit trenches and had a keek at the soil they were made of'[23]; but nonetheless he is changed, 'Chae himself, thin, his fine eyes queered and strained somehow' . . . 'his old laugh queerly crippled'.[24] Another who is cruelly changed by the war is Ewan Tavendale—too abruptly so, perhaps, for all the care that Gibbon has taken to show the darker side of his character beforehand.[25] Nonetheless, if there is some initial straining of credibility, the episode as a whole—the image of Ewan with his 'coarse hair . . . like short bristles all over his head, the neck with its red and angry circle about the collar of the khaki jacket, a great half-healed scar across the back of his hand',[26] and the later moving account of his desperate and futile attempts to return to Chris and restore their prewar harmony—is a potent symbol both of the irrevocability of the passing of the crofter's way of life and of the shattering, alienating impact of war. The third person to show the war's relentless effects is Long Rob of the Mill, the rationalist whose sardonic comments thread the story. His initial reaction to the hostilities is one of jeering mockery, but gradually the realities of the inflamed militarism around him take their toll. After enduring punishment, imprisonment, and ostracism, he finally realises the futility of this kind of individual pacifist protest in a society which will give him no peace or livelihood until he goes: ' . . . all the world had gone daft and well he might go with the rest . . .'.[27]

Towering over all these characters, however, is Chris Tavendale herself, as she moves from childhood to widowhood, a sensitive and passionate young girl who grows into a young woman, still emotional and impulsive, but developing within her a stoicism to counteract the bitterness she sees life can bring. From her father she has inherited a hatred of 'rulers and gentry', but it is, needless to say, an instinctive, not an ideological hatred. Thus, although she admires Chae Strachan, his creed, with its dogmatic division into Rich and Poor, seems irrelevant to her, for 'she was neither one nor the other herself'.[28] This does not mean, of course, that her allegiance is to the present system. Indeed, as she recalls the events of the story, significantly from her favourite haven, the ancient Standing Stones of Blawearie, we learn of her growing conviction, which assumes the strength of a choric commentary on these events and points forward to *Cloud Howe*, that sadness, joy, beliefs and creeds, all must change and all must eventually pass, 'that nothing endured at all, nothing but the land she passed across, tossed and turned and perpetually changed below the hands of the crofter folk since the oldest of them had set the Standing Stones by the loch of Blawearie. . . . Sea and sky and the folk who wrote and fought and were learnéd, teaching and saying and praying, they lasted but as a breath, a mist of fog in the hills . . .'.[29] Only in the concluding section of the book does Gibbon give to this theme of change an explicit touch of hope, as the Reverend Colquohoun echoes Chris's words, but also expresses his liberal conviction that change can involve progress: '. . . *here in Kinraddie where we watch the building of those little prides and those little fortunes . . . we must give heed that these also do not abide, that a new spirit shall come to the land with the greater herd and the great machines'.*[30]

III

Sunset Song thus closes on a note of muted optimism, an optimism which lingers on for a while into the second volume of the trilogy, *Cloud Howe*, where the Reverend Colquohoun and Chris leave the shattered peasant economic structure of Kinraddie and, significantly, move on to a further stage of Capitalist development, the small weaving town of Segget. A town of 'less than a thousand souls . . . and most of them lost',[31] Segget is uneasily poised between the urban and the rural, tolerating its spinning mills for the trade they bring, but half-fearing, half-despising the Spinners for the alien element they represent. It is on the non-spinning section of the town—the small shopkeepers, joiners, and smiths, the barmen, the roadmen, and those still working on the land—that Gibbon concentrates: they form the bulk of the characters, and theirs are predominantly the voice of the 'speak'. While some of them, such as Ake Ogilvie, a joiner and embittered poet, have retained the fierce and impassioned independence that distinguishes the crofters, there are many others, as the 'speak' makes only too clear, who have not, and who occasionally adopt what can only be called a fawning attitude towards the gentry. It is noticeable too that the gossip and hypocrisy of *Sunset Song* have considerably increased, and, while the 'speak' remains as strong and ribald as ever, the satire is now far more often directed inwards than outwards:

> Behind them the Segget band played up. Ake Ogilvie there at the head of it, fair thinking himself of importance, like, with Jim that served in the bar of the Arms and folk called the Sourock because of his face, tooting on his flute like a duck half-choked, and Newlands the stationy cuddling his fiddle a damn sight closer than ever his mistress, or else she'd have had a bairn ere this—not that you blamed him, she'd a face like a greip, and an ill greip at that, though you don't cuddle faces. And Feet was there, he was playing the bassoon, he sat well back to have room for his boots and looked as red as a cock with convulsions. God ay! it was worth going up to the board if only to take a laugh at the band.

But not a childe or a quean would venture up on the thing till at last Jock Cronin, that tink of a porter that came of the spinners, was seen going up and pulling up a quean. She laughed, and turned her face round at last, and folk fair had a shock, it was Miss Jeannie Grant, she was one of the teachers, what was she doing with a porter, eh?—and a tink at that, that called himself a socialist, and said that folk should aye vote for labour, God knew you got plenty without voting for't.

Socialists with queans—well, you knew what they did, they didn't believe in homes or in bairns, they'd have had all the bairns locked up in poor houses; and the coarse brutes said that marriage was daft—that fair made a body right wild to read that, what was coarse about marriage you would like to know? . . . And you'd stop from your reading and say to the wife, *For Heaven's sake, woman, keep the bairns quiet. Do you think I want to live in a menagerie?* And she'd answer you back, *By your face I aye thought that was where you came from*, and start off again about *her* having no peace . . . and whenever were your wages going to be raised? And you'd get in a rage and stride out of the house, and finish the paper down at the Arms, reading about the dirt that so miscalled marriage—why shouldn't they have to get married as well?[32]

The 'speak' remains Gibbon's main seedbed of satire, but as in *Sunset Song* it is by no means the only centre of consciousness in the book. *Cloud Howe* is also the continuing story of Chris, of her husband, and of her son Ewan: of their own development, their reactions to Segget, and to the social events that form the background of *Cloud Howe*. These social events—the General Strike and the spreading slump—are never thrust upon us as 'historical events', but are woven into the very texture of their lives, and are always subordinate to their personal reactions, just as they naturally interlace the thoughts of the 'speak'.

For Ewan, uprooted from his background before he has had a chance to absorb it or feel allegiance to it, Segget is a place to be coolly explored, its gossip, its faiths—even that of his stepfather—rejected. Chris finds him in his coolness and hardness a 'stranger whom slow through the years she had grown to half-know as a traveller half-knows the face of another on a lone road at night'[33]; for in fact Ewan is in many ways a reflection of Chris in his capacity for self-analysis, his instinctive rejection of supernatural beliefs, and his interest in and awareness of the ancient past of Scotland. Like her he has little confidence in the Socialist activities of his stepfather: 'Robert was fun, when he wasn't at work, with the kirk or the spinners, or his Labour plans . . .'.[34] The quality of Chris's that he most noticeably lacks is, of course, the emotional side of her nature: the deep love of which she is capable, and the passionate identification she feels with the land and the people. But Gibbon gives us one important indication in *Cloud Howe* that he may be finding a way out of the limbo in which he is poised. After hearing an account of conditions in the spinners' section of the town from a childhood friend, Charlie Cronin, he is suddenly and violently sick. Later Chris visits his bedroom, and finds him

> staring out at the fall of sleet, a pelt and a hiss in the moving dark. . . .
> She touched him, quiet, and he started a little.
>   *Oh, nothing*, he said, *I'm fine, don't worry, I was trying to remember old Cronin's face.*
> He was turning to look in the face of Life.[35]

The Reverend Colquohoun is another who, in Gibbon's words, turns to 'look in the face of Life'. One interview with the dissipated mill-owner, Mowatt, convinces him that he should abandon his plans of forming a League of the middle and upper-classes to improve conditions in Segget: instead he turns to the Labour Party Socialism of the spinners. But here again his hopes are short-lived. For a double blow—the collapse of the Strike, and the stillbirth of his son—turns him away from any direct action, turns him inward, indeed, to a weak mysticism where he sees again and again a Presence, the figure, as he believes, of Christ. Only in the closing stages of the book is he shocked out of this mystic retreat when the plight of one evicted spinner family reminds him once more of the basically unChristian nature of the society he lives in. Realising that the effects of a gas-attack suffered in the World War are nearing their fatal conclusion, he struggles to the church to make one final impassioned sermon, expressing the hope that there will be found a '*stark, sure creed that will cut like a knife, a surgeon's knife through the doubt and disease—men with unclouded eyes may yet find it, and far off yet in the time to be, on an earth at peace, living and joyous, the Christ come back . . .*'.[36]

In this cry, in the ignominious collapse of the General Strike and the disillusionment of those involved in it, and in his glimpses of the personal tragedies involved in the economic chaos of Capitalism in crisis, Gibbon is preparing the ground for the Communism of *Grey Granite*. In a different way, too, Chris is preparing the ground. Still the central focus of most of the events, as she recalls them from high in the ancient Kaimes, she is an older, maturer Chris than the young woman of *Sunset Song*. Her passionate, but not blind love of the common people is still present: indeed, she it is who provides one of their most heartfelt defences, when, after listening to the young mill-owner, Mowatt, outline his plans for a revival of Nationalist Scotland on the model of Fascist Italy, in her thoughts she sees all the common people together, ground down over centuries by the gentry, 'the rule and the way of life that had left them the pitiful gossiping clowns that they were . . . the kindly souls of them twisted awry and veiled from men with a dirty jest; and this snippet of a fop with an English voice would bring back worse, and ask her to help!'[37] But for all this she remains an obstinately unideological figure, convinced that Colquohoun's Socialism will prove as transitional as his Christianity, involved in the General Strike

only at the personal level—as she runs to help prevent a bridge being
blown up by some hot-headed strikers, she causes her child to be
stillborn—her heart going out in sympathy to the strikers, but seeing no
hope in their attempts. For her certitude has grown that men

> followed and fought and toiled in the wake of each whirling pillar that
> rose from the heights, clouds by day to darken men's minds—loyalty
> and fealty, patriotism, love, the mumbling chants of the old dead gods
> that once were worshipped in the circles of stones, christianity, socialism,
> nationalism—all—Clouds that swept through the Howe of the world,
> with men that took them for gods: just clouds, they passed and finished,
> dissolved and were done, nothing endured but the Seeker himself, him
> and the everlasting Hills.[38]

Only in Ewan does she see any hope, 'who hadn't a God and hadn't a faith
and took not a thing on the earth for granted. And she thought as she held
him . . . he was one of the few who might save the times, watching the Ice
and the winter come, unflustered, unfrightened, with quiet, cold eyes'.[39]
These words point forward to the Communism of the last book: but also
implicit in them is the basis for the possible eventual rejection of the 'last
faith', by Chris, and by what she seems increasingly to symbolise, history,
time itself.

IV

In *Grey Granite* the themes of the trilogy at last reach their conclusion. We
move on to the most advanced stage of Capitalism, to the industrial city of
Duncairn, and to a further stage of the Capitalist crisis. For the first time
the voices of the industrial proletariat are heard, some grumbling aimlessly
in discontent, others showing signs of more firm political attitudes. Young
Ewan is now more and more the central viewpoint, first working in a steel-
mill, where he gains the 'keelies' admiration and respect, then as a
labourer, moving from Socialism to a hardened revolutionary Communism, a figure having his moments of mystic communion with all the
workers: 'And a kind of stinging bliss came upon him, knowledge that he
was that army itself—that army of pain and blood and torment that was
yet but the raggedest van of the hordes of the Last of the Classes, the
Ancient Lowly, trampling the ways behind it unstayable . . .'.[40] Chris
meanwhile lives on with a resigned acceptance, working as a partner in a
boarding house until the other owner dies, and then attempting a short-
lived marriage of convenience with Ake Ogilvie, the joiner from Segget. At
the close of the book, Ewan is about to leave on a Communist-inspired
hunger march to London, while Chris is returning alone to her birthplace
in Echt, delivering before she goes her final estimation of Ewan's new

faith: '*Yours is just another dark cloud to me—or a great rock you're trying to push up a hill*'.[41] Obdurately apolitical to the last, she is given the concluding words, sitting on the hillside beside her croft, expressing her belief 'that that Change who ruled the earth and the sky and the waters underneath the earth, Change . . . whose right hand was Death and whose left hand Life, might be stayed by none of the dreams of men, love, hate, compassion, anger or pity, gods or devils or wild crying to the sky. He passed and repassed in the ways of the wind, Deliverer, Destroyer and Friend in one'.[42]

One finishes *Grey Granite* moved by Gibbon's passion and saddened by the reminder that he was to die only a few months after the completion of this work: but at the same time this should not blind us to the fact often commented upon that by the standards of its predecessors it contains some disappointing artistic flaws, which should—even at the risk of anticlimax—be enumerated. One is very much aware, in the first place, that though Gibbon conveys something of its murk and grime, Duncairn is a city seen through the eyes of an emigré countryman: the acute sense of background, of atmosphere, which characterised his treatment of Kinraddie and Segget, has somehow eluded him. Then, too, the bite of the prose, the pungent satire, has noticeably diminished: several of the characters, indeed, such as the Reverend MacShillock and Baillie Brown, seem crude caricatures, refugees from other, lesser revolutionary novels. Nor are the workers, through whose eyes much of the action should logically be seen, ever evoked with the same power and vividness that distinguished the crofters of *Sunset Song*, the shopkeepers of Segget. It is symptomatic that Ewan should establish a relationship with the keelies by fighting with them: though this is a feasible enough process, it is nonetheless an artistic short cut, a revelation of Gibbon's own uncertainty, and of his handicapping lack of a really intimate knowledge of the industrial proletariat. Part of the problem here, however, would seem to arise not just from the circumstances of Gibbon's upbringing, but from the fact that the 'speak', so effective in rendering the voices and feel of a small community, is incapable of suggesting the immensity of an industrial population; hence it is only when the workers are gathered together in a compact unit—as in the unemployment demonstration—that the power of the technique reasserts itself. This hardly explains the noticeably diminished humour, but it does perhaps explain why the city of Duncairn seems so underpopulated, and why characters such as Brown and MacShillock seem so crudely drawn. Seen through Gibbon's eyes, and not through those of the community, isolated, apparently without roots, they inevitably seem feeble indeed—and the attacks on them somewhat gratuitous—beside the Reverend Gibbon of *Sunset Song*.[43]

For all these obvious, and indeed, serious defects, *Grey Granite* still remains a moving and in many respects eloquent ending to the trilogy. It is on the work as a whole—for *A Scots Quair* should be viewed as one work— that the final judgement should be passed, but one can still delineate here some of the virtues that give this volume, flawed as it is, a superiority over the works we have been discussing.

If the prose has lost some of its bite, and if there do seem to be more passages where Gibbon slips into a style which is virtually a parody of the real thing, it retains, nonetheless, much of its singing zest, whether in a more lighthearted mood, as when a young keelie reluctantly attends his first political meeting:

> . . . there was a piano up in the corner with a lad sitting at it, and he started to play and you all got up and sang about England arising, the long, long night was over, though the damn thing had barely yet set in, God what a perfect fool you felt not knowing the words, a quean next to you pushed a book in your hands, smirked at you, trying to get off, would you say? So you made on to sing, glowering about, there was Alick Watson, bawling like a bellows, if England didn't awake she must be stone deaf . . . .[44]

or, in a more serious vein, as the unemployed of Duncairn start their protest march:

> And on and up you rumbled through Paldy, clatter of boots on the calsay stones, the sun was shining through drifts of rain, shining you saw it fall on the roofs in long, wavering lines and floodings of rain. . . .
> . . . .
> . . . and you all felt kittled up and high by then and looked back by your shoulder and saw behind the birn of billies marching like you, you forgot the wife, that you hadn't a meck, the hunger and dirt, you'd alter that. They couldn't deny you, you and the rest of the Broo folk here, the right to lay bare your grievances. Flutter, flutter, the banner over your head, your feet beginning to stound a wee, long since the boots held out the water, shining the drift of rain going by.[45]

And, if the number and vivacity of Gibbon's minor characters has diminished, there is still the solid Ake Ogilvie, 'Long-moustered, green-eyed, with his ploughman's swagger', whose 'coming had brought to Duncairn something clean and crude as the smell of rain',[46] and there is, too, the inimitable Ma Cleghorn, Chris's partner, whose death scene, as David Craig has commented, is 'sheer folk-story, the old devastating irreverence of Burns now linked to a passionate rationalism'[47]:

> And suddenly Ma's lips ceased to twist and slobber with their blowings of brownish spume, her hand in Chris's slackened with a little jerk; and she stepped from the bed and out of the house and up long stairs that went wandering to Heaven like the stairs on Windmill Brae. And she met at the Gates St. Peter himself, in a lum hat and leggings, looking

awful stern, the father of all the Wee Free Ministers, and he held up his hand and snuffled through his nose and asked in GAWD'S name was she one of the Blessed? And Ma Cleghorn said she was blest if she knew— *Let's have a look at this Heaven of yours*. And she pushed him aside and took a keek in, and there was God with a plague in one hand and a war and a thunderbolt in the other and the Christ in glory with the angels bowing, and a scraping and banging of harps and drums, ministers thick as a swarm of blue-bottles, no sight of Jim and no sight of Jesus, only the Christ, and she wasn't impressed. And she said to St. Peter *This is no place for me*, and turned and went striding into the mists and across the fire-tipped clouds to her home.[48]

But *Grey Granite* is more than ever before primarily the story of two people: Chris and her son Ewan; and it is in their development, and what they finally seem to become, that much of the effectiveness of *Grey Granite*, and, indeed, of the trilogy as a whole rests. An earlier novel by Gibbon, *Spartacus*, had featured a protagonist similar in some ways to Ewan: in his moments of mystic communion with the 'hungered dispossessed of all time', and in the elements of 'superhero' in his make-up. More ominously, there is, in Ewan's cold rejection of anything that does not advance the Communist cause, in the impressive physical and intellectual stature attributed to him, and even in certain turns of phrasing ('Bunk symbolism was a blunted tool'[49]) a tang of the obnoxious Jock MacKelvie. But the character as a whole coheres, and if there does linger about him something of the superhero, there is enough else in Gibbon's handling of him to make him a strangely compelling figure. One should note in the first place that he does not spring up, Phoenix-like, armed with his granitic qualities, and with no explanation offered: his development, as we have seen, has been carefully traced from childhood, and his background and the traits he has inherited from his mother and grandfather, go some way towards establishing his reality. Nor is he, like MacKelvie, or like most of the other revolutionary characters, presented blankly for our approval: Gibbon has few illusions about what he has become by the end of *Grey Granite*. There is sufficient in his character and circumstances to involve the reader sympathetically in his struggles to break away from the workers' problems, to forget the conditions they live in, and in his final refusal to take the easy way out and get a 'respectable' job. We know enough of his background, too, to involve ourselves in his realisation at the Socialist dance, that

in a sudden minute . . . he would never be himself again, he'd never be ought but a bit of them, the flush on a thin white mill-girl's face, the arm and hand and the downbent face of a keelie from the reek of the Gallowgate, the blood and bones and flesh of them all, their thoughts and their doubts and their loves were his, all that they thought and lived in were his. And that Ewan Tavendale that once had been, the cool boy

with the haughty soul and cool hands . . . slipped away out of the room
as he stared, slipped away and was lost from his life forever.[50]

Part of any such emotional involvement that the reader may feel at this
point will, of course, have arisen from the accumulated core of sympathy
established earlier by Gibbon for the common people: but part, too, is
accorded to Ewan in his own right, for the rootlessness of his feelings has
been brought home so vividly to us. The keelies and the Cause are his
equivalent of Chris's roots in the land. At the same time, however, he is
presented as utterly ruthless and sectarian in his devotion to the cause. His
sneering rejection of his girlfriend Ellen when she shows a desire to
compromise and settle for the easy way, is only a practical application of
the awareness he—and Gibbon—have shown of what the revolutionary
cause can bring in its wake:

> And Ewan sat and looked on and spoke now and then, and liked them
> well enough, knowing that if it suited the Party purpose Trease would
> betray him to the police to-morrow, use anything and everything that
> might happen to him as propaganda and publicity, without caring a fig
> for liking or ought else. So he'd deal with Mrs. Trease, if it came to
> that . . . And Ewan nodded to that, to Trease, to himself, commonsense,
> no other way to hack out the road ahead. Neither friends nor scruples
> nor honour nor hope for the folk who took the workers' road . . .[51]

There may, it is true, be an element of 'romanticised fatalism'[52] in this, but
the statement itself stripped to its essentials is one that is sorely lacking in so
many other novels of the time: the recognition that if the revolutionary
cause has its rich compensations, it also has its debilitating effect on human
personality and human relationships. There is never any doubt about the
real strength of Gibbon's support for the workers' cause, but neither is
there any doubt about his honesty. It is this honesty which helps to draw us
to Ewan, for all our misgivings.

One final facet of Ewan's role in the novel has yet to be examined, but this
can be discussed more usefully after a consideration of Chris, for, despite
her lesser role in this final volume, she still remains of crucial importance.
Now middle-aged, some of her beauty gone, she retains her passionate
independence. She can be moved by the conditions in the Duncairn slums,
but her instinctive allegiance remains with the peasantry; to a workman
who tells her to enjoy her money while her class still survives, she flares
out: '*My class? It was digging its living in sweat while yours lay down with a whine
in the dirt*'.[53] Her marriage to Ake Ogilvie makes her realise after the first
few hours of 'shivering disgust'[54] that life now holds no terrors for her at all,
and when the marriage is terminated by mutual agreement shortly
afterwards, she decides 'She'd finished with men or the need for them . . .
That dreadful storm she'd once visioned stripping her bare was all about

her, and she feared it no longer, eager to be naked, alone and unfriended, facing the last realities with a cool, clear wonder, an unhating desire'.[55] And so she completes the cycle, by returning to her birthplace, to the 'last realities' of unceasing, unstaying Change.

What then, finally, is the connection between Chris's last words and the decision made by Ewan? On one level *A Scots Quair* is concerned with man's striving for personal fulfilment: in the struggles of Long Rob to retain his independence, in the desperate break made by the first Ewan to return to Kinraddie, in the mental struggles of the Reverend Colquohoun leading to his disavowal of Christianity, and, pre-eminently, in the struggles of the young Ewan and Chris. And, though the latter pair choose divergent paths, their quest for reality does not end in quite such a divergent manner as might first appear. Both are seeking to recapture some of the simplicity of that Golden Age referred to again and again in *A Scots Quair*: Chris by returning to the ways of her peasant forbears, Ewan by striding into the future. But clearly we can hardly ignore Chris's final bedrock affirmation; nor can we ignore the fact that she has assumed by the conclusion of *A Scots Quair* a more than individual status, and seems in one sense anyway, the 'personification of life', as Walter Allen would have it,[56] or even the personification of time itself.

Indeed, throughout the book Chris's rejection of creeds has about it the instinctive wisdom of the ages, and her awareness of the past seems as real as her awareness of the present. She goes through the cycle of life's experiences, and through the stages of civilisation, from the croft, to the town, to the city, and back to the croft again, where at the last she seems literally to become part of the enduring land itself. And in concert with her is an ever-present awareness of history: in the Standing Stones of Blawearie, the Kaimes of Segget, and the Pict tunnel buried deeply below Duncairn. Ever present too, in her mind or in the background which seems part of her, are reminders of the transitory nature of beliefs, feelings, attitudes and way of life: the accent throughout is on change, 'nothing endures but the land'.

But, accompanying this accent on change, is throughout a passionate sympathy for the common people, a rage for the wrongs they have suffered down the centuries, and a hope for their life in the future. And accompanying our sense that Gibbon's indictment of Christianity, Nationalism, and Capitalism is a confirmation of the view of Chris that all creeds are but clouds, is our sense that it is also a confirmation of Ewan's view that the stark sure creed of Communism is both urgently needed, and will inevitably arrive by the process of Change. And, finally, if we feel that Ewan's faith has led to a sectarian hardness, in much the same way do we feel that Chris's rejection of all faiths has led to a bleakness, a granitic hopeless quality, never more harshly expressed than when she realises: '. . . SHE HAD NOTHING AT ALL, she had never had anything, nothing in the world she'd believed in but change . . .'.[57] Thus, though much of our commitment goes with Chris, much too goes with Ewan, and is meant to go with Ewan, in his belief that his actions—the actions of *living history* itself[58]—will lead not to the dissolving clouds visualised by Chris, but into 'first life as it never yet had been lived',[59] 'the shining ways of to-morrow'.[60]

What finally emerges, however, is not so much a clash of irreconcilable opposites, as a dual tension, a philosophy which can see Communism both as necessary, inevitable, and the only possible hope for the future, and at the same time can draw back in resignation and see it as but one part in a larger cycle of history which will in its turn be superseded—possibly having accomplished no more than the revolutionary creeds of the past. It is, surely, an appropriately undogmatic conclusion to a trilogy which, while never shedding its revolutionary purpose, for most of its length has laid the emphasis—often humorously, sometimes tragically, but always movingly—on life rather than dogma.

The question that was asked at the beginning of this examination of *A Scots Quair* has, it is hoped, been answered, but a few words remain to be said with reference to the opening remarks of this chapter. Gibbon was from the peasantry, and he was thus somewhat more fortunately situated than members of the middle class in that his beliefs arose partly from the facts of life rather than from statistics. But the gap between peasantry and proletariat was in many ways fully as wide as the more obvious gap between proletariat and middle class. Gibbon can certainly not be said to have bridged this gap completely, but it can be said that he has with a large degree of artistic success moulded his experience and his peasant consciousness to his revolutionary purpose. Moreover, he has achieved this with little more benefit of education than most of the working-class writers: a native genius, coupled with a rigorous self-education, has in fact resulted in one of the most imaginative and skilfully constructed of all the novels of the thirties. Finally, faced with the limitations of belief that plagued so many of the books we have studied, he has made of these limitations, these doubts, an integral artistic aspect of his theme, a positive, rather than a confusing presence in the novel.

9 Blighted Spring

I

In May 1938, complete with May Day messages from Sean O'Casey, Sybil Thorndike, and the Dean of Canterbury, *Left Review*—in which three years earlier Grassic Gibbon had proclaimed his revolutionary intentions—appeared for the last time. 'Not', as its farewell editorial hastened to add, 'because it has proved a failure. . . . Paradoxically it comes to an end at the height of its success, and because of that success. . . . Now it is felt by the Editorial Board that the present basis of editorial work, production and distribution, is too narrow to cope adequately with the job and the opportunities that press so urgently upon us.'[1]

According to its editor, Randall Swingler, all this was a euphemistic way of saying that too great control by the Communist Party, and inadequate funds, had brought *Left Review* to a grinding halt.[2] Whatever the reason, it can be seen now that the closing of *Left Review* was one of the first signs of a slight decline in strength of the already struggling revolutionary literary movement: a decline which became more apparent six months later with the departure of Auden (and Isherwood) to America, and which ended less than eighteen months later with the movement in a state of virtual collapse.

It was a decline which was paralleled in part at least by the fortunes of the British Communist Party itself. Although the Party was still gaining supporters throughout much of 1938, the first eight months of 1939 saw a distinct curbing of expansion as the membership figures hovered uneasily around the 18000 mark.[3] The publication of details about the mass Soviet trials of 1937–38, and some rather disquieting stories about the role of the Communists in Spain,[4] had undoubtedly contributed towards this. So too, and perhaps more strongly, had the withdrawal of the International Brigade from Spain in January 1939, and the complete surrender of the Republican Government to Franco two months later. Not only was the one cause which had inspired so much hope now lost, but history, it seemed to many, was not moving in a Marxist direction.

Far more dramatic in its effect on the Communist Party, however—and particularly in its effect on the Party's intellectual supporters—was the chain of events beginning in August 1939, with the announcement of a Russo–German Non-aggression Pact. While the Party leaders were still trying to work out this Pact's mind-wrenching implications came further startling news—Germany's invasion of Poland, swiftly followed by Britain's declaration of war. The Party executive hastily announced full support for this 'anti-Fascist' war and then only two weeks later, as Russia herself moved into Poland, hastily decided to retract. Pollitt, temporarily divested of leadership, was exiled to the provinces, and the war was denounced as 'unjust and imperialist', one in which Britain should play no part.[5] Later, after Russia's invasion of Finland at the end of the year, the Party's line seemed to harden into Lenin's classical policy of 'revolutionary defeatism'.[6]

While these events were taking place thousands of members and supporters of the Party were leaving its orbit, unable to digest or comprehend this apparent switch after so many years of anti-Fascist propaganda. There was by no means a Party collapse, but Pelling has estimated that for a while in 1940 the membership figures had sunk to about half their prewar total.[7] And, far more importantly, although there still remained a fairly strong core of intellectual supporters, there were enough sympathisers like John Strachey and Party members like Ralph Bates and Tom Wintringham who publicly announced their disaffiliation to make it clear that there had been a significant revision of opinion amongst a large section of them. It is reasonable to assume, furthermore, that most of the intellectuals alienated were irretrievably lost. For when after June 1941 (the date of Russia's involvement in the war against Germany), the Party's membership and popularity once more went surging upwards to reach a dramatic peak in 1942, not only were the vast majority of the new recruits manual workers in the large war factories, but also a fair measure of the support proved to be less ideological than a gesture of solidarity with the magnificent Russian War efforts.[8]

But by 1942 the future of the Communist Party at least held some promise: there was—to return to our opening remarks—little corresponding promise about the future of the revolutionary literary movement. In fact it had almost ceased to exist. As far as full-scale fiction was concerned, there was, with the prominent exception of Jack Lindsay's efforts, a fairly protracted silence from the end of 1939 onwards. Of the literary periodicals, the only one with a Party political link remaining was the general review *Our Time*, a former offshoot of the *Left Book Club*.[9] The Club itself, after severing most of its Communist connections, survived, and indeed struggled on until 1948, but with a greatly reduced membership. John Lehmann's *New Writing*, under a series of slighly changed names,[10] was another rather more healthy survivor, but again it was a survivor with a difference. *New Writing* had admittedly never been tied to the Communist Party line, but its anti-Fascist and Communist sympathies had nonetheless frequently emerged. Now, not only had 'the old political assumptions' largely disappeared, and 'the predominance of the "victims of oppression" . . . faded',[11] but even more significantly there was an actual note of critical hostility towards the political art of the thirties.[12]

Although the exigencies of the war must have been in part responsible for the collapse of the movement, there is little doubt that this collapse was in large measure a reflection of the political reorientation of 1938–40. So too was the note of critical hostility towards political writing: a hostility, as we shall see, expressed even more forcibly in *New Writing*'s main rival, *Horizon*. It was not at this stage a hostility towards radicalism as such. Some intellectuals moved in this direction, no doubt with the feeling that the decade's closing disappointments and apparent betrayals had rendered all political optimism childish or at best irrelevant. There was too an understandable revival of Christian belief in certain quarters: at at least one university, according to John Wain, 'every figure who radiated intellectual glamour of any kind, was in the Christian camp'.[13] But there was also throughout these years an extremely powerful, if fluctuating, tide of parliamentary left-wing feeling—as Gallup Polls, by-elections and the convincing Labour Party victory of 1945 clearly illustrated[14]—and George Orwell was probably right when he said in 1943 that the disenchanted Communist of the thirties would now vote Labour.[15] Disenchantment with Communism, however, if not leading to political despair, inevitably did lead to a reappraisal of that which many of the Communists had so strongly stressed: the necessity for a writer *as a writer* to align himself with a political group. For quite apart from the obvious point that the Labour Party itself made no such demands, and quite apart too from the fact that support for the Party still did not necessarily entail anything more than a vague desire to see fair play, there was the instructive example of the sheer mediocrity of much of the political writing of the thirties, a quality perhaps more clearly revealed now that many of its most passionate premises were thought to be invalid. One may surmise, in short, that many writers, though still feeling that political action for social justice was essential, also felt that to link themselves too closely as a writer to any political programme, however worthwhile, was to harness themselves to the ephemeral, that literature should deal with more eternal, more universal subjects than any political programme. This latter attitude was most strikingly revealed in the pages of *Horizon*, founded in January 1940, under the editorship of Cyril Connolly and (initially) Stephen Spender. From the outset *Horizon* made clear its editors' continuing belief in progressive aims, frequently published articles dealing with the question of social reconstruction after the war, and more than once implied or expressed its continuing belief in the idea of a 'benevolent world socialism'.[16] At the same time it made quite clear that its imaginative writing was not to be harnessed to any political aims at all.[17] 'The Marxist attack on the Ivory Tower dwellers', its second number editorialised,

> . . . set fire to a lot of rotten timber. But the fire grew out of hand, and, now that it is burning itself out, we can see that many green young saplings have been damaged, and the desolation is hardly compensated

for by the poems of Swingler and Rickword, or the novels of Upward and Alec Brown. . . . it must be restated that writing is an art, that it is an end in itself as well as a means to an end, and that good writing, like all art, is capable of producing a deep and satisfying emotion in the reader whether it is about Mozart, the fate of Austria, or the habits of bees.[18]

If by no means all writers accepted these sentiments entirely it is nonetheless true that *Horizon*'s emphasis on the writer as an artist rather than the writer as political prophet struck the dominant note during the war years. And this emphasis continued to dominate in the postwar period. There was no return to the thirties mood, and certainly little sign that the setback of 1938–40 was, in one Communist's words, 'deceptive and momentary'.[19] Even before the end of the war a decline in the Communist Party's membership from the peak of 1942 showed, as we have already implied, that much of the immense enthusiasm generated by the Russian defence of Stalingrad was a transitory affair, and despite the Party's impressive gains in the Trade Unions this overall decline continued after 1945. By this time, indeed, other limiting factors were at work, such as the apparently imperialist direction of Soviet foreign policy, the desire to let the Labour Party show its mettle, and, above all, an ever-increasing awareness of the authoritarian nature of Stalinist Russia. For the intellectuals in particular there were the disturbing stories of the ideological rigidities demanded by Zhdanov, whose regimentation of the Russian writers impressed few people—as it did *Our Time*—as 'the opening of a vast landscape of opportunity to the writer'[20]; rather did it confirm their impression that there was a 'fundamental hostility between the wintry political will and the creative imagination'.[21] As a result of all these factors, by the time the Cold War set in after 1948, further polarising such attitudes, the Communist Party, though numerically much larger than it had ever been in the thirties, was nonetheless a Party on the decline and its intellectuals, though still by no means negligible in number, essentially an isolated and defensive group.

But by 1948 there were increasing signs of a development which was, if anything, to make the postwar climate even less propitious for Socialist propaganda: a growing indifference, even hostility amongst formerly left-inclining intellectuals towards radicalism in any form. Cyril Connolly had early given expression to one mood of disenchantment when in 1947 in *Horizon*—now rapidly divesting itself of its editorial Socialist sympathies—he had complained that the Labour Government had done nothing for artists and able writers and had 'failed to stir up either intellect or imagination . . .'.[22] Others were quick to see in the numerous controls set up by the Labour Government signs of a parallel to Stalinism, an indication, according to one former Socialist, of a 'comprehensive failure of the human element by which Socialism created not a universal brotherhood but a clogging, spreading weed of bureaucracy, leading logically perhaps to an authoritarian state'.[23] To such people George Orwell's last 'strangled cry',[24] *Nineteen Eighty-Four*, with its near hysterical warning about the dangers of bureaucratic state control and its unfortunate use of the word 'IngSoc'[25] came as a confirmation and as a gospel. But the reactions we are concerned with were not simply those of antagonism: they more often took the form—especially after 1949, when the energies of the Labour Government were obviously running down— either of a passive acceptance or, conversely, of a demoralised apathy. For the very considerable reforms of the Government had in the first place been amply sufficient to soften the hard edge of the thirties: there were 'No more millions out of work, no more hunger-marches, no more strikes; none at least that the rebel can take an interest in . . .'.[26] At the same time, to others the reforms had been too little to prevent the growing feeling that *plus ça change, plus c'est la même chose*; class distinctions and inequalities were still apparent, while the cautious attitude of many Labour Party leaders seemed to suggest that instead of 'realising that their work was only beginning . . . [they] thought it was at an end'.[27]

It might be thought that one beneficiary of such a reaction would be the Communist Party, and no doubt it did absorb some disaffected Labour supporters at this time. But, still hampered by the totalitarian image of Russia, and by internal problems, it continued to be too unattractive a proposition to most. Indeed, despite its adoption in 1951 of a policy of parliamentary revolution,[28] and despite the relaxation after 1953 of Cold War tensions, its overall membership continued up to 1956, like the enthusiasm for Socialism itself, slowly to decline . . .

II

It was against this inhospitable artistic and political backdrop that what remained of the genre we have been examining struggled fitfully on. From what has been said so far it would seem to be not merely a genre in eclipse, but even, indeed, in its death-throes. Without denying the truth of this, one can say that novels have continued sporadically to appear, even if the number and variety have drastically decreased, and the individual authors been confined to a handful.

As would be expected, it has been the Communists who, despite their waning influence, have in the main kept the tradition alive. Indeed it is worth noting at this point that the writer who is most often thought of as a literary supporter of the Labour Party during these years was one whose views were so stripped of dogma that they barely emerge as Socialism at all. This was J. B. Priestley, who was later to share in some of the disillusionment of the postwar years, and move to a position in the 'wilderness' (although he remained, as he expressed it, 'pink'[29]), but who at the high noon of his hopes wrote three left-wing propaganda novels,

Daylight on Saturday (1943), *Three Men in New Suits* (1945), and *Bright Day* (1946).

Of these, *Three Men in New Suits* delivers the least diluted message, primarily perhaps because Priestley gives his characters so little chance to demonstrate in depth what their views really are. Apparently written hurriedly as the war drew to an end,[30] this short and flimsy tract can in fact be most charitably viewed as an extended manifesto for the 1945 elections. Three demobilised servicemen—of upper, middle, and lower-class extraction—return to what they hope will be a new life, and, after a series of swift disillusionments, gather together to express the resolution that they at least will try to change things. In the final pages the pervading suggestion of soap-box oratory becomes explicit, as the upper-class Alan Strete is transformed into a spokesman for national regeneration. 'We stop trying for some easy money', he declaims. 'We do an honest job of work for the community for what the community thinks we're worth. We stop being lazy and stupid, greedy and callous. We try to remember that it's much more important—and much more fun—to create than to possess . . . Instead of guessing and grabbing, we plan. Instead of competing, we co-operate. We come out of the nursery—and begin to grow up.'[31]

The element of paternalism in this novel—it is Alan who takes the initiative and to whom the others look instinctively for guidance—is also present in the earlier, rather better *Daylight on Saturday*. Indeed this book, despite an almost token reference to the future as 'a world of socialism and engineering',[32] and a comment on the factories after the war: 'What we don't know yet is for whose sake their power will be operated. We can only hope',[33] finally resolves itself through the pattern of its development into nothing more demanding than a rejection of inefficient upper-class Tories and a call for national unity and decency. In a similar fashion, *Bright Day*, the story of a successful screen writer who turns away from the easy money of Hollywood to join a trade union film group, instead of becoming an effective metaphor for a wholesale censure of Capitalism, limits its conclusions to the moralistic message that those who think solely in terms of money are less happy than those who do not. In both these books Priestley was undoubtedly capturing and appealing to some of the rather vague idealism of the war years,[34] and in addition was getting to the heart of the strong ethical strain in the support for the Labour Party; but he was hardly advocating a very full-blooded Socialism.

Apart from Priestley's contribution, the bulk of the novels have been, as we have said, from the Communists, or rather, to qualify this, the bulk of them have been the work of one man: the indefatigible Jack Lindsay. Through the upsets of the Russo–German Pact days and the Cold War period, he has clung tenaciously to his faith, and what is more, has continued to propagate this faith in his novels.

Lest his position of comparatively lonely prominence suggests a significant contribution, however, it should be said at once that this tenacity has not always been accompanied by a corresponding degree of literary merit. Because of this, and because of a certain repetitive quality in his output, some selective examination is necessary. Certainly his few historical novels of the forties—and he has moved away from his earlier concentration on illuminating the present by exploring the past—need not detain us here. These four books—*Light in Italy* (the problem of a revolutionary painter in 1816), *Hannibal Takes a Hand* (the betrayal of ancient Carthage), *Stormy Violence* (a novel of the Elizabethan era) and *The Barriers Are Down* (the collapse of the Roman Empire)—all bear strong signs of their common hurried gestation,[35] and, despite the energy of their narrative, are very much inferior in structure and characterisation to *1649*. Much the same, unfortunately, could be said for his first two approaches to contemporary affairs in the forties, *We Shall Return* (1942) and *Beyond Terror* (1943). However, despite their minimal literary qualities, they are the only English war novels written from a Communist viewpoint and for this reason do deserve some slight examination.

Set in France, *We Shall Return* focuses on a group of British soldiers in the closing days of the 'phoney war'. Hugh Evans, the middle-class Communist 'Hamletian hero' (Lindsay's phrase), ploughs through interminable soliloquies debating his reasons for involvement in the war, and finally comes to the conclusion on the beach at Dunkirk—apparently impervious to the shells bursting and the blood flowing around him—that 'the people have their own time, and that is history, and the first necessary humility is to know that and to live in the daily struggle, the daily liberation, and not to lose the sense of ultimates, of human freedom as a whole, the whole which is becoming possible and when possible is fact, is burstingly achieved'.[36] The thoughts of the minor characters, from private to captain, parallel his thoughts and indeed all achieve an astonishing degree of unanimity in their conclusions that they are about to crush Fascism and achieve a world of peace and brotherhood. Similar conclusions are iterated even more fervently in *Beyond Terror*, as British soldiers fight a last-ditch battle against the Germans in Crete—even more fervently, and, it must be said, even more incredibly. One could, for example, perhaps imagine Gunner Arnold chanting, 'Hell. Do 'em in, the whole bloody lot, every one of 'em, here, there and everywhere. Stamp it out. Yeh, fascism'[37], but when he shortly afterwards throws his grenades to the accompaniment: 'That's for my old woman. . . . That's for me. That's for my trade union. Again. That's for the people of England. And again. That's for the Russians',[38] the thin thread of belief snaps.

There is in fact very little sense of reality in either of these novels, despite Lindsay's eye for detail and his ability to convey an energetic sense of action. To the Germans he has merely transferred the epithets formerly reserved for the evil capitalists or Franco's soldiers in the thirties: they are *en masse*—except in the opening pages of *We Shall Return*—the 'Fascists'. Nor, ultimately, does he seem very much concerned with the lives of his

English soldiers, beyond propping them up to spout rhetorically on the stages of Dunkirk and Crete. There is much blood, and there are many severed limbs, but there is little imaginative involvement. It is sympto- matic that death is often a gratuitous detail, as when we are introduced to Gunner Arnold, 'whose wife lives in Stepney waiting for the plaster to fall down and the roof to fall in and the house itself to fall over, and who bore her fourth in an air-raid shelter. . . . (as a matter of fact she died of peritonitis last week, but the gunner doesn't know that)'[39], or else is blurred under grandiloquent prose: '. . . . a rifle cracked over on the right, and he fell forward, as if his pain had whipped round him, had gone clean through and out, and left only that, the pure echo of his cry, infinitely returning'.[40] Lindsay has, in fact, treated the war as he and many other poets treated the Spanish Civil War: as a battleground for abstractions, in which the human actors and their personal fate seem of subsidiary importance.

And it has been this problem, of preventing his characters from being dwarfed or unnaturally distorted by his ideological message, which has, needless to say, remained one of Lindsay's greatest difficulties since this date. In one sense this is because the turn away from the situations of the past has brought him face to face with the—for him—despondent realities of contemporary England, and he has consequently found himself resorting to even more obviously authorial manipulation and heavy- handed didacticism. But inextricably involved with this and exacerbating the difficulty have been his own creative deficiencies as a writer: primarily his inability to express convincingly the emotional attitudes of people and their relationship one with another. In *Hullo Stranger* (1945), for example, an unpretentious novel written shortly before the end of the war, Lindsay found a suitable milieu for his revolutionary message: a factory at the height of the pro-Russian feeling. Here the heroine, Kathy Cowell, takes a job when her husband of a few months leaves for the front, and her growth of pride in her work coupled with her slowly increasing political consciousness is described fairly effectively, and, it is important to note, with little of that breathless attitude to the working class present in *End of Cornwall*.[41] But when we are also expected to believe that Kathy finds herself becoming emotionally involved with one of the Communist workers, Ken Williams, our measure of sympathetic co-operation lapses. Ken's protestations of love we have to take at their face value—for we know nothing of what he thinks—while Kathy's involvement is super- ficially treated in such phrases as 'At moments . . . she'd felt very powerfully drawn towards him . . .'.[42] The situation further deteriorates when Kathy's husband returns. She welcomes him as a stranger, partly because of their long estrangement, but primarily because she feels that her own political beliefs have advanced so far beyond his essentially oppor- tunist and apolitical attitudes. In the final pages of the book, however, we learn from his thoughts that he no longer holds these views: that now he is aware that 'the bastards are in power everywhere, not only in Germany. Call it what you like. Fascism, that's it. I'm with you'.[43] So, tentatively, aware of possible problems ahead, they become reunited as man and wife. But here the husband has been present for too short a time either for us to feel the relationship between them in the first place, or for us to place any credence in his newly acquired political beliefs. The empty rhetorical flourishes of *Beyond Terror* have been toned down, but life still trickles out of the book long before it has reached its conclusion.

Rather more successful, however, was the novel which followed *Hullo Stranger*, *Time to Live* (1946). This is partly because of more careful structural planning and partly too because Lindsay has eschewed the directly political approach and tempered his impatience for the full political consciousness evidenced by the Fascist-haters of the previous three books. This is not to say that *Time To Live* does not make a political comment. Indeed, the book is clearly an expression of Lindsay's view, as expressed in *After the Thirties*, that 'unless the people are everywhere and all the time participating in the work of forming their own society; there cannot be even the beginnings of socialism: there can only be a bureaucratic State in which the strengthening of the central powers works out for the benefit of the monopolists'.[44] Set entirely in Holly Street in London immediately after the war, the novel relates the efforts of Mr Wylie and his growing band of supporters to have a street concert party in an attempt—although this they only dimly realise—to keep up the spirit of comradeship and communal art established during the war years. During this time there had sprung up numerous factory bands, choirs and drama-groups, a 'widening participation', to quote *After the Thirties* once more, 'of the people in both enjoyment and creation',[45] and it is this participation that the Holly Street inhabitants—or some of them— are trying to preserve. Opposed to them are such people as Mr Tulse, who sees the Party as one more threat to his system of life, already crumbling as his small shop fails and his daughters revolt. Others in the street remain neutral, such as Mrs Cunnington, yearning desperately for a fuller life than that provided by her money-dominated husband or that represented by her seedy, corrupt brother. Towards the end of the book she has a foretaste of this fullness as she sings at the concert, and finds with her audience, 'though they could not have given words to their feelings', that her voice and the music becomes 'a call to a new level of life, a new conception of peace and happiness, a new gentle strength of comradeship'.[46] The success of the concert party makes its leading supporters decide to fight to continue such activities in the future, and establish a permanent community centre.

But the novel is also in a sense a novel within a novel, for observing all this, and at the same time participating in it, is a young journalist, Philip Smith, presumably representing aspects of Lindsay himself. As the story progresses, he too is trying to write a novel, but apparently never gets beyond the opening paragraphs, phrases from which occur in the actual story. At first he feels that nothing 'really happened in this dull street, in the dull houses, among these dull people who passed him lymphatically in the roadway'.[47] Unsure either of his style or of his subject-matter, he experiments momentarily with a study of suburban madness along the lines of Julian Green, an outpouring of the unconscious à la Joyce, and even a Kafkaesque allegory in which the evil aspects of life predominate. But gradually he realises that his proper theme is the people in the street, and that when he writes of them his style will sort itself out. There is evil, and conflict in life, but there is also, he feels, a unity as expressed by the people in their search for communal living, a unity in which he himself is involved: and so he begins his novel, which we finally realise is the novel we have been reading.

One certainly would not wish to make any very high claims for *Time to Live*. Many of the characters are still shadowy sketches rather than creations, while the central character of Philip in particular is far too obviously an authorial puppet ever to attain much credibility. Indeed, as this unbearably solemn young man preaches to his latest girlfriend towards the close of the book—'At the moment I feel I want to get down on my knees and kiss the common earth, in gratitude for the unutterable fount of goodness I feel in people'[48]—one is sure that unity with these same 'people' is the last thing he would ever be able to achieve. But one can say that some of the worst excesses of the war novels have gone, and that, if the bones of Lindsay's thesis do at moments project a little too prominently, the novel is at least an interesting attempt to solve the problem of the fusion of message and content.

Clearly, however, to go very much further along this path would take Lindsay away from the political novel altogether, to the territory, say, occupied by Priestley in *Bright Day*. And, indeed, it was in this direction, or in the direction of silence, that he moved for the next five years, as the Cold War reached its height. *The Subtle Knot,* for example, a novel-cum-psychological treatise published in 1947, explores the efforts of various people to know themselves, 'to knit that subtle knot which makes us man', to struggle towards the Marxist unitary consciousness. Its emphasis falls almost entirely on the psychological aspect of Lindsay's ideas about man, and the relevance of this to the political and social aspects is only rarely—and then vaguely—implied: it is symptomatic that when Philip Smith of *Time to Live* appears, it is for three lines, and as 'Philip Something, from Reuter's'.[49] Following *The Subtle Knot* there appeared at intervals: *Men of Forty-Eight* (1948—actually written in 1939, and discussed previously); one almost 'straight' historical novel, *Fires in Smithfield* (1950), concerned with the last year of Mary Tudor's reign when she was trying to restore Catholicism to England[50]; and, finally, one much more light-hearted historical novel, *The Passionate Pastoral* (1951).[51]

But Lindsay, contrary to all appearances, had not in fact abandoned political writing. In 1952, excited by the recent formation of the Authors'

World Peace Appeal[52] and by what seemed to be promising cultural stirrings in the Party, he informed the readers of the American magazine *Masses and Mainstream* that after the 'dullest and deadliest interregnum in our cultural history'[53] there is a 'rapidly-maturing demand for a party literature which has been showing itself in the Communist Party here. A party literature, I said, but the phrase must not be taken in a narrow sense: it means a literature aimed also at the broad masses of the organized Labor [*sic*] movement, and so reaching out further to all progressive sections of the community'.[54] Ignoring—or perhaps spurred on by—such disquieting details as the continually decreasing Party membership, and such baleful warnings as that expressed in the *Times Literary Supplement* that year which spoke of the 'uncommitted talents' of the young contemporary writers,[55] Lindsay immediately set out to show that his words were not without substance, and the following year published the first of a series of novels to be known collectively as the 'British Way'. This series—not entirely, as will be seen shortly, the only answer to the 'rapidly maturing demand' he spoke of—has now in fact reached nine volumes, but the three which appeared before 1956 can be conveniently and logically considered here on their own, for the novels which follow both introduce a large number of new characters and also change in technique and mood.

The technique used in these three books—*Betrayed Spring* (1953), *Rising Tide* (1953) and *The Moment of Choice* (1955)—is in fact similar to that employed in Lindsay's historical fiction, namely the setting of individual lives against a wide-scale picture in an attempt to bring out the historical structure beneath the apparently unconnected events and lives. But whereas his historical fiction relied on historical documents, Lindsay has here used the active aid of the workers; like Naomi Mitchison in the thirties—but with somewhat more successful results—Lindsay discussed many of the incidents with workers while actually writing the book, and then later had relevant sections read by workers best in a position to assess their accuracy.[56]

This technique is seen most clearly—and most effectively—in the first novel of the series, *Betrayed Spring*, which is set in Britain during the period September 1946 to March 1947. This was a momentous and troubled time for Britain, the time of the homeless squatters, the nationalising of the pits, and, as a cruel climax, the worst winter for fifty years, which ravaged the already depleted coal supplies, forced the closure of thousands of factories, and brought the life of the nation almost to a standstill. It was also, according to Lindsay, the time of betrayal, for although people responded to this emergency, the Labour Government, instead of implementing further measures of Socialism—such as greater worker's control—and thus drawing fully upon this response, chose instead to stand still, and thus 'betray' its trust. This is Lindsay's thesis, but he has succeeded to a large extent, as in *1649*, in giving life to it.

There are four separate strands to the story of *Betrayed Spring*, and by weaving back and forth between these strands—which are all linked, both at a personal and at an historical level—Lindsay is able to convey something of a national as well as an individual background. In London the central character is Phyl Tremaine, the daughter of an unemployed plasterer, a naive young girl only just emerging from the world of love-films and American-dressed spivs. It is, indeed, almost for the sake of excitement alone that she finds herself involved in a large strike of hotel-workers, but the excitement changes to a deeper, more purposeful feeling when she senses something which drives out all thoughts of the misery of the Tremaines' one-roomed existence, a sense, she later recognises, of 'the world within the world, the deep struggle of change as well as the everyday adaptation'.[57] However, although she resolves henceforth to turn away from the corrupt complicity represented by the party black-marketeers, the spivs, and the goodtime girls around her, and although she comes to mingle with such Communists as Harry Manson, her growing class-consciousness remains primarily at the level of intuition. To the last she is envious of the Communists' confidence and comradeship; but to the last she finds their conversations bewildering and alien: 'Some key-understanding was absent; and until she gained it, she'd go on being bewildered'.[58]

Little more a Communist theoretician is Dick Baxter, who forms the main thread in the Lancashire strand of the story. Only just demobilised at the outset of the book, he has to decide whether to go back into the pit where his father works, or to make use of his skills in some more profitable enterprise. When he finally decides on the former—and in the process parts company with his fiancée, Patricia Hemans—it is mainly to avoid the same petty corruption that Phyl has rejected, for he senses that the newly nationalised pits will 'give him the chance of self-betterment harmoniously . . . so that he wouldn't feel the blood of the war-dead crying out against him'.[59] He is thus plunged into the very thick of the fuel crisis, a crisis which leaves him momentarily dulled with 'fatigue and confusion',[60] uncertain of its meaning. It is the chance image of a girl framed against a bedroom window, an image which breaks into him 'with a sudden warmth, as if for the first time he had realised how piercingly happy and rich life could be',[61] which restores him to a sense of faith in himself and in the future. He ends the book no more a political animal than Phyl, but like Phyl sensing at moments—as when he listens to Harry Manson, an ex-war comrade—an intimation 'of opening horizons, of great movements'.[62]

The link with Harry Manson is in fact the main link—at a personal level—with London; and it is also the link with the remaining two strands of the novel: the story of Kit Swinton and that of William Emery, who represent—although the book is rather less mechanical than this short summary would seem to suggest—the 'betrayal' aspects of *Betrayed Spring*. Emery—whose wife's dead brother, Gavin, was a war companion of Kit

Swinton, Baxter, and Manson—is a successful trade union leader in the Tyneside. He is sincere enough in his hatred of the rich, but he has reached the stage where he can no longer bear the thought of relinquishing his job, where his very surroundings seem to symbolise his fear of failure, his fear of a decline back to the poverty from which he sprang. However, when he strikes up an uneasy acquaintance with Clayton, one of the local mill-owners, it is, he tells himself, for the ultimate good of his trade union principles, and he continues to have his moments of turning in outright disgust from Clayton and what he represents, when he recalls the England of the thirties, 'burnt-out furnaces charred with their own black fires of death, derelict steel mills falling into scrap, coke-ovens with the weeds creeping closer, slag-heaps scurfed with grey-green weeds. Aye, that was your England, Clayton, that was Tory England. To hell with it'.[63] Despite these moments he finds himself, impelled by his own sense of insecurity, moving almost unwittingly into closer and closer collaboration with the employers, until by the end of the book, his marriage in ruins, he has compromised beyond the point of no return. And yet he can still say, and believe: 'I've begun to get the knack of this job of mine. I've begun to find out how to get all that's possible from the managements and give away the least. They don't like me, but they respect me . . . And I'll go on fighting 'em on their own ground, and winning'.[64]

The fourth, and final character is Kit Swinton, the young son of a Yorkshire mill-owner. His war experiences, and latterly the university, have loosened the old family beliefs: Kit now calls himself a Socialist, and is even contemplating joining the Labour Party. Although he is uneasily aware that his views are in part an instinctive act of rebellion against his domineering father, they are genuine enough: his problem is to throw aside the last family ties, and act upon his belief that his father's way of life is 'wrong, unworthy of human dignity'.[65] When he yields to his father's pressure and enters the mill on an experimental basis, it is still, he tells himself, as a Socialist, although he remains unsure whether he had 'beaten his father, or had . . . fallen into a trap from which there was henceforth no escape'.[66] For a while, however, he is able to escape this trap, attends a radical discussion group and strikes up a friendship with a Communist factory girl, Jill Wethers. But life and the moral issues he has to face prove too complicated for him, as he alternates between loyalty to his father and loyalty to his ideas, as he learns of the various corrupt practices in the mill, and as his friendship for Jill grows into love. The bleak winter and his consequent illness force the issue: in an effort to find some kind of stability he decides to enter the mill fully, as his father's right-hand man. He tells his father he is still a Socialist, and that he intends joining the Labour Party, but exactly how far he has compromised, exactly what has emerged from his 'wintry withdrawal',[67] is soon made clear. When his father shows him a list of troublemakers that he intends to sack for 'redundancy'—a list which includes Jill and most of the discussion group—he feels a moment of nausea, and then expresses agreement.

It should be clear, even from this short summary, that there is rather more complexity in the portraits of Kit and Emery than there is in those of Phyl and Dick, who move in a rather set, stereotyped pattern, and about whose decision there is never any real doubt. Nevertheless, there is a sense of movement in *Betrayed Spring*, paralleling the historical events which form its background. Kit and Emery compromise, move almost unknowingly into the 'dark snare'[68]; while Phyl and Dick, if in a somewhat more pat way, show the other side, the response to the events of the winter, the movement forward, slow but sure, into the new life. And if there is a lack of depth about the latter pair, they are certainly not over-romanticised or turned into dogmatic machines; they are, rather, recognisable English people coming to identify themselves with their own class. Finally—and this is a virtue of *Betrayed Spring* not readily evoked by any summary—the four main characters move constantly against a vividly realised backdrop of the England of the time, the conflicting hopes and disappointments, the shortages and fuel queues, the spivs and the homeless squatters. By showing us glimpses of the docks, the mines, and the factories, by letting us hear snatches of overheard conversation and lyrical reminiscences—'. . . when I say beer, I mean beer, and not this piss and chemicals that isn't strong enough to drown a mouse. Why, drinking it is like talking to yourself. In those days you could get sozzled by walking along the promenade and being breathed on'[69]—Lindsay guarantees that we see the radical side of working-class England in some depth.

To say this, of course, is not to say that the book does not have its serious faults. The insubstantiality of Phyl and Dick has already been mentioned, and there are moments, too, when characters are abruptly dropped for the sake of momentum—as, for example, is Jill—raising serious doubts once more about Lindsay's concern for these people as people. But the book's most obvious faults arise in part out of its very virtues. Lindsay is dealing in the main with non-Communist characters, people who are at most only half-aware—according to Lindsay—of the issues in which they are swept up. Because he wants us to be fully aware of these, and has to have his Communist commentary, this comes at intervals in jargoned conversations, usually carried on by peripheral characters such as Harry Manson: ' "Well, they've made certain gains, but the challenge to the old ways hasn't been carried out", Harry went on, mixing his delight in rhetoric with a kind of inverted-comma picking-out of the cant phrases. "The rot of compromise and class collaboration goes too deep in the Labour leaders." '[70] Despite the repudiation implied in the words 'cant phrases', Harry is in fact regarded with a non-ironic awe by the other characters, and thus his jargoned summary—so inadequate for the development seen in Will Emery—inevitably acquires a measure of authority. This kind of commentary comes most heavily towards the end, when the Communists gather like political vultures to debate the significance of the events of the winter. Phyl does not understand their conversation, but it is directed towards the reader, and as they comment that the crisis was the 'crisis of British Capitalism, spotlighted by nature', and that now 'monopoly forms will emerge all the stronger',[71] one has the sense that Lindsay is impatiently trying to talk out the issues, not all of which have emerged in the book.

But at least—and this is some indication of the solidity of *Betrayed Spring*—many of the issues do emerge: in the novels which follow the gap between what happens and what is preached grows far more obvious. The disappointing drop in quality between *Betrayed Spring* and *The Moment of Choice* and *Rising Tide* parallels, indeed, the drop in quality between *1649* and the two historical novels following it: it is as if Lindsay's creative powers last only for short bursts, or perhaps, as he grew aware that the optimism expressed in *Masses and Mainstream* was illusory, he was growing more impatient. In *Rising Tide*, for example, a novel centring on the great dock strike of 1949, there is a much greater predominance of set speeches by the Communists, and far less attempt to humanise them. It is true that the central story and background of Phyl Tremaine and her docker husband, Jeff Burrows—whom she met towards the end of *Betrayed Spring*—remains interesting and lively in its evocation of the squatters' and the dockers' lives of the time. It is also true that Lindsay makes some attempt to link their personal lives to the political theme by showing the deterioration of their marriage as Phyl finds that being married to a docker is rather different from seeing them as an abstract force: 'A strike now wasn't just an exciting event she could cheer from the sidelines; she had to reckon it in terms of lost earnings, hardships, frayed tempers, troubles of all sorts'.[72] But unfortunately these 'frayed tempers'—which result in their growing estrangement as Jeff involves himself more and more onesidedly in the strike—are frequently almost swamped by a series of virtually documentary accounts of the progress and of the complex worldwide background of the strike. At the last, indeed, when Phyl resolves their personal problem by engaging herself as militantly as her husband, this resolution seems cursory and abrupt, sandwiched as it is between more progress reports and a final Communist summing-up. The latter, further-more, seems little linked with what has gone before. 'I say the whole CSU dispute [concludes Harry Manson] and its offshoots are part of a deliberate plan by U.S.A. imperialism, in which our Government and capitalists humbly and gratefully concur, to smash the militant sections of the seamen and dockers all over the world––to make possible the war they plan against the Soviet Union. The fight we've been waging has been in its deepest sense a fight for peace.' The position of this conclusion, and the following comment: 'They had a feeling they'd got to bedrock . . .',[73] indicate that this is the author's own conclusion: but in fact there has been no sense at all in which one could say that the book has revealed that the strike has been a fight for peace.

A similar imbalance and at times an even greater and more shrill amount of preaching badly mar *The Moment of Choice*, which takes place two years later in 1951 and returns to the story of Kit Swinton. By this point in time, Lindsay was aware that hopes of a broadly based working-class Communist movement were rapidly receding, and to give him his due he does at least communicate this awareness. The characters, indeed, are now predominantly middle class: even Jill Wethers has, in fact, come from a middle-class background. But if he shows his working class as in the main reluctant to engage in political activities, he wildly overcompensates by excesses with his middle-class characters. His businessmen all talk with knowing cynicism of the Capitalist system, as, for example, does Bannister, the General Manager of the Swinton Mill, who tells Kit: 'The pace is madder than it's ever been. Without the profits from the colonies the system would jam in no time'.[74] A May Day peace march, where the middle-class Jane Dacres has her moment of revolutionary awareness, is described without any suggestion that there may be any apathy or hostility amongst the watching crowd; while the police are seen as the stereotyped 'Fascists' of the thirties. And Kit's sister, Margaret, introduced without any explanation at the beginning as a near Communist, gives a straight *Daily Worker* style report of a Peace Congress held in London and Moscow. Nor is the central story of Kit and Jane Dacres, for all its superficial complexity, ultimately on a very much higher level. Kit, now with a mistress called Val, is at the outset of the book thoroughly immersed in the running of the mill, but holding himself aloof, he feels, from the excesses of business corruption by maintaining 'an ironic detachment'.[75] When he meets Jane Dacres, shortly after her experience at the peace march, he recognises in her and feels the need for her 'goodness of heart'.[76] Their friendship rapidly blossoms into love, and they marry. But on their honeymoon news comes of the invasion of Korea: 'Well, your Red friends seem to be showing their hand at last',[77] says Kit inexplicably—inexplicably because he knows nothing of her peace march experience, and, indeed, she has done nothing about this since. Their relationship further deteriorates, as he finds that Jane has become involved with the Peace Movement through Jill Wethers. But exactly what Kit does feel becomes unclear from this moment onwards—as unclear as it is, one uneasily suspects, to Lindsay. Suggestions are thrown out that his violent reaction to the Korean War is a reaction against 'the local Communist branch and Jill in particular' and, too, that it is a reaction against 'economic pressures which at moments recently had seemed liable to topple down the Swinton Mill'.[78] Later it is suggested that his hostility towards Jane's involvement in the Peace Movement in particular is, in fact, a reaction against her goodness, that 'His relations with Val seemed to fit harmoniously with his position in the mill, the whole philosophy he had been building up to express and justify that position—whereas his relations with Jane had jarred and kept jarring with it'.[79] But there are also other long moments when his awareness—and Lindsay's too, for that matter—seems to lapse altogether, when he sneeringly attacks Jane with no remorse, and when he immerses himself in financial skullduggery with Bannister, partly, one cannot help feeling, because Lindsay wants to lay before us exactly what kind of corruption goes on in business.

Finally Jane leaves him, solemnly telling him before she goes that no relationship can be divorced from the wider issues:

> 'I tell you, Kit, that every relationship, every emotion, every work of art, every institution is being judged at this moment by the extent to which it impedes or helps the horror of murder that is going on in Korea.' . . .
> 'Is judged, judged!' he repeated pettishly. 'Who judges?'
> 'Christ,' she said, 'Lenin, myself, William Blake, Mao Tse-tung, Edith Sitwell.'[80]

With the departure of Jane, business pressures build up, until Kit learns that a taxation inspection is to be made of the firm. He now discovers that his former position of ironic detachment is no longer an adequate defence. 'He was trapped in a mechanism that went on moving faster and faster, every moment escaping a crash by sheer chance. What's the use of pretending to lead, to be master, inside this blind heaving mechanism? No, no, he thought, what I want is to get out of it, get out of it at all costs.'[81] Thus when Jane is persuaded by Jill to return to him, he is ready to plead with her to 'Help me to live a decent life'.[82] Their new relationship would, he thinks, mean 'more than the sacking of Bannister . . . though it included all that. It meant a new relation to people everywhere, in the mill and in the Labour Movement; it meant ceaseless effort always to find the ways and means that truly advanced the cause of life'.[83] Alick West, in the only full-length essay on Lindsay, is right to point out here that Jane has still not said anything to Kit about the peace march, and that his vague words could mean anything that one chooses them to mean. However, my criticism would be not only that, in West's words, 'the stress falls upon the subjective emotion of an unflawed unity',[84] but that the 'unity' itself seems very flawed and precarious indeed. There is, in fact, a sense in which Kit seems to be seeking a momentary refuge from business worries in Jane's arms, and because his own motives and thoughts have been so blurred and shifting throughout, this is a reasonable deduction to make. However, Lindsay wants the book to end optimistically, with progress recorded, and therefore tries to make far more of their reconciliation than is actually warranted. Once again, as in so many of Lindsay's novels, the gap between what he wants us to believe, and what we feel, is distressingly large.

Before making any final, summarising comments on Lindsay's work— which will be reserved for the conclusion of this study—I would like at this point to return to 1952, and the optimistic statement he made in *Masses and Mainstream*. Enough has been said so far to indicate that the chances of his 'rapidly maturing demand' being answered to any significant extent were very slim, and such, indeed, proved to be the case. The great mass of writers, for the reasons already given, continued to fit the description given them in the *Times Literary Supplement* that year of the 'uncommitted'. Nor did the burst of new dissenting and more socially aware novels appearing from 1953 onwards, though often written by people of professed left sentiments, show any greater degree of commitment—Socialist or Communist. Indeed, as has often been pointed out, the political attitudes in such novels as Kingsley Amis's *Lucky Jim* (1954) and John Wain's *Hurry on Down* (1953) were marked by their ambivalence more than by their conviction.

But if there was no very significant response to this demand, it was at least answered: up to 1956, in fact, four novels had appeared. Two of these can be quickly dismissed with a brief mention: the Anglo-Australian James Aldridge's *Heroes of the Empty View* (1954), which leans so heavily on the Lawrence of Arabia legend that it virtually becomes a revolutionary historical novel in the Lindsay tradition; and David Lambert's *He Must So Live* (1956), a solid, but hardly exciting working-class novel set in the Clydeside of the late thirties. The other two, which were of rather more interest, and do deserve an examination in this concluding section of our study, were *A Miner's Sons* (1955) by Len Doherty, himself a former miner, and Doris Lessing's *Retreat to Innocence* (1956).

Doherty's novel is chiefly concerned with the story of Robert Mellers, a miner from the village of Mainworth who has just completed a jail sentence for the manslaughter of a former trade union official. Although he decides not to return to mining, he is at once involved in the activities of Mainworth's tiny Communist branch. During the course of the book he successfully converts his own brother, Herbert, persuades his father, riddled with silicosis, to leave the mines, and finally returns to the mines himself. To complete the picture of Communism triumphant, the local trade union leader, Barratt, who has twice been a Party member and has twice resigned his Party card, realises the dangers facing the individual alone, and will, the ending implies, return once more to the Party.

Written in a plain, rather graceless style, and resembling in some ways Heslop's work in the thirties, *A Miner's Sons* does, nonetheless, sustain interest throughout, and at moments is extremely effective. Much of this interest derives from its central character, Robert Mellers, who, if not presented with any profound psychological insights, is certainly far from being a proletarian cardboard cutout. Although he is looked upon as a hero by the other, younger branch members, and although he is effective in persuading his father and converting his brother, inwardly he is plagued by a sense of indirection and a lack of confidence. Partly because of the stigma of his jail sentence, partly because of tendencies already present within himself, he is apt to react with disillusionment or cynicism at any sign of a slight to himself or of a setback to the cause. In much the same way he is unable to achieve any kind of finality in his relationship with his girlfriend, Irene. Ironically, it is just that advice that he gives to others that he is in most need of himself. When, for example, his father says that he is going to stay on in the mines till he dies, to prevent his becoming a burden on others, Robert retorts:

> 'You've only really thought about yourself yet. . . . What about the others who've got a stake in this? What about the ones that might—need you. Me? Herbert? The old lady?' It took an effort to say the words. He was fighting against inhibitions that from childhood had made him hold this kind of talk and emotion as effeminate and unmanly.
>
> Mellers stared at him. Distaste flickered in his eyes and his features showed acute discomfort. He fidgeted in the chair and looked down at his unsteady hands . . .
>
> 'We've never been—' his hands gestured vaguely 'tha knows—we were never ones for fussing o'er each other. I don't see as I've been so much to you as you'd be losing a lot.' His voice held a mixture of half-regret and revolting pride, as though he didn't know which way he wanted to be answered.[85]

Only gradually does Robert realise that it is this very isolated pride inculcated in him, his inability to admit that he could be in any way dependent upon others, that is at fault. When Irene points out that he has always shied away from references to marriage, even before his prison sentence and before joining the Party, he reflects that he can hardly deny this:

> That [any references by him to marriage] would be to admit that he wanted her wholly for his own sake—that without her he was incomplete—and he couldn't sacrifice his only security of independence by admitting that he needed anyone. Even the Party he unconsciously interpreted to himself as a moving force rather than a mass of living men and women. And rather than feel that he needed the Party, he had always felt that the Party needed him if he could find the right way to give truly what was in him.[86]

Despite this self-realisation, however, Robert is still prone to doubts, and is actually on the point of leaving Mainworth altogether when the area organiser comes to him and persuades him to act out what he has been preaching. In one of the least convincing scenes of the book—least convincing because the man who persuades him has been at most a peripheral character up to this point—Robert accepts the fact that 'every man's problem's a problem for all on us',[87] resolves to return to the mines, to the comradeship and help of the Mainworth branch, to marry Irene, and to prove to her that what he is doing is 'a fine thing and win her to the Party'.[88]

This attempt to show Communism not as a set of static beliefs, but as something a man lives out in his actions and thoughts, gives to *A Miner's Sons* an energy which goes some way towards counteracting its very real weaknesses. It also gives to Mellers' propaganda speeches a certain tension and depth: a process aided by the fact that these speeches are frequently abusively interrupted by the other miners. But this energy is not solely confined to Mellers, for the characters grouped around him add to this sense of movement by being all at varying stages of belief. Apart from Mellers senior himself, who is certainly the most convincing, there is Robert's brother, Herbert, seeking—and failing—to find the answers to his dissatisfaction in books on How to Live Successfully and You Can Be Happy; Barratt, a Communist by instinct, but never too happy to submit to the discipline of the Party; Mainwaring, the middle-class intellectual Communist; Frank Wells, the thoroughly confident Communist organiser; and finally Jud Rodgers and Taylor, the two young new members, naive, breathless in their awe of Robert, beaming at him 'with delight and admiration'[89] whenever he makes a suggestion.

What might well be seriously objected, however, is that Rodgers and Taylor are a little too naive and breathless, that there is indeed about all these Communists a faint whiff of carbolic soap, as if they have been freshly scrubbed and brushed for the occasion. This impression doubtless partly arises from the fact that all the Communists we do see are presented as such basically good people—whatever inner or domestic problems they may have—and that the book in fact reads at times like a manual on how the good Communist Party member should behave. More significantly, however, it arises from the omissions or distortions in Doherty's presentation of the state and nature of contemporary Communism. In the first place, although he says the branch is small, the impression conveyed—by concentrating on all the Party members, and having such a thoroughly rousing ending—is precisely the opposite, just as Lindsay's admission in *Moment of Choice* that the working-class members of England are declining in numbers is swamped by the rather ludicrous impression that a large proportion of the middle class of England are Communists, or nearly so. In the second place, there is absolutely no suggestion, from Mellers, from any other character, or from the author himself, that there might be anything seriously remiss in the Socialist world which might have caused these declining numbers: that there were growing murmurs even in the Communist Party itself about Soviet bureaucracy and Stalinism. Doherty's viewpoint, in short, despite the gestures towards contemporaneity, is rosy and wishful, fundamentally blurring the issues, and undermining the positive aspects of the book.[90]

Whatever else might be said of the final novel we have to consider here—Doris Lessing's *Retreat to Innocence* (1956)—that particular accusation at least cannot be made. Mrs Lessing, who spent the early part of her life in Rhodesia, had an early opportunity of seeing the possible deficiencies of ideology, of recognising the fact that beliefs do not always square with circumstances. Her novels set in Africa, indeed, though mainly written while she was a member of the British Communist Party, are fundamentally humanist rather than Communist. *Martha Quest* (1953) and *A Proper Marriage* (1954)—the first two volumes of *Children of Violence*—certainly strongly assert Martha's instinctive aversion for the colour bar, and towards the end of *A Proper Marriage* she has her moment of revelation, when for the first time she becomes aware of the Russian Revolution, and hastens, with others, to form a Communist Party. But there is a remarkable objectivity and lack of enthusiasm in Mrs Lessing's description of the formation of this Party, a forewarning of its eventual disintegration described so effectively in *A Ripple from the Storm* (1958). There, certainly, her attitude becomes clearer, but it is implicit in the early volumes. Assuredly she wants freedom and brotherhood for all, and her Communists, however much satirised, are never cruelly so: but she is poignantly aware, too aware, in fact, to be a propagandist at any level, of their human limitations and, more importantly, of the irrelevance of their ideology to the complexities of African society.[91]

In *Retreat to Innocence*, while by no means relaxing her stress on the deficiencies and irrelevancies of Communist ideology, Mrs Lessing does provide a far stronger counterbalance, to make this book come as close as any of her novels to delivering a direct, positive political message. Set in a London summer of 1955, it relates the meeting and involvement of Julia Barr, a young upper-class representative of Britain's 'uncommitted generation', with Jan Brod, an ageing Communist writer who was a wartime refugee from Czechoslovakia. Julia almost immediately falls in love with Brod. But it is seemingly in spite of herself, for his views, his politics, appear repulsive to her. Politics are all 'that filth and dirt and heroics',[92] fundamentally dehumanising, and meaningless and irrelevant in contemporary, comparatively comfortable Britain. They are part of history, part of the thirties in which her parents were involved, and they seem to have—as with all the other young people in the novel—no personal relevance to her whatsoever. When she undertakes some research for a novel Jan is writing, she tries to summon up images in connection with the notes she is making:

> And she could not. At the end of that day, she had succeeded in forming a picture: it was of wastes of dirty snow, men in ragged coats struggling, a stumpy corpse lying face downwards, arms flung out, outside a gate guarded by a man with a rifle. 'I must have seen a film, it's from a film,' she told herself at last; and was discouraged because she could create no images for herself, was dependent on ideas fed into her from outside. She

went back to Jan with 1917, 1918, 1919, 1920 (years, apparently of the most appalling hardships for the whole of Europe) reduced to five pages of notes and that single picture in her mind, the shot from an old film.[93]

To Jan, on the other hand—and in his personality lies the real strength of the book—politics, or rather, political beliefs, are his lifeblood. This is in no sectarian sense: he has certainly not allowed his faith in Communism to blind him to reality. England he has grown to like and view with 'exasperated admiration'[94]; it is, he tells his brother Franz, 'a very corrupt country. They have habeas corpus, and people have passports, and if someone gets kicked around, questions are asked'.[95] Nor has he any illusions about the nature of the Communist régimes in Europe. He himself has been declared an enemy of the people in Czechoslovakia, his friends have been killed, and his own brother has been imprisoned for a course of Marxist 're-education'. 'The word traitor. . . .' he says to Franz, 'You people have made it so that when one hears it, one has an instinct to get to one's feet in respect. That's what you've done.'[96]

And yet in spite of all this, his basic faith remains untouched. To him the revolution was and is 'holy',[97] and the formation of the Party was a time 'when people formed themselves together . . . for the first time in history, without God, without excuses, relying on themselves, saying: We accept the responsibility for what we do, we accept all the good and evil of the past, we reject nothing. . . '.[98] To Julia's bitter complaint that politics dehumanise, that they mean for her mother only Town Councils and Birth Control Clinics, and that they have nothing relevant to say to people in Britain, he responds:

'There is a poor peasant. Let's take one peasant, it's simpler. And this peasant is in his hut, thinking. . . . He is hungry—the rains have failed this season. He has been hungry so long that he has forgotten what not being hungry is. And that peasant, Julia, represents nearly all the people in the world. He is the norm, not you.'

'It's not my fault.'

'No. But now, Julia Barr, who has been motoring through his country on a nice pleasure trip comes into his hut. And he doesn't feel at all affectionate towards this Julia Barr. He says to the nice clean English girl who will live to be eighty-five and will have four healthy children: Change places with me. Otherwise I shall die when I'm forty, and I'm tired of having children who die before they are a year old.'

'But it wouldn't be possible.'

'Of course. And that's why—the Party is always right,' he said, laughing.[99]

Under the influence of his arguments, and the force of his personality—for it is, of course, his very involvement which had really attracted her in the first place—Julia gradually finds her complacency not shattered, but certainly disturbed. She is affected, too, by other events in connection with their relationship. When she tries to assist him to get his British citizenship papers, the unpleasant nature of some aspects of British democracy and politics is revealed to her, as she finds herself blundering helplessly up against a bureaucracy which does not want the Jan Brods of this world. Her father is a charming liberal, who works for the Labour Party, and who seems on the surface to want to help. But when he succumbs weakly to the forces of bureaucracy, her attitude towards him changes. 'When it boils down, you behave just as *they* do. You don't really believe in the things you say you do. . . . He believes in what he says. . . . And they all do. And that's why you're just nothing. When it comes to the point, you'd do all the things you blame *them* for, and laugh.'[100]

But Julia's realisation is not so much a realisation of the validity of Jan's ideas, as of the strength of them, a realisation that her mother and father were 'like charming, perpetually-gesticulating wraiths' while Jan was 'four-square, solid as an army'.[101] Thus when Jan departs for Czechoslovakia towards the end of the book, leaving Julia behind, there is never any suggestion that Julia should join the Communist Party or start mouthing Communist ideas; rather, does she start making preparations for marriage with the young man she had known before meeting Jan, uneasily looking forward to a lifetime of happiness 'out of the rain'.[102] The novel ends, indeed, on the renewed note of uncertainty that perhaps Jan himself will be an anachronism even in Czechoslovakia; that perhaps the youth there only want to get 'out of the rain'. But for all this, there is no doubt that at least one corner of Julia's indifference has been eroded, that she will never again be able to be quite so complacent about the nature of her particular retreat to innocence.

If this novel seems an extraordinarily hesitant and uncertain one to be included in a study of Socialist propaganda, then one can only say that by 1956 any fundamentally different approach, any more emphatic insistence on the immediate future of Socialism would have been to blind oneself to the nature of British politics, and, for that matter, to world politics generally. *Retreat to Innocence* is by no means an exemplary novel: Doris Lessing's sympathy for Jan's ideas and her own uncertain grasp of the English background are reflected too obviously in the thinness of the other characters and in certain stereotyped scene-settings for it to be that. But it does at least steer skilfully and successfully in between the Scylla of wishful thinking and the Charybdis of disillusionment, and in so doing makes its political point effectively and intelligently.

III

Barely a few months after the publication of *Retreat to Innocence* the beliefs of

Jan Brod and his kind were to be put to their severest test. In February the Twentieth Congress of the Russian Communist Party had been held: in secret session, Khrushchev had outlined the full extent of the Stalinist terror of the thirties. When the report of this speech was finally published in June—by the US Department of State—the effect was shattering and immediate on Communist Parties throughout the world. In Britain it brought renewed and urgent demands for more airing of opinion within the Party, rising resentment, and more resignations: by September, in the words of one of Doris Lessing's characters, people were 'reeling off from the C.P. in dozens, broken-hearted'.[103] But on the 23 November 1956 came far more disillusioning news, as the Hungarian Revolution was put down in Stalinist fashion by the Red Army.[104] The resignations increased to a flood: by February 1957, some 7000 members had left the Party,[105] either in shock about Hungary or in disgust with the British Party's failure to condemn it. But it was amongst the intellectuals—whether the stalwarts from the thirties or the new recruits since—that the furore was at its greatest. As with the revision period of 1938–41, it is impossible to say with any accuracy how many did resign, but when one considers that those known to have done so at this time included such well-known names as Doris Lessing, Randall Swingler, Edward P. Thompson, Rodney Hilton, Rutland Boughton, and John Sommerfield,[106] some indication of its magnitude is revealed.

These events did not of course mark the final death of Socialist propaganda in Britain—any more than 1906 marked its birth. But they did, to say the least, sound a final death-knell to hopes of a revival of anything closely approximating to the thirties movement. They most assuredly made it unlikely that there would in the near future be many more novels in which final solutions were blithely found in the Party. Socialist activity and hopes continued, indeed flourished in the following years, particularly in the new left movement, with its accompanying *New Left Review*.[107] But this movement—which had for its initial basis many of the ex-Communist Party members—was one which collectively paid allegiance to no particular party on the left, while one of the more notable causes connected with it—the CND campaign—was a largely non-political activity. It was, in addition, a movement whose premises were less economic or historical laws, or any body of ideology, than a humanist concern for the quality of life. It is significant that when the New Left writers and critics, such as Raymond Williams, John Mander, and Stuart Hall, did revive for a while the controversial notion of literary commit-ment, it was in a form noticeably different from that of the thirties. They did not in fact speak with one tongue, but certain points were clear from the outset: generally, they were 'wary of involvement in parliamentary and party politics',[108] and they were concerned, in theory at least, less with the writer's politics than with the depth of his response to life. As Stuart Hall wrote of D. H. Lawrence: 'Lawrence wrote "for life's sake". This is not a weak emotionalism. It restores literature to its proper function—serving life, serving our humanity, saving us from the abstractions which, in the name of humanity, can be exalted over man'.[109] Even the most politically committed of the novels which can be said to be loosely connected with this movement, such as John Berger's *A Painter of Our Time* (1958) and Margot Heinemann's *The Adventurers* (1960), are strongly tinged with political uncertainty and doubt; while Raymond Williams' *Border Country* (1960), despite its resurrection in new guise of the journey and frontier symbols of the thirties, ultimately implies that political action is irrelevant: what is needed is a change of heart.

Of course there have been a few exceptions to this prevailing caution: Alan Sillitoe is a name which springs most readily to mind here. And certainly there is a strong strain of Socialist sympathy running through both his *Key to the Door* (1961) and the trilogy of novels which followed: *The Death of William Posters* (1965), *A Tree on Fire* (1967), and *The Flame of Life* (1974). But it is a sympathy which can have meaning only in the context of the Third World—in Malaya, in Algeria; within Britain his characters flounder helplessly, their zeal for revolution capable of expression only in talk and at times comic fantasy, while if any political parties are mentioned, they are mentioned with contempt.

As a final indication of the extent of this climate of suspicion in Britain of party politics and easy ideological solutions one needs only to turn to the post-1956 work of that most inveterate of Communist believers, Jack Lindsay. He has certainly not abandoned his faith or left the Party, but his novels since have reflected in varying degrees his belief that the revolutionary working-class movement in Britain has run down, that 'the Spring was definitely blighted . . . the Tide had ceased to rise', and also— although this is part of the same problem—that the buttressing effect of the Welfare State and the distortions practised elsewhere in the name of Socialism have made political solutions appear much less simple, that the 'Choice', in effect, has 'become confused and evaded'.[110] *A Local Habitation*, appearing in the year following Hungary, admittedly but faintly reflects this, but the novels since have shown an increasing propensity to ignore the Party, to fail, indeed, to give anything but the most elementary political consciousness to his characters, so that in his latest (and what appears to be his last) contemporary novel, *Choice of Times* (1964), his hero, Colin, ends on a note of unanswered desperation: 'Everything must be different, I can't live this way any longer. But how can I change it, how?'[111]

It was a question similar in some ways to that asked by Tressell, and by most of the writers in this study, and, no doubt, it will continue to be asked. For the issues of Socialism, needless to say, are most certainly not dead, and nor, despite some premature funeral announcements,[112] is ideology. But, partly because the nature of the question has changed, and partly because many of the answers have proved to be misleading, it is unlikely that it will in Britain—in the near future, at least—often be answered with quite that blend of passion and hopefulness that has characterised most of the better Socialist propaganda novels of the past.

Conclusion

The self-proclaimed 'committed' author-narrator-hero of David Caute's *The Occupation* (1971) ends that novel reading a book he has just written about the committed novel: 'He reads the book, always meaning to stop at the next section, but continually drawn by the magic of his own prose, of his own thoughts—of himself. Print is so pretty. It really is a long time since he has felt so contented, just sitting and reading himself'.[1]

In this attempt at the 'de-mystification'[2] of the novel, and particularly of the committed novel, we seem to be light years away from the thirties, and I certainly would not try to assert that Caute's novel is necessarily the worse for that. Nor, furthermore, would I deny that a fair proportion of the works examined in this study have escaped the aptness of Orwell's previously quoted dismissive phrase—'dull, tasteless and bad'—only by a hair's breadth. Very often, in fact, these attempts to breathe life and conviction into political beliefs have tended to ossify rather than vivify such beliefs.

But if in the main this has been a study of literary ephemera, if time and again one felt that the authors simply should have been doing something else—writing tracts, for example, or standing on soap-boxes—this is certainly not to reject everything that has been written. Quite apart from their often considerable sociological value—as in the way they consciously or unconsciously reflect political attitudes or draw attention explicitly or implicitly to the effects of the English class structure—quite apart from this I would assert that in the very best of the novels examined the authors have produced something unique to our literature.

Theoretically the literary propagandist, at whatever level he is working, should never assume for a moment that he is addressing an audience of the already converted. Thus in the Socialist tract *Merrie England*, for example, Blatchford imagines throughout an intelligent working-class reader who must be continually reasoned with and who must be allowed to see no weak links in the argument. At the same time, however, Blatchford is under no necessity to embody his arguments in anything more demanding than anecdotal illustrations, or to place his ideals against any harsher reality than the imaginary attacks of his opponents. In the novel, though the imaginary audience remains the same, the problem confronting the writer is vastly increased. Now his ideas have to be given life, to spring organically from the body of the work; now his ideals have to be placed against the unflattering reality of the world and the people in it. Now he has to show, to borrow Irving Howe's words about the political novel, 'the relation between theory and experience, between the ideology that has been preconceived and the tangle of feelings and relationships he is trying to present'.[3] His responsibilities as propagandist remain, but are now infinitely increased and accompanied by his responsibilities as novelist.

His attempt to fulfil these responsibilities may end in various ways. He may, like Dorris Lessing in the *Martha Quest* series, have decided beforehand that the ideology will not stand against the wayward intractable realities, and make his novel the clash between the two: something other than, but not necessarily better than, propaganda. He may, like Harold Heslop, in considerably less control of his material, show an unconscious preference for the devil, and shatter the already thin surface of his art. He may, like Ralph Bates towards the end of *The Olive Field*, momentarily allow his propagandist intentions to prevail over his artistic responsibilities, and thus do harm to both. He may like Jack Lindsay in far too many of his novels, impatiently abandon the struggle and produce what is virtually a tract masquerading as a novel. But finally he may, in the very best of these works, as in *The Ragged Trousered Philanthropists* and *A Scots Quair*, produce something which does not transcend propaganda, but which is *both* a work of art *and* propaganda: where the ideology neither takes over nor is submerged; where reality is allowed its fullest expression, but where, nonetheless, the Socialist ideals arise inevitably and organically from within the body of the work. We may reject these ideals, but we can do nothing more but concede that in the terms of the world presented, which *is* accepted by us, they seem inevitable and necessary.

References and Notes

Introduction

1. *The Road to Wigan Pier* (1937), p. 215.
2. 'Why I Write' (1946) reprinted in *The Collected Essays, Journalism and Letters of George Orwell*, i: *An Age Like This, 1920–1940* (1968), p. 5.
3. The word 'Socialist' was actually first used in print in 1837 to designate the followers of Robert Owen's Co-operative doctrines. (G. D. H. Cole, *A History of Socialist Thought*, i: *The Forerunners, 1789–1850* (1953), p. 1).
4. See Y. V. Kovalev, *An Anthology of Chartist Literature* (1956), pp. 213–92, for excerpts from these novels, which include Thomas Martin Wheeler's *Sunshine and Shadow* (1849–50, *Northern Star*) and Thomas Frost's *De Brassier: A Democratic Romance* (1851–52). For critical discussion of these books see Jack Mitchell, *Robert Tressell and The Ragged Trousered Philanthropists* (1969), pp. 30–33, Jack Mitchell, 'Aesthetic Problems of the Development of the Proletarian–Revolutionary Novel in Nineteenth-century Britain' in *Marxists on Literature*, ed. David Craig (1975), pp. 245–66, and Martha Vicunas, *The Industrial Muse* (1974), Chapter 3.
5. [Mrs Lynn Linton], *The True History of Joshua Davidson* (1872), p. 263.
6. P. J. Keating, *The Working Classes in Victorian Fiction* (1971), makes reference to Constance Howell's *A More Excellent Way* (1888), W. E. Tirebuck's *Miss Grace of All Souls* (1895), and Margaret Harkness' three novels of the late 1880s—but concludes that they belong to a 'very minor' tradition in the nineteenth century (see Keating, pp. 235–42, and 285, no. 37).
7. Bart Kennedy, *Slavery: Pictures from the Depths* (1905), p. 363.

Chapter 1

1. Robert Tressell [Robert Noonan], *The Ragged Trousered Philanthropists*, (unabridged ed. 1955), pp. 11–12.
2. Noted in T. A. Jackson, *Solo Trumpet* (1953), p. 77.
3. Balfour to Lady Salisbury (January 1906); quoted in Frank Bealey and Henry Pelling, *Labour and Politics 1900–1906* (1958), p. 277.
4. Quoted in Chushichi Tsuzuki, *H. M. Hyndman and British Socialism* (1961), p. 154.
5. G. D. H. Cole, *A History of Socialist Thought*, iii, Pt. 1: *The Second International 1889–1914* (1956), p. 159
6. 'The Labour Party and the Books That Helped to Make It', *Review of Reviews*, xxxiii (June (1906), pp. 568–82.
7. *Labour and Politics*, p. 277.
8. Robert E. Dowse, *Left in the Centre* (1966), p. 6.

9. Tsuzuki, p. 284.
10. Tsuzuki, pp. 158–9.
11. Tsuzuki, p. 123.
12. Hyndman in fact ended his days as one of the most bitter opponents of the Marxist–Leninists, whom he referred to scornfully in 1918 as 'these Petrograd Butchers' (quoted in Tsuzuki, p. 240)
13. Tsuzuki, p. 168.
14. They did not always confine themselves to such gradualist, peaceful anticipations, however. See, for example, 'The Second English Revolution', a three-part sketch by the Fabian, Holbrook Jackson, in *The New Age* of 1908. This sketch, in the form of a letter supposedly written by 'John Faraday' in 1950, describes with great enthusiasm the bloody revolution of 1920 which eventually ushered in the 'Commonwealth of Britain' (*The New Age*, III (May 2, May 9, May 16, (1908), pp. 12–13, 31–2, 51–2). But such revolutionary protestations by a Fabian were very rare indeed. Much closer to the Fabian spirit was Beatrice Webb's request of Harley Granville Barker in 1909 that he write a play propagandising her Minority Report: a request he politely declined on the grounds that he might end up eulogising Lloyd George, the author of the Majority Report! (Noted in Samuel Hynes, *The Edwardian Turn of Mind* (1968), pp. 126–31).
15. A. M. McBriar, *Fabian Socialism and English Politics, 1884–1918* (1966), p. 348.
16. For example, three of the successful Liberal candidates in 1906 were Fabians (Bealey and Pelling, pp. 169–70), a situation which probably prompted Arnold Bennett, in the course of explaining rather unconvincingly 'Why I Am a Socialist', to point out that 'Socialist has become the most convenient and effective name for the left wing of the Liberal Party' (*The New Age*, II (30 November 1907), 90).
17. Quoted in Paul Thompson, *Socialists, Liberals and Labour: The Struggle for London, 1885–1914* (1967), p. 237
18. *The Case Against Socialism* (1908), p. 87.
19. Ibid., p. 89
20. Ibid., p. 168.
21. Ibid., p. 150
22. Ibid., p. 154.
23. Ibid., p. 180.
24. Ibid., p. 187.
25. Ibid., p. 370.
26. Ibid., p. 397.
27. Ibid., p. 402.
28. A search of the *Times Literary Supplement* revealed a total of twenty-two anti-Socialist tales in these six years; many more, however, may be buried there.

Chapter 2

1. James Adderley, *Behold the Days Come* (1907), p. ix.
2. Adderley, pp. x–xi.
3. James Adderley, *In Slums and Society* (1916), pp. 197–9.
4. Peter d'A. Jones, *The Christian Socialist Revival 1877–1914* (1968), pp. 99–163.

5. Jones, pp. 225–302.
6. *In Slums and Society*, p. 209
7. Adderley, p. 169.
8. Presumably based on Adderley, who was nicknamed 'Father' by the Protestant Press (*In Slums and Society*, p. 128), and perhaps suggested by William Morris's *A Dream of John Ball* (1888).
9. *Behold the Days Come*, p. 42–3.
10. Ibid., p. 38.
11. Ibid., p. 222.
12. Ibid., p. 86.
13. Ibid., p. 110.
14. Richard Whiteing, *My Harvest* (1915), pp. 1 and 24.
15. *No. 5 John Street* (new ed., 1907), p. 12. The islands themselves were the subject of an earlier Whiteing novel, *The Island* (1888).
16. *No. 5 John Street*, p. 280.
17. *No. 5 John Street*, p. 232.
18. In *My Harvest* Whiteing praises Dickens for bringing to the novel 'the apotheosis of the common man, till then but a low-comedy super for the background of the piece . . .' (p. 260).
19. Amongst which are *Tales of Mean Streets* (1894), *A Child of the Jago* (1896), and *The Hole in the Wall* (1902). I am thinking not so much of Morrison's hostility to Socialism and Trade Unionism—which emerges clearly in *Tales of Mean Streets*—as of the impression he often conveys of dealing with something subhuman. For example, in *Child of the Jago* when the Parson stops the slum-dwellers from stealing, 'he flung them back, commanded them, cowed them with his hard, intelligent eyes, like a tamer among beasts' (new edition, 1969, p. 82).
20. *Ring in the New*, p. 115.
21. Ibid., p. 200. There are several other characters closely modelled on contemporary figures, including Bernard Shaw and Dr Furnivall, the Shakespearian critic.
22. Ibid., pp. 204–5.
23. Ibid., p. 263.
24. Ibid., p. 293.
25. Ibid., p. 309.
26. *Putman's Monthly*, 1 (March 1907), 112. Noted in Wendell V. Harris, 'The Novels of Richard Whiteing', *English Literature in Transition*, VIII, no. 1 (1965), 36–43.
27. Edith Moore, *A Wilful Widow* (1913), p. 194.
28. The fullest account of this may be found in Henry David, *The History of the Haymarket Affair* (2nd edition, 1958).
29. Hugh Kingsmill, *Frank Harris* (new edition, 1949), p. 50.
30. David, pp. 338 and 141.
31. Frank Harris, *The Bomb* (new edition, 1963), p. 286.
32. Ibid., p. 181.
33. Afterword to *The Bomb* (1920), reprinted in the 1963 edition, p. 324.
34. *Times Literary Supplement*, February 16, 1906, p. 53.
35. Maxwell Gray [Mary Gleed Tuttiett], *The Great Refusal* (new edition, [1907]), p. 241.

36. Promulgated by him in *Fors Clavigera*, a series of letters to the Workmen and Labourers of Great Britain, 1871–1884. (See W. H. G. Armytage, *Heavens Below* (1961), pp. 289–384, for an account both of the practical results of this, and also of the innumerable little co-operative colonies or communities set up in late Victorian and Edwardian England.)
37. *The Great Refusal*, p. 438.
38. *An Amazing Revolution and After* (1909), p. 84.
39. Ibid., p. 101.
40. Ibid., p. 159.
41. Harry Pollitt, *Serving My Time* (1940), p. 34.
42. The most balanced account of his life is to be found in Laurence Thompson, *Robert Blatchford* (1951).
43. G. D. H. Cole, *The Second International*, Pt 1 (1956), p. 167.
44. Alexander M. Thompson's Preface to Robert Blatchford's *My Eighty Years* (1931), p. xiii.
45. *Merrie England* (1894), p. 104.
46. But not his only attempt at fiction. He wrote numerous short stories which were mainly concerned with military life, and several novels, none of which is concerned basically with Socialism.
47. *The Sorcery Shop* (1907), p. 2.
48. Ibid., p. 13.
49. Ibid., p. 17.
50. Ibid., p. 63.
51. Ibid., p. 59.
52. Ibid., p. 63.
53. Ibid., p. 100.
54. Ibid., p. 127.
55. Ibid., p. 177.
56. Ibid., p. 189.
57. It is a subtitle which is possibly hopefully following the precedent of Walter Beasant's *All Sorts and Conditions of Men: An Impossible Story* (1882), an extremely popular social novel which visualised the creation of a free, working-class 'Palace of Delight' in the East End of London, complete with theatre, library, gymnasium, and schoolrooms. Such a Palace, the 'People's Palace'—eventually prosaically transformed into Queen Mary College of London University—was in fact established in Mile End Road in 1887, as a partial result of the public interest aroused by Besant's novel.
58. *The Sorcery Shop*, pp. 190–1.
59. He is the old soldier, and therefore, according to Blatchford, more open to persuasion. For in the army Blatchford nostalgically saw the seeds of Socialism. Socialism 'meant the collective action of the army. It meant *esprit de corps*, a larger, deeper, nobler *esprit de corps*' (*My Eighty Years*, p. 37).
60. *News From Nowhere* in *The Collected Works of William Morris*, Vol. XVI (1912), pp. 47–8 (Chapter vii).
61. Blatchford shared with Ruskin and Morris a belief that agriculture should be the basis of England's existence, and that England could be self-supporting. However, he envisaged a rather larger role for machinery than Ruskin would grant it.
62. *News From Nowhere*, pp. 103–30 (Chapter xvii), pp. 88–9, 87 (Chapter xiv), p.

39 (Chapter vi).

63. Margaret Cole, *Growing up into Revolution* (1949), p. 42.
64. *New Worlds for Old* (revised edition, 1909), p. 23.
65. Ibid., p. 277.
66. Ibid., p. 291.
67. Ibid., p. 347.
68. Ibid., p. 353.
69. *Experiment in Autobiography*, II (1934), p. 752.
70. Ibid., I (1934), p. 265. For a comprehensive account of Wells's evolution as a prophet of World Order, see W. Warren Wagar, *H. G. Wells and the World State* (1961).
71. *Studies in a Dying Culture* (1938), pp. 82–3, 93. See also A. L. Morton, *The English Utopia* (1952), pp. 183–94.
72. On the grounds that neither are concerned to any significant extent with 'Socialism', both *The War in the Air* (1908) and *The History of Mr Polly* (1910) have been excluded from the following discussion.
73. *Ann Veronica* (1909), p. 147 (vii, 4).
74. Ibid., p. 221 (x, 1).
75. Ibid., p. 147 (vii, 4).
76. *Tono-Bungay* (new edition, 1911), p. 110 (II, i, 4).
77. Ibid., p. 268 (III, iii, 1).
78. Ibid., p. 194 (II, iv, 10).
79. *Language of Fiction* (1966), p. 242.
80. *The New Machiavelli* (1911), p. 145 (I, iv, 10).
81. Ibid., p. 320 (III, i, 8).
82. Ibid., p. 330 (III i, 9).
83. Ibid., p. 334 (III, ii, 1).
84. *Marriage* (1912), p. 378 (III, ii, i).
85. Ibid., p. 526 (III, iv, 16).
86. Ibid., pp. 528–9 (III, iv, 16).
87. Ibid., p. 531 (III, iv, 17).
88. *The Passionate Friends* (1913), p. 237 (viii, 5).
89. Anthony West, *Principles and Persuasions* (1958), p. 14.
90. *The Passionate Friends*, p. 269 (ix, 10).
91. Ibid., pp. 355–6 (xii, 3).
92. *The World Set Free* (1914), p. 68 (i, 6).
93. Ibid., p. 154 (iii, 2).
94. *In the Days of the Comet* (new edition, 1963), p. 89 (iii, 4).
95. Ibid., p. 38 (i, 3).
96. *New Worlds for Old* pp. 256–8.
97. Exactly how ambiguous may be gauged from the fact that Wells commented in *New Worlds for Old* that the state envisaged in *The Days of the Comet* was, like Morris's *Nowhere*, 'a glorious anarchism', 'free from property, free from jealousy, and "above the law"' (pp. 256 and 254). And yet, as J. Kagarlitski points out, there is a strong suggestion that apart from the collective ownership of the land, the system would continue to be a form of modified capitalism, where 'The capitalist and the worker work together for the common good' (*The Life and Thought of H. G. Wells* (1966), p. 95).
98. *In the Days of the Comet*, p. 236 (xi, 1) (italics in original).

99. So much attention was in fact focused on this aspect of the book that Wells eventually felt bound to issue a public denial that the views on marriage expressed in this novel were representative of official Socialism: 'The book is a dream, is intended to be a beautiful dream, and it ends with an epilogue that makes that intention perfectly clear. If the book is immoral and indecent, then the New Testament is equally so. The story has just as much to do with current politics and ordinary social relations as Michaelangelo's Last Judgment or the well-known picture of "Love and Life"'. ('Mr. Wells and Free Love', *The New Age*, I (17 October 1907), 392). For further details of reactions to this event and Well's own, somewhat ambiguous attitudes see Ingvald Raknem, *H. G. Wells and His Critics* (1962), pp. 76–77.

100. *In the Days of the Comet*, p. 171 (vi, 6).

101. Guy Thorne (C. A. E. R. Gull), *The Socialist* (1909), pp. 53–71.

Chapter 3

1. Grant Richards, *Author Hunting* (new edition, 1960), p. 222 (1st edition, 1934).

2. In the abridged form his name was actually given as 'Tressall'. I have throughout used the complete version rather than the edited version, for time has shown that the reinsertion of the deleted portions has in no way detracted from the success of the book. Indeed, despite Miss Pope's claim (in the Preface to the first edition) that she had 'cut away superfluous matter only', and despite Grant Richard's statement that the second edition was in no way expurgated for political reasons (quoted in R. W. Postgate, *The Builders' History* (1923), p. 391), part of the editing did in fact reflect a conservative political and moral bias, which seriously blurred Tressell's message. (A discussion of the differences between the two versions can be found in an article by Jack Beeching: 'The Ragged Trousered Philanthropists', *Our Time*, VII (May 1948), 196–9.)

3. Frank Swinnerton, *The Adventures of a Manuscript* (1956), pp. 20–1.

4. *Tressell of Mugsborough* (1951).

5. F. C. Ball, 'More Light on Tressell', *Marxism Today*, XI (June 1967), 177–82, and F. C. Ball, *One of the Damned* (1973).

6. See 'Sold Rights to Classic for £25', *The Times* (5 June 1967), p. 3; and 'Talking to Kathleen Tressell', *Labour Monthly*, L (June 1968), 261–3.

7. In a letter to the present writer (9 July 1969), Kathleen Lynne (née Noonan) insists that her grandfather, according to family conversations, was a *Sir* Samuel Croker, and points out that the dates of F. C. Ball's plain 'Samuel Croker' are incorrect. 'I always understood', she continues, 'that my father left home and worked his way to South Africa because he would not live on the family income derived largely from absentee landlordism in Ireland'.

8. *The Ragged Trousered Philanthropists*, pp. 507–40 (hereinafter cited in the notes as *The Philanthropists*).

9. Whether directly borrowed, it is impossible to say. Bellamy's influence, though declining after the turn of the century, had been very widespread, and his ideas had been incorporated into many other Socialist tracts of the time (see *Bellamy Abroad*, edited by Sylvia E. Bowman (1962), pp. 86–118).

However, there is no particular reason to suppose that Tressell had not read the book. It is recommended reading in one of his favourite tracts, *Merrie England*, and there were cheap editions available.

10. For a discussion of the influence of Morris on Tressell see the only book-length study of Tressell's novel by Jack Mitchell: *Robert Tressell and the Ragged Trousered Philanthropists* (1969), pp. 156–62.

11. *The Philanthropists*, pp. 297–9.

12. Ball, *Tressell of Mugsborough*, p. 56.

13. *The Philanthropists*, p. 508.

14. Ibid., p. 527.

15. Ibid., p. 218.

16. Ibid., p. 244.

17. This is not to say that their beliefs were identical; they were certainly not. Tressell seems to have cherished no illusions about making Britain's agriculture the basis of its economy: nor is his conception of the future Socialist State in any way anarchic.

18. As has already been noted Blatchford did not actually attack Christian theology until the appearance of *God and My Neighbour* (1903).

19. *Britain for the British* (1902), pp. 41–2.

20. *The Philanthropists*, p. 12.

21. Alan Sillitoe makes a similar point about Morrison in his Introduction to the Panther edition of *The Ragged Trousered Philanthropists* (1965), p. 8.

22. *The Philanthropists*, pp. 449–50.

23. Ibid., p. 46.

24. Ibid., p. 225.

25. Ibid., p. 152.

26. Although, as Humphrey House has said, 'Nearly everybody in Dickens has a job: there is a passionate interest in what people do for a living and how they make do' (*The Dickens World* (new edition, 1960), p. 55), this interest has its limitations, and there are no characters—and certainly no proletarian characters—whose working-life forms the central pivot of the novel. Even Joe Gargery's blacksmith shop in *Great Expectations* is important for what it represents, rather than for what actually goes on inside it.

Perhaps the only two English novels before the appearance of *The Ragged Trousered Philanthropists* to focus so intensely on work are Defoe's *Robinson Crusoe* (1719) and George Gissing's *New Grub Street* (1891). Defoe's novel of course was written, as Jack Mitchell comments (p. 146), when the working middle classes were still relatively close to and even active—as Defoe was— in the actual process of production; while Gissing's novel concentrates on the fundamentally middle-class occupation of writing.

27. *The Philanthropists*, p. 47.

28. Ibid., p. 172. One is reminded here of William Morris's comments in his lecture 'The Art of the People' (1879) of the few 'right-minded men' 'the salt of the earth' who will 'in despite of irksomeness and hopelessness, drive right through their work'.

29. But to say, as the Marxist critic Jack Beeching does, that 'they grow towards a fuller understanding of each other, their values and their characters deepen' ('The Uncensoring of *The Ragged Trousered Philanthropists*', *The Marxist Quarterly*, II (October 1955), 219) is surely absurdly to overstate the case.

Eastman's change of attitude towards Ruth is only briefly dealt with, and we never actually see them together after he has decided to return to her.

30. *The Philanthropists*, p. 27.

31 and 32. *The Philanthropists*, p. 471. For a more extended discussion of this element of 'what might be' and particularly of the 'Beano', a feast which recalls the feast in William Morris's *News from Nowhere*, see Jack Mitchell, pp. 162–88.

33. He was a character omitted altogether in the Jessie Pope abridgement. According to Kathleen Lynne he and Owen 'form a composite picture of the author, though I do not think Dad ever had recourse to any family money' (letter to the present writer, 9 July 1969). Mitchell, pp. 138–42, defends the character of Barrington partly on the grounds of historical accuracy, saying that he represents the middle-class Socialist theorist, so prominent in the early labour movement; while Brian Mayne in '*The Ragged Trousered Philanthropists*: an Appraisal of an Edwardian Novel of Social Protest', *Twentieth Century Literature*, XIII, No. 2 (July 1967), 80, sees him as providing 'a more sophisticated context for the discussion of Socialism than could credibly be allowed to the self-educated Owen'. Neither critic, however, answers the charge that in the context of the novel Barrington is inevitably seen primarily as a piece of wish-fulfilment on Tressell's part.

34. *The Philanthropists*, p. 164. A similar illustration occurs in Blatchford's *Merrie England*, but it is interesting to note the different uses the two men make of it. Discussing the private ownership of land, Blatchford says:

> It would be just as reasonable for a few families to claim possession of the sea and the air, and charge their fellow creatures rent for breathing or bathing, as it is for those few families to grab the land and call it theirs. As a matter of fact we *are* charged for breathing, for without a sufficient space of land to breathe on we cannot get good air to breathe.
>
> If a man claimed the sea, or the air, or the light as his, you would laugh at his presumption. Now, I ask you to point out to me any reason for private ownership of land which will not act as well as a reason for private ownership of sea and air (pp. 67–8).

For all his emotional and humorous appeal, Blatchford could never forget that he was also appealing to the sound common sense of the British workman. Tressell, however, called for an imaginative involvement of a quite different order.

35. *The Philanthropists*, p. 251.

36. It continued, however, in 'folk-song' (for example, 'Harry was a Bolshie/One of Lenin's lads'), in middle-class revolutionary poetic parody, and in the satirical reviews put on by the London Unity Theatre, Glasgow Unity Theatre, etc.

37. Beeching, 'The Uncensoring of *The Ragged Trousered Philanthropists*', p. 225.

38. It would be pointless to enumerate this in any detail, for the debt is obviously a fairly general one, ranging from Dickens's spontaneous combustion of Mr Krook in *Bleak House* (although even he justifies this by precedent) to his series of reports on the 'Mudfog Association for the Advancement of Everything'

(cf. the meeting of the Organised Benevolence Society in *The Philanthropists*, pp. 365–70).

39. Irving Howe, *Politics and the Novel* (1961), p. 219.
40. *The Writer and Politics* (1948), p. 162.

Chapter 4

1. Quoted in Henry Pelling, *A Short History of the Labour Party*, (3rd edition, 1968), p. 44.
2. Again, the converts to Labour were by no means always very sure about the extent of their Socialism: 'A few, mostly Fabians like Money and Webb, had clear and precise aims which included, ultimately, a socialist commonwealth. The other, larger group, though jolted by the experiences of the war into a receptivity to certain socialistic schemes, were less enthusiastic about a totally socialist economy' (Catherine Ann Cline, *Recruits to Labour, 1914–1931* (1963), p. 42).
3. Quoted in L. J. Macfarlane, *The British Communist Party* (1966), p. 278. The same Congress eventually passed a resolution repudiating the 'reformist' view that a social revolution could be achieved through Parliament, but conceding that Parliamentary and electoral action was a valuable means of 'propaganda and agitation towards the revolution' (ibid., p. 56).
4. 1926 and 1930 figures from Henry Pelling, *The British Communist Party* (1958), p. 192. Macfarlane (p. 58) makes the calculation that there were 4000 represented at the Foundation Congress.
5. Purportedly coming from the Third International, and addressed to the British Communist Party, this letter — now generally accepted as probably a forgery—called for armed insurrection in Britain. In the excitement of the moment it was easily used to fan suspicion of the Labour Party.
6. Quoted in Stephen Richards Graubard, *British Labour and the Russian Revolution, 1917–1924* (1956), p. 275.
7. Philip Gibbs, *Ten Years After* (1924), p.v.
8. H. Hessell Tiltman, *Poverty Lane* (1926), p. 309.
9. Quoted in Graubard, p. 246.
10. This author's solution of the class struggle and revolution leads her upper-class hero, Lord Peter Forelands, to pitch all his property—and persuade as many other friends as he can to do the same—into a pool of capital for the future Commonweal.
11. Her father was a University Professor. See *Remembering My Good Friends* (1944), pp. 8–9.
12. *Follow My Leader* (1921), p. 79.
13. Ibid., p. 300.
14. Ibid., p. 311.
15. He also enjoyed a brief period of renown as a 'miner poet', his *Songs of a Miner* (1917) selling some 5000 copies in its first month of publication.
16. S. Dynamov, 'Stacey Hyde: An Artist of English Social Fascism', *International Literature*, 2–3 (1932), 116. For a much more meaningful and interesting discussion of Welsh by a Marxist critic see Jack Mitchell, 'The Struggle for

the Working-Class Novel in Scotland—Part 1, *Scottish Marxist*, 6 (April 1974), 40–52. (Two later articles by Mitchell in the same magazine deal with Lewis Grassic Gibbon and James Barke: 7 [October 1974], 46–54, and 8 [January 1975], 39–48).

17. *The Underworld* (1920), pp. 163–4.
18. Ibid., p. 242.
19. Ibid., p. 256.
20. The title is, of course, derived from the cannibalistic underground workers of H. G. Wells's *The Time Machine* (1895).
21. *Norman Dale, MP* (1928), p. 97.
22. Ibid., p. 98.
23. Ibid., p. 174.
24. Ibid., p. 311.
25. *Clash* (1929), p. 68.
26. Ethel Mannin, *Confessions and Impressions* (1930), p. 168.
27. *Clash*, p. 51.
28. Ibid., p. 309.
29. *Men Like Gods* (1923), p. 291 (III.iv.3).
30. *The Life and Thought of H. G. Wells*, pp. 142–3.
31. *Men Like Gods*, p. 264 (III.ii.6).
32. A political party—the Labour Party—is viewed favourably in one Utopia of the period, Duncan Campbell's *The Last Millionaire* (1923), although this hybrid adventure story-tract can hardly be called Socialist. Feeling the need for social justice, but disliking complete Socialism, or Communism, which 'he regarded as a nightmare of homicidal maniacs, and the last resource of disappointed failures' (p. 207), a millionaire, Wallace McCrae, enters public life in support of the Labour Party. The Party finally comes to power in 1959—backed by Wallace's airfleets—and proceeds to nationalise the land and levy a tax on capital. Wallace, however, 'resisted the great pressure brought to bear by his own followers in favour of extending socialistic ideals into every department of business; and it is undoubtedly to him that Englishmen owe it, that they still retain so much of that personal freedom and power of initiative, which have always been characteristic of the nation' (p. 243).
    There would have been one other, genuinely Socialist Utopia, presumably supporting a political party, had H. M. Hyndman finished his planned *The Life to Come*, but unfortunately he died in 1921, with only the Introduction completed (noted in Tsuzuki, *Hyndman*, p. 269).
33. 'Unitas', *A Dream City* (1920), p. 39.
34. Ibid., p. 57.
35. Ibid., p. 80.
36. *Against the Red Sky* (1922), p. 270.
37. *Apparition* (1928), p. 360.
38. I. T. Blundell, 'Man Who Took to "the Masses" as He Would to Drink', *The Sunday Worker* (17 June 1928), p. 8.

Chapter 5

1. Figures from Charles Loch Mowat, *Britain Between the Wars, 1918–1940* (revised edition, 1956), pp. 357 and 379.
2. Oswald Mosley, *The Greater Britain* (1932), pp. 149 and 22 (italics in original).
3. Mowat, p. 432.
4. It will be seen later that it was from these areas—and London—that most of the working-class revolutionary novels came.
5. *The Condition of Britain* (1937), p. 217.
6. Some indication of the awakening interest in Socialism at the universities— where, in 1922, according to Leonard Woolf, 'if you wanted to do well for yourself academically it was safer to conceal the fact that you were left of centre' (*Downhill All the Way* (1967), p. 46)—is afforded by the fact that in 1933 the revolutionary student Socialists under the leadership of the young Cambridge Communist, John Cornford, were strong enough to found a Federation of Socialist Societies, comprising ten affiliated organisations in England and Scotland (Neal Wood, *Communism and British Intellectuals* (1959), p. 52).
7. Allen Hutt, *The Condition of the Working Class in Britain* (1933), p. 244.
8. The British Union of Fascists was claiming 20000 members by 1934, although Colin Cross (*The Fascists in Britain* (1963), p. 131) estimates that the active membership was nearer 5000.
9. Maxim Litvinoff.
10. Wood, p. 38.
11. Edward Upward, *In the Thirties* (1962), pp. 281–2.
12. (1932; four editions in just over a year). With its emphasis on the way Capitalism would give way to Fascism, which in turn would give way to social revolution and the dictatorship of the proletariat, 'It appealed because it read like a true interpretation of the period . . .' (Kingsley Martin, *Editor* (1968), p. 58).
13. The question mark was removed for the second edition of *Soviet Communism* in 1937.
14. Ethel Mannin, *Privileged Spectator* (1939), p. 75.
15. Naomi Mitchison, *The Kingdom of Heaven* (1939), p. 151n.
16. 'Inside the Whale' (1940) reprinted in *The Collected Essays, Journalism and Letters of George Orwell*, I: *An Age Like This, 1920–1940* (1968), p. 515.
17. Pelling, *The British Communist Party* (1958), p. 95.
18. Both figures from Pelling, p. 104.
19. I have tried to make this short account as brief as possible, and as relevant as possible to the issues that will later be raised. For a more general account of the attractions of Communism for the British Intellectuals, see Neal Wood, and for the activities involving university students see Peter Stansky and William Abrahams, *Journey to the Frontier* (1966).
20. *Literature of the World Revolution*, [3] (1931), 193 and 226. (The International Union of Revolutionary Writers had been founded somewhat casually in 1927 by a group of individual authors who were in Moscow to attend the Tenth Anniversary of the October Revolution. A minimal political pro- gramme had been adopted at that time. At this second Conference in 1930, however, the union was placed on a rather more organised basis, and the

writers were given a political programme of a 'broader and more concrete character' [Walter B. Rideout, *The Radical Novel in the United States* (1956), p. 309n]).

21. In 'Stacey Hyde: An Artist of English Social Fascism', *International Literature*, 2–3 (1932), S. Dynamov explained that the social-fascist writer, 'while pretending to write about the real life of the proletariat . . . really employs the labor [sic] themes as a means of "bourgeoisifying" the working class'' (p. 116). Thus James Welsh came under attack primarily for *The Morlocks*, while Stacey Hyde was abused for a series of novels on labour themes: *Shopmates* (1924), *Simple Annals* (1925), *The Blank Wall* (1929) and *The Blackleg* (1930).

22. The issues of this London-based magazine included poems by T. H. Wintringham ('The Immortal Tractor') and revolutionary stories by Rayner Heppenstall, Rhys J. Williams, A. P. Roley, and Gore Graham. In the editorial of the first issue ('Storm and the Struggle', [February 1933], 2) it was stated that '*Storm* is the first magazine of Socialist Fiction to be published in this country. We intend it to contain stories, sketches, poems and illustrations depicting all phases of the struggle, a virile and progressive counter-blast to the reams of counter-revolutionary dope that are contained in other organs of popular fiction'. In general, however, the magazine dismally failed to live up to this optimistic introduction. An attempt was made to stave off collapse by offering Maxim Gorky's *Short Stories* as a prize for the best contribution, and by appealing for regional 'Storm Shock-Brigades' to boost circulation, but after four (?) issues in 1933, the magazine appeared no more.

23. Hugh MacDiarmid's two *Hymns to Lenin* had appeared in 1931 and 1932, but the first clear indication of a growing revolutionary poetic movement came with the publication of *New Country: Prose and Poetry* in 1933. Although the latter work, and particularly the prose, is by no means as uniformly revolutionary as the introduction by Michael Roberts implies, the poems by W. H. Auden, C. Day Lewis, Charles Madge, Rex Warner *et al.* certainly show strong signs of impatience for radical social change. (For an interesting analysis of the political attitudes of this volume see Samuel Hynes, *The Auden Generation* (1976), pp. 102–10).

24. 'New Life for the Novel', *Viewpoint*, 1 (April–June 1934), 12.

25. *Revolution in Writing* (2nd edition, 1938), pp. 29 and 27.

26. 'American Authors Popular in Soviet Russia', *International Literature*, 3 (1936), 103.

27. 'The British Are Coming', *New Masses*, XXI (15 December 1936), 23–4.

28. 'A Letter from London', *New Masses*, XXVII (7 June 1938), 21.

29. Rideout, pp. 295–8.

30. Apparent in his novels, but explicitly expressed in his documentary survey of the depressed areas of Wales, *Grey Children* (1937), where he says of the various political parties: 'One listens patiently or impatiently to all the ideas, suggestions, hopes and threats, and one listens in vain for the faintest echo of that rapidly receding voice of Reason . . .' (p. 169).

31. In *Pie in the Sky* (1937).

32. *The English Catalogue of Books for 1937*, edited by James D. Stewart (1938), p. vi.

33. And, for those intellectuals who were disenchanted with its lack of radical

zeal, there was the short-lived Socialist League, which aimed at radicalisation within the Party, and attracted such writers as Storm Jameson, Walter Greenwood, and Naomi Mitchison.

34. Pelling, p. 192.
35. Rideout, p. 243.
36. Pelling, p. 104.
37. This is undoubtedly the most important factor, but there were others, among the most prominent being the trial of Sacco and Vanzetti and their execution in 1927. A vast number of American writers had desperately tried to prevent this apparently flagrant violation of justice, but had found themselves powerless. As Robert Morse Lovett commented the following year, nothing had 'so shaken the Liberal's belief in the working for equal justice of free institutions' (quoted in Rideout, p. 133). The only event remotely comparable in Britain during the twenties was the General Strike, and more particularly the long-drawnout miners' strike that followed, and, indeed, as has already been mentioned, this did bring a momentary rise in the Communist Party's ranks. But the issues here were nowhere near so clearcut or so intensely focussed: wrong-headedness could be seen on both sides.
38. Rideout, p. 131.
39. Ibid., pp. 144–5. The John Reed Club was formed in October, 1929, by a group of writers and artists—many of whom were contributors to *New Masses*—and named after John Reed, a former editor of *The Masses*, and author of that classic work on the 1917 Revolution: *Ten Days That Shook the World* (1919).
40. Rideout, pp. 145–7 (see also Daniel Aaron, *Writers on the Left* (1961), pp. 219–21; 280–1; and 431n).
41. Indeed, if the experiences of William Holt, an English Communist Councillor, workingman, and writer, are at all typical, there would seem to have been an active hostility in certain quarters to any individual efforts to set up a proletarian movement. Holt claims that in early 1930:

> I drew up a manifesto for a League for the Liberation of Proletarian Arts and sent it to the *Daily Worker*, hoping to get in touch with other kindred spirits and fight on this more congenial front. The document was returned unpublished, together with a letter from the party centre pointing out that it was contrary to party discipline to launch unofficial united-front organizations. Our appeal for party sanction was turned down with derision. 'There can be no proletarian art until after the revolution,' they said. 'To the factories—the masses! That's our job now.' (*I Haven't Unpacked* (1939, new edition, 1942), p. 235).

Holt has stated subsequently that 'by "league for the Liberation of Proletarian Arts" I meant working-class art pure and simple without "orientation" from anyone' (letter to the present writer, 31 June 1969), and it may well be that his attempts were rebuffed because of this very fact; but it is significant all the same that as a Communist he was rebuffed, and that no attempt was made to put him in touch with other writers. (His first novel, *Backwaters*, was as we shall see later, most certainly Communist 'orientated'.)

42. Victor Gollancz, 'Editorial', *The Left News*, 19 (November 1937), 556. It should be noted here that the *Book Club* also branched out into other activities, such as a Readers' and Writers' Group, a Poetry Group with its attendant magazine, *Poetry and the People*, and a Theatre Guild, which acted in co-operation with the left-wing Unity Theatre. (See Stuart Samuels, 'The Left Book Club', *Journal of Contemporary History*, 1, no. 2 (1966), 65–86).
43. Founded in 1936.
44. 'Manifesto', *New Writing*, 1 (Spring 1936), [v].
45. He went as a stretcher-bearer, but would appear never to have actually served in that capacity. For a summary of the evidence of what he actually did do, see C. K. Stead, 'Auden's "Spain"', *London Magazine*, VII (March 1968), 46–7.
46. Julian Symons, *The Thirties* (1960), p. 124.
47. *Left Review*, III (March 1937), 79–86.
48. It will be seen later that there were in fact no English revolutionary novels *about* the Spanish War, although there were several—for example C. Day Lewis's *Starting Point* (1937), James Barke's *Land of the Leal* (1939), and Lewis Jones's *We Live* (1939)—which end with the hero's departure for Spain.
49. See the comments by Michael Gold and John Lehmann in *Ralph Fox: A Writer in Arms* (edited by John Lehmann *et al.*, 1937), pp. 10–11 and 109–10. According to Lehmann, Fox—who died in the Spanish War, and is chiefly remembered as the author of *The Novel and the People* (1937)—might, 'if he had given himself a chance among all his other activities, have written one or two of the finest revolutionary novels of our generation' (p. 109).
50. Charlotte Haldane, *Truth Will Out* (1949), p. 289.
51. And in his essay 'Sketch for a Marxist Interpretation of Literature' in *The Mind in Chains* (1937), where he says that the newly converted Communist writer will find himself involved in political work just at the time when he needs all his energy to create a new style. It is one of the burdens he will have to bear if he wishes eventually 'to tell the truth about reality' (p. 52). A heartfelt plea for the recruitment of more political workers so that radical writers would have more time to write was made by the English novelist and editor of *Left Review*, Amabel Williams-Ellis at the International Congress of Writers for the Defence of Culture, Paris, 1935 ('Paris Congress Speeches', *Left Review*, 1 (August 1935), 474–5).
52. *Revolution in Writing*, p. 23.
53. Calder-Marshall, letter to the present writer (28 February 1968). From this one might branch out into an examination of the possible inherent conservatism of the British booksellers and publishers in the thirties. Unfortunately, however, Victor Gollancz's claim that when he started the *Left Book Club* in 1936 the booksellers constituted 'an invisible barrier across which it was almost impossible to get progressive literature into the hands of the general public' ('*The Left Book Club* and the Labour Victory', *The Left News*, 110 (August 1945), 3252), can no more be verified than Harold Heslop's statement at the Kharkov Writers' Conference in 1930 that his novel *The Gate of a Strange Field* was cut drastically by the deletion of anti-capitalist references (*Literature of the World Revolution*, [3], (1931), 226). Certainly it should be noted that from the outset the publishers of the revolutionary books were not confined to such recognised radical publishers as Victor Gollancz,

Martin Lawrence or Wishart and Company (the latter two, amalgamated in 1936, became the official Communist publishing house).

54. C. Day Lewis, *Revolution in Writing*, p. 22.
55. Arthur Calder-Marshall, 'The Pink Decade', *New Statesman and Nation*, XXI (15 February 1941), 157.

    For an indication of exactly how wide this class-gulf was, one has only to turn to George Orwell's well-intentioned discussion in *The Road to Wigan Pier* (1937) about the question of whether the working classes 'smell' (pp. 159–63).

Chapter 6

1. *Revolt* (1933), pp. 92–3.
2. Ibid., p. 126.
3. Ibid., pp. 178–9.
4. *The Left Heresy—in Literature and Life* (1939), p. 151.
5. 'A Lancs Worker Seeks the Way Out', *Daily Worker* (21 February 1934), p. 4.
6. *Backwaters* (1934), p. 30.
7. Ibid., pp. 114–5.
8. Ibid., p. 272.
9. Ibid., p. 287.
10. This is, of course, no reflection on the sincerity of Holt's views, for which, in 1932, he was sentenced to nine months' imprisonment (*I Haven't Unpacked*, p. 256.) But evidence seems to suggest that at the time of writing *Backwaters* his faith—which was anyway in large part an act of rebellion, an expression of defiant individuality—had practically withered away. He narrates in his autobiography how he was forced to resign from the Communist Party at the end of 1934; but he seems far less concerned about this than he does about losing the managing directorship of a travelling Book Company shortly afterwards. It is significant too that only a few months after *Backwaters* was published, another novel by Holt appeared, *The Price of Adventure* (1934), which featured a character who was almost identical to Stone, but who conspicuously lacked his radical views.
11. *Ten-a-Penny People* (1938), p. 260.
12. Ibid., p. 262.
13. Ibid., p. 284.
14. See his autobiography, *The Name's Phelan* (1948).
15. 'Sketch for a Marxist Interpretation of Literature', *The Mind in Chains*, p. 46.
16. *The British Communist Party*, p. 85.
17. *Jew Boy* (1935), p. 30.
18. Ibid., p. 96.
19. Ibid., p. 189.
20. Noted by E. Elistratova in 'The Work of Harold Heslop', *International Literature* I (1932), 99. This writer has her own solution for Heslop's apparent political confusion: 'It is not for nothing that Harold Heslop was once a member of the Independent Labor [*sic*] Party, a party which Lenin used to speak of as being "independent of socialism". His novels show how very deeply the social fascist bacteria had penetrated into his psychology and infected his work' (p. 101).

21. The phrase is perhaps borrowed from H. G. Wells's novel, *Meanwhile* (1927), where it is used in a similar fashion to describe the General Strike (p. 148 in 1962 edition).

22. This may be an unfair judgement on Heslop's ideological uncertainty; it has already been mentioned how he claimed at Kharkov that *The Gate of a Strange Field* had been cut drastically by his publishers.

23. *Journey Beyond* (1930), p. 252. Another novel, *The Crime of Peter Ropner* (1934), is little more than a conventional tale of love and murder.

24. *Last Cage Down* (1935), p. 80.

25. Ibid., pp. 185–6 (italics in original).

26. Ibid., p. 312.

27. *The Gate of a Strange Field*, pp. 205–27. See also the Marxist critic Alick West's discussion of *The Gate of a Strange Field* in *Crisis and Criticism* (1937) where he argues that Tarrant's delay in London with his wife 'conveys at least negatively a feeling of the determination it needs to fight in the class-war instead of compromising' (p. 195). West does, however, go on to say that Tarrant's later passionate address to a Trade Union meeting 'conveys nothing, because in the depths of his being, as shown by the action, is the desire for success and a woman' (p. 196).

28. The point is confirmed by Heslop's only other novel after *Last Cage Down*, *The Earth Beneath*, published in 1946, but apparently written in the thirties (see *International Literature*, 8–9 (1939), 28–52). This is again set on a northern coalfield, but at an earlier period and the apolitical hero John Dakers is never 'tamed' in the sense that Joe Cameron is: in consequence he comes as close to life as anything in Heslop.

29. *Last Cage Down*, p. 133.

30. Now chiefly remembered for his postwar series of novels on Burns.

31. Perhaps suggested by C. Day Lewis's poem, *The Magnetic Mountain* (1933):

    It is now or never, the hour of the knife,
    The break with the past, the major operation.

(From Section 25, 'Consider these, for we have condemned them'.)

32. *Major Operation* (1936), p. 363.

33. Ibid., pp. 387–8.

34. Sommerfield, who was later to fight in the Spanish Civil War and to remain a supporter of the Communist Party till the mid-fifties, did, however, contribute to the Key Books series a 64-page novelette called *Trouble in Porter Street* (1939), a simplistic story of Communist work in a London street.

35. *May Day* (1936), p. 18.

36. Ibid., p. 70.

37. Ibid., p. 145.

38. Ibid., p. 30.

39. As one of James Hanley's miners claimed: 'All Communists down there now, you know. Whole place is full of them. Communists and policemen. Aye' (*Grey Children*, p. 47). Pelling in *The British Communist Party* notes that in 1935 there were sixteen Communist Councillors serving in South Wales (p. 85).

40. He died in January, 1939, in Cardiff, shortly after addressing some street meetings for Spain (*Dictionary of Welsh Biography* (1959), pp. 493–4).

41. *Cwmardy*, (1937), p. vii.
42. This strike is an example of Jones's telescoping of events. It seems to be based partly on the actual strike that took place in the Rhondda in 1910, the long Cambrian Combine Strike, when the police and troops sent in were widely criticised for unnecessary violence (R. Page Arnot, *The Miners: Years of Struggle* (1953), pp. 59–66), and partly on the shooting incident in another area altogether, at Featherstone in Yorkshire in 1893, when during the Great Lock-out the military fired on a crowd that would not disperse, killed two, and wounded sixteen (R. Page Arnot, *The Miners* (1949), pp. 236–41). This telescoping has the presumably desired effect of highlighting even more the clash of proletariat – capitalist.
43. *We Live* (1939), p. 309.
44. *We Live*, p. 332. Cf. the young English Communist John Cornford's letter to Margot Heinemann when he was at the front in Aragon, December 1936: 'Loving you has been the most perfect experience, and in a way, the biggest achievement of my life.

    'The party was my only other love. Until I see you again, bless you my love, my strength. Be happy. I worked for the party with all my strength, and loved you as much as I was capable of. If I am killed, my life won't be wasted' (quoted in Peter Stansky and William Abrahams, *Journey to the Frontier* (1966), p. 384).
45. *Cwmardy*, p. 78.
46. Ibid., p. 310.
47. See his autobiography of these days, *The Green Hills Far Away* (1940).
48. *The Land of the Leal* (1939), p. 101.
49. Ibid., p. 258.
50. Ibid., p. 389.
51. Ibid., p. 436.
52. Ibid., p. 499.
53. Ibid., p. 568.
54. Ibid., p. 596.
55. Ibid., p. 608.
56. Ibid., p. 634.
57. *Last Cage Down*, pp. 61–2.
58. Stanley J. Kunitz and Howard Haycraft, *Twentieth Century Authors* (1942), p. 88.
59. It is worth noting at this point that there was one other English working-class writer who had had experiences similar to Bates. This was Charles Ashleigh, who after several turbulent years spent with the International Workers of the World in America, returned to England in the early twenties. However, his only novel, *Rambling Kid* (1930), a semi-autobiographical work of historical rather than literary importance, is based almost solely on his American activities, went almost unnoticed in England, and is fully discussed in Rideout, pp. 94–5.
60. *Lean Men* (1934), p. 329.
61. Ibid., p. 224.
62. Ibid., p. 437.
63. Ibid., p. 555.
64. Ibid., p. 483.

65. Ibid., p. 91.
66. Ibid., p. 67.
67. Ibid., p. 169.
68. Ibid., p. 209.
69. Ibid., p. 193.
70. *The Olive Field* (1936), p. 66.
71. Ibid., p. 58.
72. Ibid., pp. 228–9.
73. Ibid., p. 282.
74. Ibid., p. 296.
75. Ibid., p. 340.
76. Ibid., p. 358.
77. Ibid., pp. 386–7.
78. Ibid., p. 463.
79. Ibid., p. 461.
80. Ibid., p. 470.
81. Ibid., p. 90.

Chapter 7

1. 'We're Writing a Book', *New Masses*, xx (15 September 1936), 15–17.
2. Storm Jameson, 'Writing in Revolt: Documents', *Fact*, 4 (July 1937), 9–18. 'The conditions for the growth of a socialist literature scarcely exist. We have to create them. We need documents, not, as the Naturalists needed them, to make their tuppeny-ha'penny dramas, but as charts, as timber for the fire some writer will light to-morrow morning. . . . Writers should be willing to go and live for a long enough time at one of the points of departure of the new society. To go, if you like, into exile' (p. 13). It is worth adding here that although Storm Jameson never, apparently, followed her own advice, she did publish three novels in the thirties in which there is an undercurrent of pleading for a more radical Labour Party, namely the trilogy of *The Mirror in Darkness* (1934–36). Another novel, *In the Second Year* (1936), contained an attack on 'liberal' inaction similar to that found in Rex Warner's *The Professor* (1938).
3. Nor, in fact, was it ever more than a quarter finished. In 1938 Naomi Mitchison's husband moved away from Kings Norton—where the Proletarian Committee had been established—to another constituency, where she was unable to establish the same footing. The book was to have been called *Kitch Against Caroline*: 'Kitch, short for Kitchener (which dates him), was the Marxist hero, and Caroline the Liberal intellectual heroine'. (This quotation, and all the above information from a letter by Naomi Mitchison to the present writer, 5 July 1969.)
4. *We have Been Warned* (1935), p. 227.
5. Ibid., p. 238.
6. Ibid., pp. 240–1.
7. Ibid., p. 413.
8. Ibid., p. 415.
9. Ethel Mannin, *The Pure Flame* (1936), p. 289.

10. He outlines this background and his reasons for writing revolutionary fiction in *The Fate of the Middle Classes* (1936), pp. 248–71.

11. 'Controversy', *Left Review*, 1 (December 1934), 77.

12. Ibid., 76–7 (capitals in original).

13. *Daughters of Albion* (1935), p. 672.

14. Ibid., p. 73.

15. Ibid., p. 598.

16. Ibid., p. 668.

17. Ibid., pp. 404–5.

18. Ibid., p. 116.

19. Ibid., p. 607.

20. Ibid., p. 554.

21. *Daughters of Albion*, pp. 162–3. (Note that even Brown's most admiring critic, the Marxist Philip Henderson, acknowledged in *The Novel Today* (1936), that 'A sharper and more telling effect could have been achieved in at least two-thirds of the space'—p. 263).

22. *Daughters of Albion* was the first book in which, to use Brown's words, he entered the 'camp of those who have no doubts . . . but line up definitely on the side of progress towards change' (*The Fate of the Middle Classes*, p. 269). He remained a Communist sympathiser for many years after this date, but his books became less and less concerned with expressing his Communist views. The most political of them, *Breakfast in Bed* (1937), is an attempt to portray a liberal's growing conviction that the cause of democracy is at stake in Spain. He finally makes a resolution to go out there to fight, but Brown is quite insistent that at the end he is not a Communist, but an Englishman: the book is, therefore, a reflection of the attempts to establish a 'Popular Front'.

23. Ethel Mannin would probably take exception to her inclusion in a discussion of middle-class novelists. The daughter of a post-office worker, she takes pains to emphasise her working-class upbringing in *Privileged Spectator* (1939), pp. 318–19. The sequel to *Cactus*, *The Pure Flame* (1936) takes place, in fact, in a predominantly proletarian setting in London. However, in both books the overriding consciousness is Elspeth Rodney's with her independent income and middle-class habits: the problems, therefore, are basically the same as in the other books discussed here.

It should be noted at this point, too, that Ethel Mannin was never a member of the British Communist Party, or 'a hundred per cent Marxist' (*Privileged Spectator*, p. 78); her allegiance was instead with the now miniscule ILP, which since the 1930 elections had been growing more and more revolutionary. By 1939, without deserting her belief in the need for a complete change of society, Miss Mannin was once more, like the early Elspeth Rodney, a pacifist.

24. *Cactus* (1935), pp. 230–1.

25. Ibid., p. 285.

26. *No Escape* (1937), p. 38.

27. Ibid., p. 181.

28. Ibid., p. 143.

29. Ibid., p. 181.

30. Ibid., pp. 225–6.

31. Ibid., p. 252.

32. Ibid., p. 268.
33. Tendencies carried to even more excessive lengths in Swingler's later, much inferior novel, *To Town* (1939). Here he tries to avoid the middle-class viewpoint altogether, but ends up virtually dissolving his working-class characters in a haze of rather pretentious poetising.
34. *No Escape*, p. 270.
35. Ibid., pp. 276–7.
36. Ibid., p. 286.
37. Ibid., p. 287.
38. 'Controversy', *Left Review*, I (January 1935), 129.
39. 'New Novels', *Left Review*, II (November 1936), 787.
40. *The Friendly Tree* (1936), p. 87.
41. Ibid., p. 154.
42. *The Buried Day* (1960).
43. *Starting Point* (1937), p. 54.
44. Ibid., pp. 53–4.
45. *The Buried Day*, p. 171.
46. *Starting Point*, p. 89.
47. Ibid., p. 142.
48. Ibid., p. 267.
49. Ibid., p. 304.
50. Ibid., pp. 316–17.
51. Ibid., p. 233.
52. Ibid., pp. 317–18.
53. *The Thirties*, pp. 23–31. See also John R. Reed, *Old School Ties* (1964), pp. 103–14.
54. Fenner Brockway, *Inside the Left* (1942), p. 236.
55. *Purple Plague* (1935), p. 310.
56. A point suggested by C. Day Lewis as early as 1938 when he wrote: 'It is partly this dearth of experience outside a class which they have now rejected that has turned . . . [Rex Warner and Edward Upward] to allegory' ('A Letter from London', *New Masses*, XXVII (7 June 1938), 21).
57. 'Education', *The Mind in Chains*, p. 24.
58. Ibid., p. 35. The Sedition Act was the popular name for the Incitement to Disaffection Act (1934) which specifically aimed at preventing the spread of seditious literature (presumably Communist literature) amongst the armed forces. A person could be prosecuted solely for having 'such literature in his possession, whether or not he had read it or tried to disseminate it' (Robert Graves and Alan Hodge, *The Long Week-End* (2nd edition, 1950), p. 313).
59. 'Education', p. 35
60. Ibid., p. 29.
61. Ibid., p. 36.
62. *The Wild Goose Chase* (1937), p. 174.
63. Ibid., p. 15.
64. Ibid., p. 131.
65. Ibid., pp. 133–4.
66. Ibid., p. 166.
67. Warner was not the only writer of the thirties to associate certain aspects of school life with Fascism. See, for example, the later discussion in this chapter

of Ruthven Todd's *Over the Mountain,* and also W. H. Auden's essay on
'Honour' in *The Old School,* edited by Graham Greene (1934), where he says
that 'The best reason I have for opposing Fascism is that at school I lived in a
Fascist state' (quoted in Reed, *Old School Ties,* a book which also draws
attention to similar statements by Henry Green, Alec Waugh, Derek
Verschoyle, and Cyril Connolly pp. 120–1; 303–4n.)

68. *The Wild Goose Chase,* pp. 381–2.
69. Ibid., p. 209.
70. Ibid., p. 233.
71. Ibid., p. 440.
72. Ibid., p. 442.
73. *A Reader's Guide to the Contemporary English Novel* (1963), p. 265.
74. 'Kafka—A Comparison with Rex Warner', *Focus One* (1945), 11. Richard
Gerber describes *The Wild Goose Chase* in similar terms: 'an anti-metropolitan
utopia . . . which is designed to destroy mechanical devilishness' (*Utopian
Fantasy* (1955), p. 52).
75. One must also concede, of course, that there *are* frequent echoes of Auden's
early poetry and plays in *The Wild Goose Chase,* of which the frontier and bird
symbols are perhaps the most obvious examples.
76. It is relevant to note here that an omitted portion of the published version of
The Wild Goose Chase was printed in the anthology *In Letters of Red,* edited by
E. Allan Osborne (1938). In this portion—entitled 'Visit to a Mine'—
George actually meets those who work on the fringes of the city—the
miners—on their home ground, and arranges for their revolutionary
organisation to help the peasants. This meeting, and George's comment that
'In the faces of all of them was something which distinguished them from the
peasants, some look of secretiveness, of something hard, not to be expurged
from their natures' (pp. 267–8), would probably have lent some weight to the
dichotomy between village and city. As it is, in the published version, the
difference between the miners and the peasants is underemphasised: they
merge into the 'masses'.
77. I have not considered here Warner's other novel of the thirties, *The Professor*
(1938), for this book, a more subdued, and a more tightly organised allegory
than *The Wild Goose Chase,* is concerned less with the advocacy of Socialism
than with the exploration of the dilemma of the Liberal, who, confronted by
the force and treachery of Fascism, is unable until the last moment to
relinquish his belief in the power of reason and peace.
78. *The Whispering Gallery* (1955), p. 195.
79. *The Mind in Chains,* pp. 41 and 49. A further indication of Upward's attitude
of the time is provided in Stephen Spender's essay in *The God That Failed*
(1950) where Spender relates how in 1937 he asked his friend 'Chalmers'
(presumably Upward) what he thought of the latest Russian trials: 'He
hesitated a moment, looked away at some object in the distance, blinked, and
then said: "There are so many of these trials that I have given up thinking
about them long ago" ' (p. 215 in 1965 edition).
80. *New Writing in Europe* (1940), pp. 55–6.
81. The only pure Mortmere story published (under the name of 'Allen
Chalmers') was 'The Railway Accident', written in 1928 and published in
New Directions, 11 (1949), 84–116. It was reprinted in *The Railway Accident and*

Other Stories (1969)—which also includes *Journey to the Border*.

82. *Lions and Shadows* (new edition 1953), p. 274.
83. *Journey to the Border* (1938), pp. 21 and 22.
84. Ibid., p. 48.
85. Ibid., pp. 95–6.
86. Ibid., p. 188.
87. Ibid., p. 193.
88. *Lions and Shadows*, p. 67.
89. *Journey to the Border*, p. 25.
90. Ibid., p. 221.
91. Ibid., pp. 213–14.
92. Hynes, *The Auden Generation*, p. 320.
93. Ibid., p. 230
94. Ibid., p. 231.
95. Ibid., p. 219.
96. Ibid., pp. 255–6.
97. *New Writing in Europe*, p. 57.
98. Upward's own later comment on this was that as he was in the process of writing the book, 'the influence on me of socialist-realist ideas from the Soviet Union caused me to doubt more and more whether anything at all could give validity to a modern allegory, and my loss of confidence in what I was doing is reflected I think in a decline of vividness towards the end of the book' ('Back from the Border', *London Magazine*, IX (June 1969), 8—an interview with Upward). This 'decline of vividness' is even more embarrassingly evident in Upward's postwar novels, *In the Thirties* (1962) and *The Rotten Elements* (1969). Covering the same period (and beyond) as *Journey*, they would seem to indicate that that 'new thinking, new feeling' was precisely the doctrinaire voice found at the end of *Journey to the Border*. (For an interesting discussion of these novels and their concluding volume—*No Home but the Struggle* (1977)—see Samuel Hynes, 'Between Poetry and the Party', *Times Literary Supplement*, 5 August 1977, p. 953).
99. *Over the Mountain* (new edition, 1946), p. 10.
100. Ibid., p. 64.
101. Ibid., p. 94.
102. Ibid., p. 166.
103. Ibid., p. 181.
104. Ibid., p. 121.
105. *The Freedom of Poetry* (1947), p. 234.
106. 'The Historical Novel', *New Masses*, XXII (12 January 1937), 16.
107. 'With Robin Hood in Fight with Barons', *Daily Worker* (23 May 1934), p. 4.
108. Letter from Trease to the present writer (13 January 1968). It should be noted here that Trease, who never 'got through a line of Marx except for the comparatively readable *Communist Manifesto*' *(loc. cit.)*, also wrote two revolutionary 'children's' tales set in contemporary England and South America: *Missing from Home* (1937), and *The Call to Arms* (1935). (For an amusing account of the genesis of this series of books, and particularly of *Bows Against the Barons*, see the same author's *Tales Out of School* (2nd edition, 1964), pp. 21–2.)
109. *Bows Against the Barons* (1934), p. 136.

110. *Europa* (1936), p. 451.
111. *Europa in Limbo* (1937), pp. 508–9.
112. *Summer Will Show* (1936), p. 288.
113. Ibid., p. 406.
114. But it *was* seriously intentioned, to show 'that the *Communist Manifesto* and the conclusions behind it should be taken seriously *and gratefully*' (letter from Miss Warner to the present writer, 27 February 1968).
115. Not until 1941, however, did Fast write his first revolutionary historical novel, *The Last Frontier*.
116. In conversation with the present writer (11 February 1968).
117. *Fanfrolico and After* (1962), p. 271.
118. But one children's story, *Rebels of the Goldfields* (1936), was, after being rejected by the Oxford University Press because, according to Lindsay, 'they considered an English officer [in the story] behaved in a way derogatory to an English officer'. This was, incidentally, Lindsay's only experience of rejection by a publisher on the ground of politics (conversation with Lindsay).
119. Noted in Wood, *Communism and British Intellectuals*, p. 207.
120. *Fanfrolico and After*, p. 252.
121. Richard Preston [Jack Lindsay], *End of Cornwall* (1937), p. 368.
122. Ibid., pp. 411–12.
123. *Adam of a New World* (1936), p. 119.
124. Ibid., p. 299.
125. Ibid., p. 299.
126. A point recognised by Lindsay himself in *Fanfrolico and After*, p. 257.
127. *Adam of a New World*, p. 332.
128. Ibid., p. 393.
129. Walter Laqueur, 'Literature and the Historian', *Journal of Contemporary History*, II (April 1967), 9.
130. 'The Historical Novel', p. 16.
131. Ibid., p. 16.
132. Mention should be made of *Sue Verney* (1937), which, covering the years 1644–51, is the personal story of Sue Verney, a member of the Verney Royalist family. However, although political implications seep through, and although Sue Verney is given several Lindsay apocalyptic moments when she senses and fears the strength of the people now and their potential in the future, this novel remains essentially a romance, a story of a girl for whom the political issues of these tumultuous years have scarcely more conscious relevance than the implications of the Commune have for Arnold Bennett's Sophia.
133. He was to assert in a more chauvinistic moment that 'Communism is English' (*England, My England* (1939), p. 64).
134. *1649* (1938), p. 231.
135. Ibid., p. 287.
136. Ibid., p. 521.
137. Ibid., p. 204.
138. Ibid., p. 275.
139. Ibid., p. 274.
140. Ibid., p. 331.
141. Ibid., p. 500.

142. Ibid., p. 181.
143. Ibid., p. 246.
144. Ibid., p. 57.
145. Ibid., p. 74.
146. Ibid., p. 193.
147. Ibid., p. 497.
148. *Lost Birthright* (1939), p. 406.
149. It is interesting to note Lindsay's comment on the writing of *Men of Forty-Eight*: 'In those bitter days of the phoney-war, with the feeling that at any moment hell would be let loose, I strove to let myself go and to pack my deepest emotions about alienation and the class-world into the novel' (*Fanfrolico and After*, p. 277).
150. *Men of Forty-Eight* (1948), p. 264.
151. Edith Sitwell, 'Letters to Jack Lindsay', *Meanjin Quarterly*, xxv (Autumn 1966), 77.

Chapter 8

1. Jack Lindsay, *After the Thirties* (1956), p. 52.
2. Ian S. Munro, *Leslie Mitchell: Lewis Grassic Gibbon* (1966), p. 1 (The *nom de plume* was inspired by his mother's maiden name, Lilias Grassic Gibbon: Munro, p. 3.)
3. Originally published as three separate books: *Sunset Song* (1932); *Cloud Howe* (1933); *Grey Granite* (1934). Although they will be designated as such in the notes, the edition used is the complete trilogy (1967), first published in 1946.
4. I am thinking here particularly of Kurt Wittig's essay in his *The Scottish Tradition in Literature* (1958), pp. 330–3, which dismisses the Communist element almost as an aberration.
5. 'Controversy', *Left Review*, 1 (February 1935), 179–80. (But it should be noted that of his other novels only *Spartacus* could be said to show the positive side of his Socialist beliefs.)
6. Munro comments that Gibbon's friends were unable to agree about the depth of his Communist sympathies (Munro, pp. 133–4), while Hugh MacDiarmid, in support of his contention that Gibbon was 'utterly undialectical', says that he was expelled from the Communist Party as a Trotskyist. (' "Lewis Grassic Gibbon"—James Leslie Mitchell' (1946), reprinted in *The Uncanny Scot* (1968), pp. 160–1.)
7. *Sunset Song*, p. 190.
8. Ibid., p. 193.
9. Ibid., pp. 32–3. For a discussion of the genesis of the 'Scottish Prose' of *A Scots Quair* see Douglas F. Young, *Beyond the Sunset: A Study of James Leslie Mitchell* (1973), pp. 79–84.
10. *Sunset Song*, p. 66.
11. Ibid., p. 53.
12. Ibid., p. 72.
13. Ibid., pp. 148–9.
14. Ibid., p. 149.
15. Ibid., p. 189.

16. Ibid., p. 74.
17. *Grey Granite*, p. 452.
18. *Sunset Song*, p. 95.
19. Ibid., p. 90.
20. Ibid., p. 30.
21. Ibid., p. 80.
22. Ibid., p. 147.
23. Ibid., p. 154.
24. Ibid., p. 154.
25. According to James Barke this is an instance of Gibbon's 'lack of psychological and psychical insight' ('Lewis Grassic Gibbon', *Left Review*, II (February 1936), 221), but as Ian S. Munro comments, it is not the fact of change that is at fault: '. . . better men than Ewan have been completely disintegrated and corrupted hideously by wars; but there is an artistic weakness in confronting the reader with such a totally different person without adequate explanation' (Munro, p. 86).
26. *Sunset Song*, p. 170.
27. Ibid., p. 176.
28. Ibid., p. 159.
29. Ibid., p. 97.
30. Ibid., p. 193.
31. *Cloud Howe*, p. 215.
32. Ibid., p. 247.
33. Ibid., p. 277.
34. Ibid., p. 278.
35. Ibid., p. 342.
36. Ibid., p. 350.
37. Ibid., p. 275.
38. Ibid., p. 300.
39. Ibid., p. 339.
40. *Grey Granite*, p. 452.
41. Ibid., p. 495.
42. Ibid., p. 496.
43. A difficulty apparently anticipated by Grassic Gibbon in an essay written before *Grey Granite*, 'Literary Lights' (first published in *Scottish Scene*, 1934), where, commenting upon his own work, he noted: 'Whether his technique is adequate to compass and express the life of an industrialized Scots town in all its complexity is yet to be demonstrated; whether his peculiar style may not become either intolerably mannered or degenerate, in the fashion of Joyce, into the unfortunate unintelligibilities of a literary second childhood, is also in question' (*A Scots Hairst*, edited by Ian S. Munro (1967), p. 154).
44. *Grey Granite*, pp. 412–13.
45. Ibid., p. 394.
46. Ibid., p. 401.
47. 'Scottish Literature this Century', *The Novel Today*, Programme and Notes to the Edinburgh International Writers' Conference, edited by Andrew Hook (1962), p. 28.
48. *Grey Granite*, pp. 433–4.
49. Ibid., p. 489.

50. Ibid., p. 430.
51. Ibid., p. 482.
52. Ian Milner, 'An Estimation of Lewis Grassic Gibbon's *A Scots Quair*', *Marxist Quarterly*, 1 (October 1954), 216.
53. *Grey Granite*, p. 377.
54. Ibid., p. 468.
55. Ibid., p. 487.
56. *Tradition and Dream* (1964), p. 232.
57. *Grey Granite*, p. 429.
58. Ibid., p. 459.
59. Ibid., p. 452.
60. Ibid., p. 463.

Chapter 9

1. *Left Review*, III (May 1938), 957.
2. Noted in Hugh D. Ford, *A Poet's War: British Poets and the Spanish Civil War* (1965), p. 81.
3. Pelling, *The British Communist Party*, p. 104.
4. Most notably expressed in Orwell's *Homage to Catalonia* (1938), although it should also be pointed out that the effect of this book alone was probably fairly slight: it sold badly and was scantily reviewed (see Jenni Calder, *Chronicles of Conscience* (1968), p. 109).
5. Pelling, p. 113.
6. See *The Betrayal of the Left*, edited by Victor Gollancz (1941), for evidence to support this, particularly pp. 108–53.
7. Pelling, p. 118.
8. Pelling, pp. 121 and 127.
9. When it had been called *Poetry and the People*. It actually continued publication until 1949. (Another even hardier product of the thirties worth mentioning here was the Unity Theatre.)
10. *Folios of New Writing, New Writing and Daylight*. There was also, from 1940 onwards, a *Penguin New Writing*, which, though initially republishing several of the ideologically based stories of the old *New Writing*, soon moved in the same direction as its parent magazine.
11. John Lehmann, *I Am My Brother* (1960), p. 44.
12. See, for example, Henry Reed on poetry: 'The End of an Impulse'. *New Writing and Daylight* (Summer 1943), 111–23; and Philip Toynbee on the novel: 'The Decline and Future of the English Novel', ibid., (Winter 1943–4), 35–45.
13. John Wain, *Sprightly Running* (1962), p. 142 (the university was Oxford).
14. The fullest account of the complex political climate of these years is to be found in Angus Calder's *The People's War* (1969).
15. 'Literature and the Left', *Tribune* (4 June 1943); reprinted in *The Collected Essays, Journalism and Letters of George Orwell*, II; *My Country Right or Left 1940–1943* (1968), p. 294.
16. 'Comment', *Horizon*, I (April 1940), 229.

17. It is not meant to be suggested here that Connolly (or Spender, for that matter) himself underwent a complete reversal of attitudes. His earlier *Enemies of Promise* (1938), while displaying strong left-wing sympathies, and stating that the writer 'who is not political neglects the vital issues of his time', had also warned that 'a writer whose stomach cannot assimilate with genius the starch and acid of contemporary politics had better turn down his plate' (revised edition, 1961, pp. 109 and 116).

18. 'Comment', *Horizon*, I (February 1940), 71.

19. Jack Beeching, 'Yesterday's Literature', *Our Time*, VI (September 1946), 34.

20. 'Notes and Comments', *Our Time*, VI (November 1946). 75.

21. V. S. Pritchett, 'Books in General', *New Statesman*, XXXIV (27 September 1947), 253.

22. 'Comment', *Horizon*, XVI (July 1947), 1.

23. George Scott, *Time and Place* (1956), p. 187.

24. The phrase is John Strachey's, from *The Strangled Cry*, 1962, p. 29.

25. 'Unfortunate' in the sense that although *Nineteen Eighty-Four* was 'NOT intended as an attack on Socialism or on the British Labour Party' (*The Collected Letters, Journalism and Essays of George Orwell*, IV: *In Front of Your Nose 1945–50*, p. 502), the use of this word helped to foster the contrary impression. (For an interesting, if hostile, discussion of the whole significance of Orwell and the postwar intellectual attitudes see E. P. Thompson's essay 'Outside the Whale' in *Out of Apathy* (1960), pp. 141–94.)

26. Kingsley Amis, *Socialism and the Intellectuals* (1957), p. 9.

27. Peter Townsend, 'A Society for People', *Conviction*, edited by Norman Mackenzie (1958), p. 96. See also Richard Crossman, 'The Lessons of 1945', in *Towards Socialism*, edited by Perry Anderson and Robin Blackburn (new edition 1966), pp. 150–1.

28. Or 'because of' for some Communist supporters who saw this disavowal of the necessity for militant revolution as the 'revisionist' thin end of the wedge. Edward Upward was one of those who reacted in this way. See the interview with him in *London Magazine*, IX (June 1969), 5–11.

29. *Margin Released* (1962), p. 227.

30. Ibid., p. 192.

31. *Three Men in New Suits* (new edition, 1946), p. 163.

32. *Daylight on Saturday* (1946), p. 302.

33. Ibid., p. 3.

34. A quality even more pronounced in his popular wartime Utopian play, *They Came to a City* (1943), where the Utopia is never actually seen by the audience, but is conjured up by the characters as a glowing dream-vision, whose outlines are so blurred, and whose realisation is so nebulously hinted at, that its effect is cosily comforting rather than disturbing.

35. The first three were published in 1941, and the last in 1945, but they were all actually written in the 1940–41 period (*Fanfrolico and After*, pp. 227–8).

36. *We Shall Return* (1942), p. 313.

37. *Beyond Terror* (1943), p. 291.

38. Ibid., p. 269.

39. Ibid., p. 36.

40. Ibid., p. 297.

41. One may surmise that Lindsay's war experiences in the Signals had

184 *Socialist Propaganda in the Twentieth-Century British Novel*

something to do with this, just as, for example, the Marxist poet Roy Fuller's period as an Ordinary Seaman furthered his 'proletarianization' (*The Poetry of War*, edited by Ian Hamilton (1965), p. 165).

42. *Hullo Stranger* (1945), p. 180.
43. Ibid., p. 213.
44. *After the Thirties*, p. 76.
45. Ibid., p. 76.
46. *Time to Live* (1946), p. 257.
47. Ibid., p. 32.
48. Ibid., p. 268.
49. *The Subtle Knot* (1947), p. 236.
50. Although this could of course be seen as a prophetic allegory of the McCarthy witch-hunts of 1951–52.
51. From 1949 he was also engaged in editing *Arena*, the successor to *Our Time*, which, after promising in a March 1951 editorial to discuss in future issues writers such as Grassic Gibbon and Lewis Jones, 'writers with the future in them, who represent the tradition we must put in the place of the deathly values' (p. 3), itself died quietly in June of the same year.
52. This had originated with the Communist-inspired 'British Cultural Committee for Peace' (1948). It was headed by A. E. Coppard, and included amongst its signatories such familiar names as Naomi Mitchison and C. Day Lewis, and new ones such as Doris Lessing and and Richard Mason.
53. 'British Writers for Peace', *Masses and Mainstream*, v (April 1952), 61.
54. 'London Letter', *Masses and Mainstream*, v (September 1952), 53–4.
55. 'Uncommitted Talents', *Times Literary Supplement*, Special Autumn Issue (29 August 1952), p. iii.
56. Information provided in a letter to the present writer from Jack Lindsay (20 July 1969).
57. *Betrayed Spring* (1953) p. 104.
58. Ibid., p. 399.
59. Ibid., p. 182.
60. Ibid., p. 346.
61. Ibid., p. 347.
62. Ibid., p. 413.
63. Ibid., p. 216.
64. Ibid., p. 391.
65. Ibid., p. 110.
66. Ibid., p. 120.
67. Ibid., p. 335.
68. Ibid., p. 104.
69. Ibid., p. 78.
70. Ibid., p. 83.
71. Ibid., p. 398.
72. *Rising Tide* (1953), p. 96.
73. Ibid., pp. 271–2.
74. *The Moment of Choice* (1955), p. 331.
75. Ibid., p. 65.
76. Ibid., p. 112.
77. Ibid., p. 158.

78. Ibid., p. 164.
79. Ibid., p. 276.
80. Ibid., pp. 298–9.
81. Ibid., p. 331.
82. Ibid., p. 334.
83. Ibid., p. 334.
84. Alick West, *Mountain in the Sunlight* (1958), p. 208.
85. *A Miner's Sons* (1955), p. 202.
86. Ibid., p. 222.
87. Ibid., p. 245.
88. Ibid., p. 243.
89. Ibid., p. 45.
90. It should be noted here that Doherty did write one novel which could be classified as a more muted, though still idealistic, example of Socialist propaganda: *The Man Beneath*, published in 1957 but presumably written before his departure from the Communist Party early that year.
91. Even in the novella *Hunger*, the most obviously and consciously partisan of her African stories (see the preface to *African Stories* (1964), pp. 8–9), where Jabavu, the young African boy, turns to the 'men of light', the 'We, us' which flows through him at the end is not the proletarian 'we', but the essentially humanitarian 'we', disassociated from economic or theoretical aspects. The point is made clear when Jabavu listens hard trying to understand the 'men of light': '. . . for the space of perhaps ten minutes Jabavu understands not one word, since Mr. Mizi is using such phrases as the development of industry, the working class, and historical mission' (*African Stories*, p. 451, first published in *Five*, 1953).
92. *Retreat to Innocence* (1956), p. 41.
93. Ibid., p. 218.
94. Ibid., p. 40.
95. Ibid., p. 313.
96. Ibid., p. 309.
97. Ibid., p. 43.
98. Ibid., p. 228–9.
99. Ibid., p. 225.
100. Ibid., p. 266.
101. Ibid., p. 266.
102. Ibid., p. 333.
103. *The Golden Notebook* (1962), p. 384.
104. As Doris Lessing has said: 'What sent so many Communists out of the Western Communist Parties was not Hungary, but Hungary, coming so soon after the Twentieth Congress . . . That they crushed the Hungarian uprising in the brutal and cynical way they did after the Twentieth Congress, meant that Congress was more of a safety-valve than a promise of change' (*Going Home* (revised edition, 1968), p. 312).
105. Pelling, *The British Communist Party*, p. 179.
106. Wood, *Communism and British Intellectuals*, p. 202. Information on Sommerfield provided by Jack Lindsay.
107. Initially known as *The Universities and Left Review*.
108. John Mander, *The Writer and Commitment* (1961), p. 11.

109. 'Inside the Whale Again?', *Universities and Left Review*, 4 (Summer 1958), 15.
110. Letter to the present writer (20 July 1969).
111. *Choice of Times* (1964), p. 271. (It is significant that since this date Lindsay has concentrated on writing historical, non-fiction works.)
112. Most notably in Daniel Bell's *The End of Ideology* (1960).

Conclusion

1. *The Occupation* (1971), pp. 302–3.
2. David Caute, *The Illusion* (1971), p. 265.
3. *Politics and the Novel*, p. 22.

Selected Bibliography

This bibliography contains only the works cited in this study. Books mentioned in passing without direct quotation are included only where they have a more than peripheral interest. Where an edition of a novel other than the first has been used, the date of the first edition will be found in square brackets immediately following the title.

1. *Novels and Collections of Prose and Poetry*

Adderley, James, *Beyold the Days Come: A Fancy in Christian Politics* (London, 1907).
Aldridge, James, *Heroes of the Empty View* (London, 1954).
An Amazing Revolution and After (London, 1910).
Ashleigh, Charles, *Rambling Kid* (London, 1930).
Barbor, H. R., *Against the Red Sky: Silhouettes of Revolution* (London, 1922).
Barke, James, *The Land of the Leal* (London, 1939).
Barke, James, *Major Operation: A Novel* (London, 1936).
Bates, Ralph, *Lean Men: An Episode in a Life* (London, 1934).
Bates, Ralph, *The Olive Field* (London, 1936).
Bellamy, Edward, *Looking Backward: 2000–1887* [1888] Modern Library edition, (New York, [1951]).
Berger, John, *A Painter of Our Time* (London, 1958).
Blatchford, Robert, *The Sorcery Shop: An Impossible Romance* (London, 1907).
Blumenfeld, Simon, *Jew Boy* (London, 1935).
Briffault, Robert, *Europa: A Novel of the Days of Ignorance* (London, 1936).
Briffault, Robert, *Europa in Limbo* (London, 1937).
Brockway, Fenner, *Purple Plague: A Tale of Love and Revolution* (London, 1935).
Brown, Alec, *Breakfast in Bed: A Novel* (London, 1937).
Brown, Alec, *Daughters of Albion: A Novel* (London, 1935).
Campbell, Duncan, *The Last Millionaire: A Tale of the Old World and the New* (London, 1923).
Caute, David, *The Occupation* (London, 1971).
Clark, F. Le Gros, *Apparition* (London, 1928).
Doherty, Len, *The Man Beneath* (London, 1957).
Doherty, Len, *A Miner's Sons* (London, 1955).

Gibbon, Lewis Grassic [J. Leslie Mitchell], *A Scots Quair* [Published separately as *Sunset Song* (1932), *Cloud Howe* (1933), and *Grey Granite*, 1934] (London, 1967).

Gray, Maxwell [Mary Gleed Tuttiett], *The Great Refusal* [1906]. Collins Modern Fiction edition (London, [1907]).

Thorne, Guy [C.A.E.R. Gull], *The Socialist* (London, 1909).

Hamilton, Ian, ed., *The Poetry of War: 1939–45* (London, 1965).

Hamilton, Mary Agnes, *Follow My Leader* (London, 1922).

Harris, Frank, *The Bomb* [1908] (New edition, Chicago, 1963).

Heinemann, Margot, *The Adventurers* (London, 1960).

Heslop, Harold, *The Earth Beneath* (London, 1946).

Heslop, Harold, *The Gate of a Strange Field* (London, 1929).

Heslop, Harold, *Goaf* (London, 1934).

Heslop, Harold, *Last Cage Down* (London, 1935).

Heslop, Harold, *Journey Beyond: A Novel* (London, 1930).

Holt, William, *Backwaters* (London, 1934).

Holt, William, *The Price of Adventure* (London, 1934).

Jameson, Storm, *The Mirror in Darkness*. Trilogy comprising *Company Parade, Love in Winter*, and *None Turn Back*. (London, 1934–36).

Jameson, Storm, *In the Second Year* (London, 1936).

Jones, Lewis, *Cwmardy: The Story of a Welsh Mining Valley* (London, 1937).

Jones, Lewis, *We Live: The Story of a Welsh Mining Valley* (London, 1939).

Kennedy, Bart, *Slavery: Pictures from the Depths* (London, 1905).

Kingsley, Charles, *Alton Locke: Tailor and Poet: An Autobiography* [1850] (New edition, London, 1905).

Kovalev, Y. V., *The Literature of Chartism* (Moscow, 1956).

Lambert, David, *He Must So Live* (London, 1956).

Lessing, Doris, *African Stories* (London, 1964).

Lessing, Doris, *The Golden Notebook* (London, 1962).

Lessing, Doris, *Martha Quest* (London, 1952).

Lessing, Doris, *A Proper Marriage* (London, 1954).

Lessing, Doris, *A Ripple from the Storm* (London, 1958).

Lessing, Doris, *Retreat to Innocence* (London, 1956).

Lewis, C. Day, *The Friendly Tree* (London, 1936).

Lewis, C. Day, *Starting Point* (London, 1937).

Lindsay, Jack, *Adam of a New World* (London, 1936).

Lindsay, Jack, *The Barriers are Down: A Tale of the Collapse of a Civilisation* (London, 1945).

Lindsay, Jack, *Betrayed Spring: A Novel of the British Way* (Melbourne, 1953).

Lindsay, Jack, *Beyond Terror: A Novel of the Battle of Crete* (London, 1943).

Lindsay, Jack, *Choice of Times* (London, 1964).

Lindsay, Jack, *Fires in Smithfield: A Novel of Mary Tudor's Days* (London, 1950).

Lindsay, Jack, *Hannibal Takes a Hand* (London, 1941).

Lindsay, Jack, *Hullo Stranger* (London, 1945).
Lindsay, Jack, *Light in Italy* (London, 1941).
Lindsay, Jack, *A Local Habitation: A Novel of the British Way* (London, 1957).
Lindsay, Jack, *Lost Birthright* (London, 1939).
Lindsay, Jack, *Men of Forty-Eight* (London, 1948).
Lindsay, Jack, *The Moment of Choice: A Novel of the British Way* (London, 1955).
Lindsay, Jack, *Rising Tide: A Novel of the British Way* (London, 1953).
Lindsay, Jack, *1649: A Novel of a Year* (London, 1938).
Lindsay, Jack, *The Stormy Violence* (London, 1941).
Lindsay, Jack, *The Subtle Knot* (London, 1947).
Lindsay, Jack, *Sue Verney* (London, 1937).
Lindsay, Jack, *Time to Live* (London, 1946).
Lindsay, Jack, *We Shall Return: A Novel of Dunkirk and the French Campaign* (London, 1942).
[Linton, Lynn], *The True History of Joshua Davidson* (London, 1872).
Mannin, Ethel, *Cactus* (London, 1935).
Mannin, Ethel, *The Pure Flame* (London, 1936).
Mitchell, J. Leslie [Lewis Grassic Gibbon], *Spartacus* (London, 1933).
Mitchison, Naomi, *We Have Been Warned: A Novel* (London, 1935).
Moore, Edith, *A Wilful Widow* (London, 1913).
Morris, William, *News from Nowhere* [serial publication: 1890] in *The Collected Works of William Morris*: xxi (London, 1912).
Morrison, Arthur, *A Child of the Jago* [1896] (Fitzroy edition London, 1969).
Orwell, George, *Animal Farm: A Fairy Story* (London, 1945).
Orwell, George, *Nineteen Eighty-Four: A Novel* (London, 1949).
Osborne, E. Allen, ed., *In Letters of Red* (London, 1938).
Phelan, Jim, *Ten-a-Penny People: A Novel* (London, 1938).
Preston, Richard [Jack Lindsay], *End of Cornwall* (London, 1937).
Priestley, J. B., *Bright Day* (London, 1946).
Priestley, J. B., *Daylight on Saturday: A Novel about an Aircraft Factory* (London, 1943).
Priestley, J. B., *Three Men in New Suits*. [1945]. Book Club edition (London, 1946).
Roley, A. P., *Revolt* (London, 1933).
Roberts, Michael, ed., *New Country: Prose and Poetry by the Authors of New Signatures* (London, 1933).
Rutherford, Mark [William Hale White], *The Revolution in Tanner's Lane* [1887] (New edition, London, [1913]).
Shaw, Bernard. *An Unsocial Socialist* [Serial publication: 1884.] (Standard edition, London, 1932).
Sillitoe, Alan, *The Death of William Posters* (1965).
Sillitoe, Alan, *The Flame of Life* (London, 1974)

Sillitoe, Alan, *Key to the Door* (London, 1961).

Sillitoe, Alan, *A Tree on Fire* (London, 1967).

Sommerfield, John, *May Day* (London, 1936).

Sommerfield, John, *Trouble in Porter Street* (London, [1939]).

Swingler, Randall, *No Escape* (London, 1937).

Swingler, Randall, *To Town: A Novel* (London, 1939).

Tiltman, H. Hessell, *Poverty Lane: A Novel* (London, 1926).

Todd, Ruthven, *Over the Mountain* [1939] (London, 1946).

Tressell, Robert [Robert Noonan], *The Ragged Trousered Philanthropists* (London, 1914).

Tressell, Robert [Robert Noonan], *The Ragged Trousered Philanthropists*. (1st complete edition, London, 1955).

Trease, Geoffrey, *Bows against the Barons* (London, 1934).

Trease, Geoffrey, *Comrades for the Charter* (London, 1934).

'Unitas', *The Dream City* (London, 1920).

Upward, Edward, *In the Thirties* (London, 1962).

Upward, Edward, *Journey to the Border* (London, 1938).

Upward, Edward, *The Railway Accident and other Stories* (London, 1969).

Upward, Edward, *The Rotten Elements: A Novel of Fact* (London, 1969).

Warner, Rex, *The Aerodrome: A Love Story* (London, 1941).

Warner, Rex, *The Professor: A Novel* (London, 1938).

Warner, Rex, *The Wild Goose Chase: A Novel* (London, 1937).

Warner, Sylvia Townsend, *Summer Will Show* (London, 1936).

Wells, H. G., *Ann Veronica: A Modern Love Story* (London, 1909).

Wells, H. G., *In the Days of the Comet* [1906] (Collins Classics edition, London, 1963).

Wells, H. G., *Marriage* (London, 1912).

Wells, H. G., *Meanwhile: The Picture of a Lady* [1927.] (2nd edition, London, 1962).

Wells, H. G., *The New Machiavelli* (London, 1911).

Wells, H. G., *Men Like Gods* (London, 1923).

Wells, H. G., *The Passionate Friends: A Novel* (London, 1913).

Wells, H. G., *Tono-Bungay* [1909.] (New edition, London, 1911).

Wells, H. G., *The World Set Free: A Story of Mankind* (London, 1914).

Welsh, James C., *The Morlocks* (London, 1924).

Welsh, James C., *Norman Dale, M. P.* (London, 1928).

Welsh, James C., *The Underworld: The Story of Robert Sinclair, Miner* (London, 1920).

Whiteing, Richard, *No. 5 John Street* [1899] (Nelson's Library edition, London, [1907].

Whiteing, Richard, *Ring in the New* (London, 1906).

Wilkinson, Ellen, *Clash: A Novel* (London, 1929).

Williams, Raymond, *Border Country* (London, 1960).

Wilson, Theodora Wilson, *The Last Dividend: An Economic Romance* (London, 1922).

II: *Biographies, Memoirs, and other works dealing with the Literary, Political, and Social Background*

Aaron, Daniel, *Writers on the Left: Episodes in American Literary Communism* (New York, 1961).

Adderley, James, *In Slums and Society: Reminiscences of Old Friends* (London, 1916).

Amis, Kingsley, *Socialism and the Intellectuals*. Fabian Tract 304. (London, 1957).

Anderson, Perry and Robin Blackburn, ed., *Towards Socialism* (New edition, London, 1966).

Arnot, R. Page, *The Miners: A History of the Miners' Federation of Great Britain, 1889–1910* (London, 1949).

Arnot, R. Page, *The Miners: Years of Struggle: A History of the Miners' Federation of Great Britain (from 1910 onwards)* (London, 1953).

Armytage, W. H. G., *Heavens Below: Utopian Experiments in England, 1560–1960* (London, 1961).

Ball, F. C., *One of the Damned*. (London, 1973).

Ball, F. C., *Tressell of Mugsborough* (London, 1951).

Barke, James, *The Green Hills Far Away: A Chapter in Autobiography* (London, 1940).

Bealey, Frank and Henry Pelling, *Labour and Politics 1900–1906: A History of the Labour Representation Committee* (London, 1958).

Blatchford, Robert, *My Eighty Years* (London, 1931).

Blatchford, Robert, *Britain for the British* (London, 1902).

Blatchford, Robert, *God and My Neighbour* (London, 1903).

Blatchford, Robert, *Merrie England* (London, 1894).

Blatchford, Robert, *Not Guilty: A Defence of the Bottom Dog* (London, 1906).

Bowman, Sylvia, E. ed., *Edward Bellamy Abroad: An American Prophet's Influence* (New York, 1962).

Brockway, Fenner, *Inside the Left: Thirty Years of Platform, Press, Prison and Parliament* (London, 1942).

Brown, Alec, *The Fate of the Middle Classes* (London, 1936).

Calder, Angus, *The People's War: Britain 1939–45* (London, 1969).

The Case Against Socialism: A Handbook for Speakers and Candidates (London, 1908).

Cline, Catherine Ann, *Recruits to Labour: The British Labour Party 1914–1931* (New York, 1963).

Cole, G. D. H., *A History of Socialist Thought*. Vol. I: *The Forerunners 1789–1850* (London, 1953). Vol. III, Pt. 1: *The Second International 1889–1914* (London, 1956).

Cole, G. D. H. and M. I. Cole, *The Condition of Britain* (London, 1937).

Cole, Margaret, *Growing up into Revolution* (London, 1949).

Cross, Colin, *The Fascists in Britain* (New York, 1963).

192   *Socialist Propaganda in the Twentieth-Century British Novel*

Crossman, Richard, ed., *The God That Failed* (Bantam edition, New York, 1965).
David, Henry, *The History of the Haymarket Affair: A Study in the Social-Revolutionary and Labor Movements* (2nd edition, New York, 1958).
The Dictionary of Welsh Biography down to 1940 (London, 1959).
Dowse, Robert E., *Left in the Centre: The Independent Labour Party 1893–1940* (London, 1966).
(Gibbon, Lewis Grassic) *A Scots Hairst: Essays and Short Stories: Lewis Grassic Gibbon*, ed. Ian S. Munro (London, 1967).
Gibbs, Philip, *Ten Years After: A Reminder* (London, 1924).
Gollancz, Victor, ed., *The Betrayal of the Left: An Examination and Refutation of Communist Policy from October 1939 to January 1941* (London, 1941).
Graubard, Stephen Richards, *British Labour and the Russian Revolution 1917–1924* (Cambridge (Mass.), 1956).
Graves, Robert and Alan Hodge, *The Long Week-End: A Social History of Great Britain 1918–1939* (2nd edition, London, 1950).
Haldane, Charlotte, *Truth Will Out* (London, 1949).
Hamilton, Mary Agnes, *Remembering My Good Friends* (London, 1944).
Hanley, James, *Grey Children: A Study in Humbug and Misery* (London, 1937).
Holt, William, *I Haven't Unpacked: An Autobiography* (Book Club edition, London, 1942).
Hutt, Allen, *The Condition of the Working Class in Britain* (London, 1933).
Hynes, Samuel, *The Edwardian Turn of Mind* (London, 1968).
Isherwood, Christopher, *Lions and Shadows: An Education in the Twenties* (New edition, London, 1953).
Jackson, T. A., *Solo Trumpet: Some Memories of Socialist Agitation and Propaganda* (London, 1953).
Jones, Peter d'A., *The Christian Socialist Revival 1877–1914: Religion, Class, and Social Conscience in Late-Victorian England* (New Jersey, 1968).
Kingsmill, Hugh, *Frank Harris* (New edition, London, 1949).
Kunitz, Stanley J. and Howard Haycraft, *Twentieth Century Authors: A Biographical Dictionary of Modern Literature* (New York, 1942).
Lehmann, John, *I Am My Brother: Autobiography* II. (London, 1960).
Lehmann, John, *The Whispering Gallery: Autobiography* I (London, 1955).
Lehmann, John, *et al. Ralph Fox: A Writer in Arms* (London, 1937).
Lessing, Doris, *Going Home* (Panther revised edition, London, 1968).
Lewis, C. Day, *The Buried Day* (London, 1960).
Lindsay, Jack, *England, My England . . .* (London, [1939]).
Lindsay, Jack, *Fanfrolico and After* (London, 1962).
McBriar, A. M., *Fabian Socialism and English Politics, 1884–1918* (London, 1966).
Macfarlane, L. J., *The British Communist Party: Its Origin and Development until 1929* (London, 1966).
MacKenzie, Norman, ed., *Conviction* (London, 1958).

Mannin, Ethel, *Priviliged Spectator: A Sequel to Confessions and Impressions* (London, 1939).

Mannin, Ethel, *Confessions and Impressions* (London, [1930]).

Martin, Kingsley, *Editor: A Second Volume of Autobiography, 1931–45* (London, 1968).

Mitchison, Naomi, *The Kingdom of Heaven* (London, 1939).

Mosley, Oswald, *The Greater Britain* (London, [1932]).

Mowatt, Charles Loch, *Britain Between the Wars 1918–1940* (Revised edition, London, 1956).

Orwell, George, *The Collected Essays, Journalism and Letters of George Orwell*, ed. Sonia Orwell and Ian Angus. Vol. I: *An Age Like This, 1920–1940*; Vol II: *My Country Right or Left 1940–1943*; Vol IV: *In Front of Your Nose 1945–50* (London, 1968).

Orwell, George, *The Road to Wigan Pier* (London, 1937).

Pelling, Henry, *The British Communist Party: A Historical Profile* (London, 1958).

Pelling, Henry, *A Short History of the Labour Party*. (3rd edition, London, 1968).

Phelan, Jim, *The Name's Phelan: The First Part of the Autobiography of Jim Phelan* (London, 1948).

Pollitt, Harry, *Serving My Time: An Apprenticeship to Politics* (London, 1940).

Postgate, R. W., *The Builders' History* (London, 1923).

Priestley, J. B., *Margin Released: A Writer's Reminiscences and Reflections* (London, 1962).

Richards, Grant, *Author Hunting: Memories of Years Spent Mainly in Publishing* (New edition, London, 1960).

Scott, George, *Time and Place* (London, 1956).

Stansky, Peter and William Abrahams, *Journey to the Frontier: Julian Bell and John Cornford: Their Lives and the 1930's* (London, 1966).

Stewart, James D. ed., *The English Catalogue of Books for 1937* (London, 1938).

Strachey, John, *The Coming Struggle for Power* (London, 1932).

Thompson, E. P. ed., *Out of Apathy* (London, 1960).

Thompson, Laurence, *Robert Blatchford: Portrait of an Englishman* (London, 1951).

Thompson, Paul, *Socialists, Liberals and Labour: The Struggle for London 1885–1914* (London, 1967).

Trease, Geoffrey, *Tales Out of School* (2nd edition, London, 1964).

Tsuzuki, Chuchichi, *H. M. Hyndman and British Socialism*, ed. Henry Pelling (London, 1961).

Wain, John, *Sprightly Running: Part of an Autobiography* (London, 1962).

Wells, H. G., *Experiment in Autobiography: Discoveries and Conclusions of a very Ordinary Brain (since 1866)*. 2 vols. (London, 1934).

Wells, H. G., *New Worlds for Old: A Plain Account of Modern Socialism*

(Revised edition, London, 1909).
Whiteing, Richard, *My Harvest* (London, 1915).
Wood, Neal, *Communism and British Intellectuals* (London, 1959).
Woolf, Leonard, *Downhill all the Way: An Autobiography of the Years 1919–1939* (London, 1967).

III: *Critical Works*

Allen, Walter, *Tradition and Dream: The English and American Novel from the Twenties to our Time* (London, 1964).
Calder, Jenni, *Chronicles of Conscience: A Study of George Orwell and Arthur Koestler* (London, 1968).
Caudwell, Christopher [C. St. J. Sprigg], *Studies in a Dying Culture* (London, 1938).
Caute, David, *The Illusion: An Essay on Politics, Theatre and the Novel* (London, 1971).
Connolly, Cyril, *Enemies of Promise* (Revised edition, Harmondsworth, Penguin 1961).
Craig, David, ed., *Marxists on Literature: an Anthology* (Harmondsworth, Penguin, 1975).
Ford, Hugh. D., *A Poet's War: British Poets and the Spanish Civil War* (Philadelphia, 1965).
Fox, Ralph, *The Novel and the People* (London, 1937).
Gerber, Richard, *Utopian Fantasy: A Study of English Utopian Fiction since the End of the Nineteenth Century* (London, 1955).
Henderson, Philip, *The Novel Today: Studies in Contemporary Attitudes* (London, 1936).
Hook, Andrew, ed., *The Novel Today: Programme and Notes of the International Writers' Conference* (Edinburgh, 1962).
House, Humphrey, *The Dickens World* (New edition, London, 1960).
Howe, Irving, *Politics and the Novel* (New Left Books edition, London, 1961).
Hynes, Samuel, *The Auden Generation: Literature and Politics in England in the 1930s* (London, 1976).
Kagarlitski, J., *The Life and Thought of H. G. Wells*. Translation by Moura Budberg (London, 1966).
Karl, Frederick R., *A Reader's Guide to the Contemporary English Novel* (London, 1963).
Keating, P. J., *The Working Classes in Victorian Fiction* (London, 1971).
Kemp, Harry and Laura Riding *et al.*, *The Left Heresy—in Literature and Life* (London, 1939).
Lehmann, John, *New Writing in Europe* (Harmondsworth, Penguin, 1940).
Lewis, C. Day, *Revolution in Writing* (2nd edition, London, 1938).

Lewis, C. Day, ed., *The Mind in Chains: Socialism and the Cultural Revolution* (London, 1937).

Lindsay, Jack, *After the Thirties: The Novel in Britain and its Future* (London, 1956).

Lodge, David, *Language of Fiction: Essays in Criticism and Verbal Analysis of the English Novel* (London, 1966).

MacDiarmid, Hugh [C. M. Grieve], *The Uncanny Scot: A Selection of Prose*, ed. Kenneth Buthlay (London, 1968).

Mander, John, *The Writer and Commitment* (London, 1961).

Mitchell, Jack, *Robert Tressell and The Ragged Trousered Philanthropists* (London, 1969).

Morton, A. L., *The English Utopia* (London, 1952).

Munro, Ian S., *Leslie Mitchell: Lewis Grassic Gibbon* (Edinburgh, 1966).

Raknem, Ingvald, *H. G. Wells and His Critics* ([London], 1962).

Reed, John R., *Old School Ties: The Public Schools in British Literature* (New York, 1964).

Rideout, Walter B., *The Radical Novel in the United States 1900–1954: Some Interrelations of Literature and Society* (Cambridge (Mass.), 1956).

Sillitoe, Alan, Introduction to *The Ragged Trousered Philanthropists*. (Panther edition, London, 1965).

Stanford, Derek, *The Freedom of Poetry: Studies in Contemporary Verse* (London, 1947).

Strachey, John, *The Strangled Cry and other Unparliamentary Papers* (London, 1962).

Swinnerton, Frank, *The Adventures of a Manuscript: Being the Story of The Ragged Trousered Philanthropists* (London, [1956]).

Symons, Julian, *The Thirties: A Dream Revolved* (London, 1960).

Vicunas, Martha, *The Industrial Muse* (London, 1974).

Wagar, Warren W., *H. G. Wells and the World State* (Yale, 1961).

West, Alick, *Crisis and Criticism* (London, 1937).

West, Alick, *The Mountain in the Sunlight: Studies in Conflict and Unity* (London, 1958).

West, Anthony, *Principles and Persuasions* (London, 1958).

Wittig, Kurt, *The Scottish Tradition in Literature* (Edinburgh, 1958).

Woodcock, George, *The Writer and Politics* (London, 1948).

Young, Douglas F., *Beyond the Sunset: A Study of James Leslie Mitchell (Lewis Grassic Gibbon)* (Aberdeen, 1973).

IV: *Articles in Periodicals, etc.*

'Back from the Border'. [Interview with Edward Upward] *London Magazine*, IX (June 1969), 5–11.

Ball, F. C., 'More Light on Tressell'. *Marxism Today*, XI (June 1967), 177–82.

Barke, James, 'Lewis Grassic Gibbon'. *Left Review*, II (February 1936), 220–5.

Beeching, Jack, ' *The Ragged Trousered Philanthropists*'. *Our Time*, VII (May 1948), 196–9.

Beeching, Jack, 'The Uncensoring of *The Ragged Trousered Philanthropists*'. *The Marxist Quarterly*, II (October 1955), 217–29.

Beeching, Jack, 'Yesterday's Literature'. *Our Time*, VI (September 1946), 33–34.

Bennett, Arnold, 'Why I Am a Socialist'. *The New Age*, II (30 November 1907), 90.

Blundell, I. T., 'Man Who Took to "the Masses" as He Would to Drink'. [Review of *Apparition*] *Sunday Worker* (17 June, 1928), p. 8.

Brown, Alec, *et al.*, 'Controversy'. *Left Review*, I (December 1934), 75–80.

Calder-Marshall, A[rthur], 'The Pink Decade'. *New Statesman and Nation*, XXI (15 February 1941), 157–8.

[Connolly, Cyril?], 'Comment'. *Horizon*, I (February 1940), 68–71.

[Connolly, Cyril?], 'Comment'. *Horizon*, I (April 1940), 229–37.

[Connolly, Cyril?], 'Comment'. *Horizon*, XVI (July 1947), 1–2.

Dynamov, S., 'Stacey Hyde: An Artist of English Social Fascism'. *International Literature*, 2–3 (1932), 116–21.

Elistratova, E., 'The Work of Harold Heslop'. *International Literature*, I (1932), 99–102.

Gibbon, Lewis Grassic, *et al.*, 'Controversy'. *Left Review*, I (February 1935), 179–83.

Gollancz, Victor, 'Editorial'. *The Left News*, 19 (November 1937), 557–61.

Gollancz, Victor, 'The Left Book Club and the Labour Victory'. *The Left News*, 110 (August 1945), 3251–5.

Hall, Stuart, 'Inside the Whale Again?' *Universities and Left Review*, 4 (Summer 1958), 14–15.

Harris, Wendell V., 'The Novels of Richard Whiteing'. *English Literature in Transition*, VIII, no. 1 (1965), 36–43.

Heslop, Harold, 'Sunnybank'. *International Literature*, 8–9 (1939), 28–52.

Hicks, Granville, 'The British Are Coming'. *New Masses*, XXI (15 December 1936), 23–24.

Jackson, Holbrook, 'The Second English Revolution'. *The New Age*, III (2 May, 9 May, 16 May 1908), 12–13, 31–32, 51–52.

Jameson, Storm, 'Writing in Revolt: Documents'. *Fact*, 4 (July 1937), 9–18.

Laqueur, Walter, 'Literature and the Historian'. *Journal of Contemporary History*, II (April 1967), 5–14.

[Lehmann, John], 'Manifesto'. *New Writing*, I (Spring 1936), v.

Lewis, C. Day, 'A Letter from London'. *New Masses*, XXVII (7 June 1938), 21–22.

Lewis, C. Day, *et al.*, 'Controversy'. *Left Review*, I (January 1935), 125–29.

Lindsay, Jack, 'British Writers for Peace'. *Masses and Mainstream*, v (April 1952), 61–64.

Lindsay, Jack, 'The Historical Novel'. *New Masses*, xxii (12 January 1937), 15–16.

Lindsay, Jack, 'London Letter'. *Masses and Mainstream*, v (September 1952), 52–54.

Lindsay, Jack, 'On Guard for Spain'. *Left Review*, iii (March 1937), 79–86.

Mayne, Brian, '*The Ragged Trousered Philanthropists*: An Appraisal of an Edwardian Novel of Social Protest', *Twentieth Century Literature*, xiii, no. 2 (July 1967), 73–83.

Milner, Ian, 'An Estimation of Lewis Grassic Gibbon's *A Scots Quair*'. *Marxist Quarterly*, i (October 1954), 207–18.

Mitchell, Jack 'The Struggle for the Working-Class Novel in Scotland – Part i'. *Scottish Marxist*, 6 (April 1974), 40–52.

Mitchell, Jack, 'The Struggle for the Working-Class Novel in Scotland– Part ii : *A Scots Quair*, *Scottish Marxist*, (October 1974), 46–54.

Mitchell, Jack, 'The Proletarian Novel-Part iii: James Barke'. *Scottish Marxist*, 8 (January 1975), 39–48.

Mitchison, Naomi, 'We're Writing a Book'. *New Masses*, xx (15 September 1936), 15–17.

Morton, A. L., 'New Novels'. [Review of *The Friendly Tree*] *Left Review*, ii (November 1936), 787–8.

'Notes and Comments'. *Our Time*, vi (November 1946), 75–76.

'Paris Congress Speeches'. *Left Review*, i (August 1935), 469–75.

Pollitt, Harry, 'With Robin Hood in Fight with Barons'. [Review of *Bows Against the Barons*]. *Daily Worker* (23 May 1934), p. 4.

Pritchett, V. S., 'Books in General'. *New Statesman and Nation*, xxxiv (27 September 1947), 253.

Rajan, B., 'Kafka—A Comparison with Rex Warner'. *Focus One* (1945), 7–14.

Reed, Henry, 'The End of an Impulse'. *New Writing and Daylight*. (Summer 1943), 111–23.

Samuels, Stuart, 'The Left Book Club'. *Journal of Contemporary History*, i, no. 2 (1966), 65–86.

'Second International Conference of Revolutionary Writers'. *Literature of the World Revolution*, [3], [1931].

Sitwell, Edith, 'Letters to Jack Lindsay'. *Meanjin Quarterly*, xxv (Autumn 1966), 76–80.

'Sold Rights to Classic for £25'. *The Times* (London), (5 June 1967), p. 3.

Stead, C. K., 'Auden's "Spain" '. *London Magazine*, vii (March 1968), 41–54.

[Stead, W. T.], 'The Labour Party and the Books that Helped to Make It'. *Review of Reviews*, xxxiii (June 1906), 568–82.

Stelger, Andrew J., 'American Authors Popular in Soviet Union'. *International Literature*, 3 (1936), 98–103.

'Storm and the Struggle'. *Storm*, 1 (February 1933), 2.

Swingler, Randall, 'Left Review'. *Left Review*, III (May 1938), 957–60.

'Talking to Kathleen Tressell'. *Labour Monthly*, L (June 1968) 261–3.

Toynbee, Philip, 'The Decline and Future of the English Novel'. *New Writing and Daylight* (Winter 1943–44), 35–45.

'Uncommitted Talents'. *Times Literary Supplement*, Special Autumn Issue (29 August 1952), p. iii.

Wells, H. G., 'Mr. Wells and Free Love'. *The New Age*, 1 (17 October 1907), 392.

Willis, D. A., 'New Life for the Novel'. *Viewpoint*, 1 (April–June 1934), 12–14.

Woolley, E., 'A Lancs Worker Seeks the Way Out'. [Review of *Backwaters*]. *Daily Worker* (21 February 1934), p. 4.

Index